D1605889

365
DAILY DEVOTIONS

WALKING
WITH
GOD

DAVID JEREMIAH

Christian art gifts

Visit Christian Art Gifts, Inc. at www.christianartgifts.com.

Walking with God

Published by Christian Art Gifts, Inc., under license from Tyndale House Publishers

Previously published as Discovering God: 365 Daily Devotions. First printing by Tyndale House Publishers, in 2015.

Cover and interior images used under license from Shutterstock.com

Designed by Brad Miedema

ISBN 978-1-64272-399-1

Printed in China

28 27 26 25 24 23

18 17 16 15 14 13 12 11 10

INTRODUCTION

When we think of the early explorers who left their homes and their comfortable lives to discover the New World beyond their horizons, we often think of Christopher Columbus, who sought to find the East Indies by traveling west. Interestingly enough, what he sought and what he found were quite opposite. Instead of reaching the riches of the spice trade in Asia, he opened up subsequent voyages to the American continents and the exploration of the Western Hemisphere. While Columbus's navigational projections were wrong, he was able to make a great contribution to the world. But isn't that typical of life? What we seek and what we ultimately discover are often two different things.

Looking to God each day for direction and purpose is also a time of exploration and discovery. We go to the Word of God seeking to know more about the One who created our world and everything in it. And there we find treasures that were never sought but become so precious to us. Peace, comfort, hope, consolation in disappointments, and solace in loss—all of these and more are found in a daily devotional time. This 365-day devotional—*Walking with God*—is designed to give you a starting point each day with God. It contains a Scripture, a heartwarming devotional thought, and a quote to take you through the day. Make *Walking with God* a habit—and allow God to open new horizons to you as you seek His Word daily.

Dr. David Jeremiah
Fall 2015

JANUARY

ATTENTION

Teach us to number our days,
that we may gain a heart of wisdom.

PSALM 90:12

Ever since God issued the Ten Commandments, we've understood there's something special about that number. It serves as the foundation for our numerical system. Ten is the sum of the first four numbers (1 + 2 + 3 + 4) and the first two-digit number. It brings us full circle. We view ten as complete and perfect, which is why we often say, "On a scale from one to ten . . ."

Ten years make a decade. And since we only have about seven of those, we should pay attention. Verse 10 of Psalm 90 says that our current earthly lives are zipping by. Our years are "soon cut off, and we fly away." But God is our "dwelling place in all generations," from "everlasting to everlasting" (verses 1-2).

Starting the year *without* Christ is like jumping into a dark, unknown patch of the future. But *with* our Lord, it's like taking a step with the One who holds the future.

Lord, remind us to turn our attention to the importance of each day, each year, and each decade. Help us to make our lives count for Christ.

O Father, let Thy watchful eye still
look on us in love, that we may praise Thee,
year by year, with angel hosts above.

MEAUX BREVIARY

TRADING STRESS FOR A SONG

Let us go into His tabernacle;
let us worship at His footstool.

PSALM 132:7

A Netherlands-based electronics firm created a bracelet that senses a person's emotional state and alerts the wearer when emotions rise to unhealthy levels. The product was developed chiefly for stock traders on European exchanges. When trading becomes too intense and the trader's blood pressure rises, the device issues a warning to the wearer to "take a time-out, wind down, or reconsider his actions," according to the manufacturer. The results are, hopefully, beneficial to both stockbrokers and investors.

If everyone on earth were wearing such a bracelet right now, how many devices would be sensing stress? Would yours?

The greatest antidote to stress is worship. Worship is recognizing God's greatness and glory and, in response, expressing our pleasure and praise. It's not about us, how we feel, or the kind of music we enjoy. It's about the One who is the same yesterday, today, and forever. It's about who He is and what He has done.

To control stress, we don't need a bracelet on our wrists, but simply a heart of worship that adores and praises the greatness of God's glory.

God wants worshippers before workers;
indeed the only acceptable workers are those
who have learned the lost art of worship.

A. W. TOZER

DIVINE DELAYS

Then it came to pass, when Pharaoh had let the people go, that God did not lead them by way of the land of the Philistines, although that was near; for God said, "Lest perhaps the people change their minds when they see war, and return to Egypt."

EXODUS 13:17

Not a day goes by when our plans aren't changed by circumstances beyond our control. Natural disasters, house repairs or car trouble, unexpected illness, traffic jams on the freeway, a friend or neighbor with an emergency need—the list goes on. The question is: Can we trust that God is in those unforeseen challenges?

A rarely read verse in Exodus (13:17) tells how God led the newly freed Hebrew nation into the Sinai Desert instead of along the southeast coast of the Mediterranean Sea into the Promised Land. Why? So the Hebrews wouldn't encounter the Philistines who inhabited that region, be attacked, and return to Egypt for safety. The Hebrews grumbled loud and long about the Sinai sand and sun, but at least they were alive. If they had met the Philistines, many of them might have been slaughtered.

The next time your path is changed unexpectedly, trust by faith that God is in it and that the change was for a good reason (Romans 8:28).

Hope is the foundation of patience.

JOHN CALVIN

LIFE ON PURPOSE

Though He was a Son, yet He learned obedience
by the things which He suffered.

HEBREWS 5:8

If John 3:16 is the most recognizable verse in the entire Bible, then Romans 8:28 is surely next: "We know that all things work together for good to those who love God, to those who are the called according to His purpose." Christians love this verse because it says that everything—the good and the bad—that happens in our lives will be used by God for a good purpose.

While that is comforting, Romans 8:28 doesn't tell us what the good purpose is, but we are told in the next verse: "Whom He foreknew, He also predestined to be conformed to the image of His Son, that He might be the firstborn among many brethren." God's purpose is to make us look more like His Son. Our lives follow the same pattern of testing that Jesus followed: "He learned obedience by the things which He suffered" (Hebrews 5:8). Our purpose is to obey God, as Jesus did. As we trust and obey Him, we will begin to look more and more like His Son.

Whether this day is "good" or "bad" in your sight, it has moved you closer to the image of Jesus.

God is working out His eternal purpose,
not only in spite of human and satanic
opposition, but by means of them.

A. W. PINK

GREATER AND LESSER LIGHTS

[Jesus said,] "You are the light of the world.
A city that is set on a hill cannot be hidden."
MATTHEW 5:14

Most lights get their power from another source. A fire is lit in a fireplace with a match, an ancient oil lamp was set alight by a flame from another source, and a modern lamp gets its power from an electric current. The Bible says there are two sources of spiritual light in this world—the greater source giving light to the lesser.

In one of His "I am" statements, Jesus said He was the "light of the world." So Jesus is *the* light of the world, but He also told His disciples, "You are the light of the world." In fact, He compared us to a lamp that is given light by another source. Jesus is the greater light, and as His followers we are the lesser lights. We have light in us because He lives in us. We have light to offer the world when we allow His light—the light of His glory and grace—to shine through us and push back the darkness.

Like a lamp that needs to be lit each night, make sure you connect with your spiritual Light Source every morning, through prayer or reading His Word, so that His light will shine through you to the world.

It's not necessary to blow out your
neighbor's light to let your own shine.

M. R. DEHAAN

SALTY SAINTS

*[Jesus said,] "Salt is good; but if the salt has
lost its flavor, how shall it be seasoned?"*

LUKE 14:34

Salt is essential to life. Without it, our cardiovascular and nervous systems would stop working. Long before refrigeration was invented, salt was used as a preservative to keep meat from spoiling—and to provide flavor for foods. Salt gives life, preserves life, and flavors life—it is one of the most important minerals found on planet Earth.

Jesus told His disciples that they were the "salt of the earth." They were to have a saving, preserving, and flavoring influence wherever they went and with whomever they interacted. Interestingly, much of the salt used in Israel was from the Dead Sea and was mixed with noxious minerals that spoiled its purity and flavor. In such a case, the salt was good for nothing; it was rendered useless and had to be thrown out. If our lives become polluted by the things of this world, our ability to save, preserve, and flavor life will be diluted and weakened accordingly. Our mission is not just to be salt, but to be *pure* salt.

In whose life are you serving as a saving, preserving, and flavoring influence? Don't lose your power by becoming mixed with the spoiled salts of this world.

We are the salt of the earth, mind you,
not the sugar. Our ministry is truly to cleanse
and not just to change the taste.

VANCE HAVNER

WALK WORTHY

*Walk worthy of God who calls you into
His own kingdom and glory.*
1 THESSALONIANS 2:12

For months, a runner prepared for her marathon. She exercised, ate right, and got adequate sleep. The day of the race, she started out strong, but a little over halfway to her goal, she began to doubt. Did she have the strength to finish? She slowed her pace. People along the marathon route encouraged her to continue. "Go! Go! Go!" they shouted. She ran on with her heart pounding and her breath coming in gasps until she finished the race.

We prepare ourselves for our spiritual walks by reading the Bible, praying, and fellowshipping with other believers. When we are faithful, God empowers us to live for Him. Sometimes, though, we walk through difficult places, and we can begin to doubt. That's when we need fellow Christians to come alongside and remind us that we already have the strength to walk worthy of God.

You may be struggling today. You may be wondering if you can make it. You can. Like the runner, you've prepared yourself. Don't let doubts creep in. You can finish the race. God has already given you the strength and ability to walk worthy of Him. Go! Go! Go!

You don't win on emotion. You win on execution.
TONY DUNGY

GOOD TO ALL

As we have opportunity, let us do good to all,
especially to those who are of the household of faith.
GALATIANS 6:10

God created the church for us to work together to bring others to Him, to reach out, and to serve the world as no other group will. Some say the church can be compared to a hospital because sick people go there to get better. Jesus would agree. When the Pharisees asked why Jesus ate with sinners, He told them, "Those who are well have no need of a physician, but those who are sick" (Matthew 9:12).

A hospital is a place where you can go to receive medical care, if necessary. When we go to a hospital for surgery, it's because there is no other way to correct our condition. The lost are in need of spiritual surgery. They need to meet the Great Physician and allow Him to restore them to spiritual health and vitality.

When Paul admonishes us to "do good to all," it is a reminder that our "hospital" is open to all for healing. We need to remember to care for those in our church, as well as those we are trying to reach for Christ.

If the church would only be the church—
if Christians would only be Christians—
nothing could halt our onward march.
VANCE HAVNER

WHAT DO YOU DO?

By this My Father is glorified, that you bear
much fruit; so you will be My disciples.

JOHN 15:8

Question: What is probably the most-often asked question at social gatherings when strangers meet?

Answer: "So, what do you do?"

Asking about a person's job is a time-tested icebreaker, good for a couple of minutes of chitchat—double that amount if the question is reciprocated: "And what do *you* do?"

Actually, every Christian could answer the question with the exact same template: "I serve the Lord Jesus Christ by working as a (name your position)." As slaves of Jesus Christ (Romans 1:1, CEB), we really have only one job in life: to serve Him. We might go to many different venues for our vocations, but ultimately we are working for Him. As Christ came into the world to accomplish His Father's will (John 6:38), so we go into the world to accomplish Christ's will (Matthew 28:19-20; John 20:21). When we work for the Lord, we accomplish two things: earning our daily bread through our labor and extending the Kingdom of God by manifesting Christ's love and values to others.

So, what do *you* do? And how can you serve Christ today through your work?

He who disregards his calling will never keep
the straight path in the duties of his work.

JOHN CALVIN

CONSISTENCY

Teach me, O LORD, the way of Your statutes,
and I shall keep it to the end.

PSALM 119:33

Reese Kauffman, president of Child Evangelism Fellowship, grew up in a Christian home where certain habits were instilled at a young age. For example, his mother had a bedtime ritual that Reese has never gotten away from: brush your teeth and read your Bible. Every night during his formative years, he brushed his teeth and read a chapter in his Bible. Even as a young businessman who had gotten away from the Lord, Reese didn't abandon the habit. In fact, one night while Reese was reading Psalm 139 before bed, God spoke to him and got ahold of his life. Now years later, he still maintains the same ritual: brush your teeth and read your Bible.

Perhaps the most important aspect of Bible study is consistency. It's better to study a little in God's Word every day than to try to absorb lots of the Bible in random study. Find a pattern that works for you, and stick with it. Brush your teeth and read your Bible every day.

A lack of Bible study leads to "truth" decay.

UNKNOWN

IT'S BETTER TO GIVE

You Philippians know also that in the beginning of the gospel, when I departed . . . no church shared with me concerning giving and receiving but you only.

PHILIPPIANS 4:15

Hudson Taylor, the English preacher who pioneered missions in China, never asked for money to fund his work. Rather, he deeply believed that God would supply all his needs, and he prayed every day for His provision. God answered his prayers, and people gave timely gifts, which enabled Taylor to continue his ministry. Their support of a co-laborer with Christ helped bring God's Word to the Chinese.

God honored the generosity of these believers, as He does our giving. He appreciates an open heart that responds to ministry and enables others to do His work (2 Corinthians 9:7). As the apostle Paul writes in Philippians, such gifts are a fragrant offering, an acceptable sacrifice, well pleasing to God (4:18, NIV).

Ask God for opportunities to invest in His Kingdom work. This may mean doing more for your local church or for missions in other parts of the world. You may help the next Hudson Taylor and discover a valuable truth: it's better to give than to receive.

If the church marries herself to the spirit of the times, she will find herself a widow in the next generation.

CHARLES STANLEY

CAUGHT LIKE A MONKEY!

Where your treasure is, there your heart will be also.

MATTHEW 6:21

There's an ancient parable, "The Monkey's Fist," that teaches a profound lesson. Native tribes would hollow out coconuts, fill them with bait, then tether them to trees to lure monkeys. When a monkey would reach into the small opening of a coconut, his hand would fit. But once his fist was full of the bait, the monkey couldn't get his hand out and free himself. The lesson for all of us is that the coconut was not the monkey's undoing, but rather his greedy unwillingness to let go of the bait.

I know a lot of people like that. They clutch their material possessions so tightly in the attitude of their hearts that worry handicaps them, negatively impacting their faith, their family and friends, and their future. If only they would put God first, giving Him what belongs to Him—their time, talents, and treasures—then they could quit worrying about their future.

If you are grasping something tightly right now, you're in a trap and need to release your grip. There's not a better time to let go. Open your hands now. God has incredible gifts and resources for you—more than you could ever hold in your fists.

[God] doesn't look at just what we give.
He also looks at what we keep.*

RANDY ALCORN

---

*Randy Alcorn, *The Treasure Principle* (Colorado Springs: Multnomah Books, 2001), 65.

AN ODD OFFERING

*Every man shall give as he is able, according to the
blessing of the LORD your God which He has given you.*
DEUTERONOMY 16:17

An Atlanta-area church recently faced an interesting dilemma.
An anonymous attendee dropped an unusual gift into the
offering plate. It was the winning Georgia Lottery ticket worth
$80,000. Such an offering would generate a variety of opinions
in many churches. But most of us would agree on this—the secret
to sustained stewardship isn't in lotteries but in lordship.

If Jesus is Lord of all, He is Lord over our finances. He is Lord
over our income and our spending. He is Lord over our financial
involvement in His work. When we support ministries He lays
on our hearts, we're not really giving to those ministries. We're
giving to Him.

These are critical days for the Lord's work and for His workers. In many places, progress is faltering for lack of funds.
Perhaps too many Christians are overspending on themselves
when they should be economizing for the Kingdom. The cause
of Christ isn't going to be advanced by lottery tickets or lavish
lifestyles, but by the faithfulness of those who proclaim Him Lord
of all.

Giving is an act of worship, and so every worshipper
must be one of God's givers, whether rich or poor.
The mites God values as much as the millions.

A. T. PIERSON

SUSTAINED!

Cast your burden on the LORD, and He shall sustain you;
He shall never permit the righteous to be moved.

PSALM 55:22

Today's devotion is sponsored by two simple syllables: *sus • tain*. It's a word that means "to support, to hold, to bear up from beneath, to bear the weight of." Nehemiah 9:21 says about the Israelites, "Forty years You sustained them in the wilderness; they lacked nothing." The psalmist says, "I lay down and slept; I awoke, for the LORD sustained me" (Psalm 3:5). David promises that God will sustain the generous person even on a bed of sickness (Psalm 41:3).

Isaiah 46:4 says, "Even to your old age and gray hairs . . . I am he who will sustain you. I have made you and I will carry you; I will sustain you" (NIV).

Like the giant pillars of an unshakable bridge, the promises of God bear us up from beneath. His everlasting arms sustain us through every storm. A hymn by Anne Steele provides a good prayer for today: "My great protector, and my Lord, Thy constant aid impart; O let Thy kind, Thy gracious word sustain my trembling heart."

Under every condition, in every circumstance, for every
burden, in every need, through every sorrow, Christ,
the source and sustainer of life, is more than sufficient.*

A. L. FAUST

---

* "The Origin of Life—Science and Faith," *The Methodist Review*, no. 95 (January, 1913): 134.

BACKPACK LIVING

He who loves silver will not be satisfied with silver; nor he who loves abundance, with increase. This also is vanity.

ECCLESIASTES 5:10

With airlines charging us extra fees if we want to take our suitcase with us on vacation, more people are learning to take less. Even on overseas trips, many seasoned travelers pack little more than a change of clothes and a toothbrush. Garments can be washed out in a sink at night, and other supplies can be picked up as needed. Traveling with a half-empty backpack is a liberating adventure.

The same is true of life. The more we acquire, the more we have to take care of. Everything requires attention and maintenance. Costs increase. An escalating lifestyle brings accelerating pressure. Pretty soon our possessions possess us.

Rather than being upwardly mobile, why not deliberately downsize? Constantly declutter. Pour your money into eternal investments and live simply.

In the book of Ecclesiastes, Solomon admits that he found little lasting satisfaction in his houses, vineyards, orchards, servants, herds, tools, toys, and treasures (2:4-11). Real joy was found in the simplest acts of eating, drinking, and working hard (2:24).

For a better trip, throw a Bible in your backpack and travel light.

We are traveling on with our staff in hand. . . .
We are pilgrims bound for the heavenly land.

FANNY CROSBY

THE MESSAGE AND THE METHOD

*Your conduct [should be] honorable among the
Gentiles, that when they speak against you as
evildoers, they may, by your good works which they
observe, glorify God in the day of visitation.*

1 PETER 2:12

Churches are always looking for new methods for doing their ministry, and many Christians are eager to find the newest ways to share their faith. Good for us! We need to be geared to the times as we proclaim the unchanging message of Christ. We want to reach our contemporary culture, and every generation devises its own techniques and systems.

But wait!

Sometimes the methods don't have to change. God's primary means of evangelism is for people to see the hope of Christ in our daily lives and to ask us about it. We're to be ready to give an answer when that happens (1 Peter 3:15). God's method is to let our light shine before men so they can see our good works and glorify our heavenly Father (Matthew 5:16). Peter said, "Live such good lives among the pagans that . . . they may see your good deeds and glorify God" (1 Peter 2:12, NIV).

God's message is Christ. His method is you.

Men are God's method. The Church is looking for
better methods; God is looking for better men.

E. M. BOUNDS

TO LOVE AND SUPPORT

Mercy, peace, and love be multiplied to you.

JUDE 1:2

Has anyone ever told you, "I love seeing what God is doing in your life"?

Whether the words came from a church elder, spouse, or friend, you probably felt appreciated and wanted to share this kind of encouragement with others. Receiving this kind of love and support affirms us in our faith as well as in our lives.

In his day, Jonathan offered tremendous love to David. He made a covenant with his friend and handed over his robe, tunic, and sword to him as a symbol of his friendship (1 Samuel 18:1-4). This bond secured the love David needed to live out God's calling for his life, even in hardship and peril.

We can all learn from Jonathan—to deeply love our fellow believers and support what God is doing in their lives. None of us can be loved too much.

Is there someone you know who would welcome a blessing from you today? Seek out that person and say, "I'm behind you." Share words of blessing. By becoming a Jonathan who offers love and support, you'll be making a way for that person to help expand God's Kingdom.

The smallest good deed is better
than the grandest intention.

UNKNOWN

HEART AND HANDS

The peace of God, which surpasses all understanding,
will guard your hearts and minds through Christ Jesus.

PHILIPPIANS 4:7

The phrase "working in concert" is illustrated most beautifully by a concert orchestra itself. What a cacophony would be created if a hundred musicians, playing several dozen kinds of instruments, were all playing separate pieces! But by working in concert—playing the same score—they produce a work of beauty.

In the Christian life, heart and hands must work in concert to produce a life of peace. Our desires (the heart) and our actions (the hands) must be working toward the same goal, or tension and disharmony will cause peace to vanish. In Philippians 4:6-9, Paul talks about living a prayerful life free from anxiety (verses 6-7) and gives us themes on which the heart can settle in peace: true, noble, and virtuous things (verses 8-9). It does no good to pray for peace if we are fixing our minds on the conflicts and struggles of this world.

If you are seeking peace today, spend time meditating on Paul's words. Fix your heart, and then fold your hands in prayer— and receive God's peace.

We must never settle for harmony at the expense
of holiness, nor for peace at the expense of principle.

JOHN BRADFORD

DO YOU BELIEVE IT NOW?

Do not be deceived, God is not mocked;
for whatever a man sows, that he will also reap.
GALATIANS 6:7

Evangelist D. L. Moody had just started preaching a sermon on Galatians 6:7 when a man in the audience stood up and shouted, "I don't believe it."

Moody replied, "My friend, that doesn't change the fact. Truth is truth whether you believe it or not, and a lie is a lie whether you believe it or not." When the meeting broke up, a police officer was at the door to arrest the man on an outstanding warrant. He was convicted of theft and sent to prison for twelve months. Moody observed, "I really believe that when he got to his cell, he believed that he had to reap what he sowed."*

We reap what we sow, whether our actions are harmful or helpful. A wrong word, an immoral activity, an angry look—all these will likely bring negative results. On the other hand, a wise word, a spiritual activity, a smile, a word of witness, a gift, a gospel tract will produce good fruit. God promises that His Word will not return void (Isaiah 55:11).

The principle of the harvest is true in every aspect of our lives—we reap according to what we have sown.

The evil harvest of sin and the good harvest of
righteousness are as sure to follow the sowing as the
harvest of wheat and barley. "Life is not *casual*, but *causal*."

D. L. MOODY

---

*D. L. Moody, *Sowing and Reaping* (Ada, MI: Fleming Revell, 1896), 9–10.

HOW YOUR GARDEN GROWS

But this I say: He who sows sparingly will also reap sparingly,
and he who sows bountifully will also reap bountifully.

2 CORINTHIANS 9:6

In 2005 scientists germinated a date palm seed that was recovered from Herod the Great's palace atop Masada in the Judean wilderness—making it around 2,000 years old. And a 1,300-year-old lotus seed recovered from China was germinated in 1995. These remarkable examples of preservation, however, are more the exception than the rule. Seed companies today don't normally guarantee the viability of their seed for more than a few years.

Lots of things determine the quality of a harvest: the quality of the seed, the number of seeds sown, the quality of the soil, and the amounts of moisture and nutrients provided. The same is true with a spiritual harvest. No farmer would sow haphazardly and expect a beautiful, bountiful harvest. Neither should we. As we sow seeds of good works, financial investments, prayers, studies, service, and worship, we must focus on the quality of our "seeds."

As stewards, we have been entrusted with seeds to sow. And as we sow, so shall we reap.

Anyone can count the seeds in an apple, but only
God can count the number of apples in a seed.

ROBERT H. SCHULLER

PERFECT PEACE

You will keep him in perfect peace, whose mind
is stayed on You, because he trusts in You.

ISAIAH 26:3

Isaiah 26:3 is one of the Old Testament's most beloved verses: a promise of peace made possible by remaining focused on God. But it's the context of this promise that makes it so inviting. Israel was anticipating the Day of the Lord, when God would rain down judgment upon His people's enemies. Although their present circumstances were full of turmoil, the Israelites had no reason to be anxious. Rather, they were to keep their minds "stayed" (focused steadfastly) on the strength of God.

The image of battles is a good one for all who desire to keep their hearts and minds in peace. Christians are in a battle, for sure (2 Corinthians 10:3-6; Ephesians 6:10-18). We battle against principalities and powers that would seek to take our minds off the God of our salvation. Anything the devil can do to make us doubt God's love, Christ's sufficiency, and the power of the Holy Spirit, he will do. Peace is kept by staying focused on who God is and what God says.

Today, before heading into battle, focus your mind on the great and precious promises of God by which you will be kept in perfect peace.

It is in the way of truth that real peace is found.

CHARLES H. SPURGEON

A POWERHOUSE OF PROMISES

*His divine power has given to us all things that pertain to
life and godliness, through the knowledge of Him who
called us by glory and virtue, by which have been given
to us exceedingly great and precious promises.*

2 PETER 1:3-4

Hundreds of promises are given in Scripture to believers who choose to live in obedience to God's Word. This heavenly bank of promises is powerful and purposeful for *all* our needs. When God provides for us, He gives lavishly from His riches. But we need to remember that God supplies all our needs, not our "greeds."

The apostle Paul explained God's heavenly bank this way: "My God [His promise is positive] shall supply [His promise is pointed] all your need [His promise is plentiful] according to His riches in glory by Christ Jesus" (Philippians 4:19). Notice that God doesn't supply "out of" His riches, but "according to" His riches in glory. We give our tithes and offerings "out of" available funds in the bank. God gives commensurate with His riches. His bank is colossal.

What are a couple of God's promises that are dearest to you at this point in your life? How can you live so that those you come in contact with daily will be drawn to the power and purpose of God's promises in you?

The future is as bright as the promises of God.

ADONIRAM JUDSON

LOVE CONQUERS FEAR

God has not given us a spirit of fear,
but of power and of love and of a sound mind.

2 TIMOTHY 1:7

Power, love, and a sound mind will conquer fear every time, especially when we recognize that the power and the love have their source in the God who resurrected Jesus from the dead and destroyed death forever.

Paul reminds us in 2 Timothy 1 that we can conquer fear and timidity by keeping our focus on the power and love that Jesus Christ has for us. It takes self-discipline to conquer fear, but when we step out boldly to serve Him, disciplining ourselves to think "sound" or wholesome thoughts, we are no longer driven by fear.

As you answer God's call to serve Him faithfully, discipline your thoughts to remember His strength and His love for you. Focus on the power there is in trusting every part of your life to Him. Then you can say with David, "Though war break out against me, even then I will be confident" (Psalm 27:3, NIV).

Our doubts are traitors and make us lose the
good we oft might win by fearing to attempt.

WILLIAM SHAKESPEARE

ROLL UP YOUR SLEEVES

Whatever you do, do it heartily,
as to the Lord and not to men.
COLOSSIANS 3:23

Batwing, raglan, dolman, puffed, set-in, butterfly, paned, hanging, bell—these are styles of sleeves worn throughout history. The expression of someone "having something up his sleeve" refers to an Oriental-style hanging sleeve that was also used as a pocket. Hardworking folks can be spotted by their rolled-up sleeves as they work to accomplish their tasks.

Somehow, the idea of "working hard" as a Christian is lost on many believers, as if spiritual work should never be strenuous. Such a perspective might have drawn a stern correction from a hard worker like the apostle Paul. Not only did he set an example of giving one's all in service to Christ but he also exhorted his readers to follow his example. We are to work heartily and be "steadfast, immovable, always abounding in the work of the Lord" (1 Corinthians 15:58).

Today, figuratively, if not literally, roll up your sleeves for the Kingdom's sake!

The reason some people do not recognize
opportunity when they meet it is because it
usually comes disguised as hard work.

UNKNOWN

GOOD COMPANY

Thanks be to God who puts the same earnest
care for you into the heart of Titus. . . . He is my
partner and fellow worker concerning you.

2 CORINTHIANS 8:16, 23

When mountain climbers scale a high peak, they go in teams. When scuba divers plunge into deep seas, they go in pairs. Why? They realize the necessity of sticking together in their pursuits.

The apostle Paul followed the same principle in his missionary journeys. Whether he was sailing the Mediterranean or traveling through Asia Minor, he always had someone to work with in ministry—Barnabas, Silas, Titus, Timothy. Paul made an investment in each one. He mentored and challenged them to live out God's purpose for their lives. And at the right time, these men moved on to equip others.

When it comes to ministry, we never have to go it alone. God has given us co-laborers, people whom we can take a deep interest in and spur on to great things. Take a look around you. Find someone in your church you can support and challenge as a partner in the gospel.

Through a faithful investment in others, you can partner with someone and climb higher or dive deeper into God's ministry.

The truth is that teamwork is
at the heart of great achievement.

JOHN MAXWELL

ENLIGHTENMENT

The statutes of the LORD are right,
rejoicing the heart; the commandment of
the LORD is pure, enlightening the eyes.

PSALM 19:8

In your daily Bible reading, have there been times when certain words appeared to jump off the page in neon colors? Not literally, of course, but in terms of impact. Perhaps it was just a simple phrase, but it was what you needed, and it provided a boost you've never forgotten.

The psalmist says that God's Word enlightens our eyes. Ezra 9:8 says that God gives grace to "enlighten our eyes and give us a measure of revival." Paul told his friends he was praying that their understanding would be enlightened so they would know "what is the hope of His calling" (Ephesians 1:18).

"There is nothing like reading an illuminated Bible," said Charles Spurgeon. "You may read to all eternity, and never learn anything by it, unless it is illuminated by the Spirit; and then the words shine forth like stars. The book seems made of gold leaf; every single letter glitters like a diamond. Oh, it is a blessed thing to read an illuminated Bible lit up by the radiance of the Holy Ghost."

This year, read God's Word prayerfully and expectantly.

Let me tell you a little secret:
whenever you cannot understand a text, open your
Bible, bend your knee, and pray over that text.

CHARLES H. SPURGEON

TRUE STRENGTH

He said to me, "My grace is sufficient for you,
for My strength is made perfect in weakness."
Therefore most gladly I will rather boast in my infirmities,
that the power of Christ may rest upon me.

2 CORINTHIANS 12:9

The *American Heritage Dictionary* defines a paradox as "a statement that seems to contradict itself but may nonetheless be true." And the New Testament gives us several good examples: we receive by giving, we live by dying, and we become great by becoming small.

One of the most important paradoxes for Christian living is found in the apostle Paul's experience with weakness and strength. When he found himself to be weak, he asked God to remove the weakness so he could once again be strong enough to serve. But instead of removing the weakness, God gave Paul grace to experience the strength and power of Jesus Christ in his life. It was when Paul was willing to be humanly weak that he was in the right place to experience the strength of Christ. And therein lies the paradox: we become strong (in Christ) as we recognize our own human weakness and depend more on Him and less on ourselves.

Today, exercise, eat healthily, sleep well. But remember that your true strength is the strength of Jesus.

Real true faith is man's weakness
leaning on God's strength.

D. L. MOODY

OPEN HANDS

Remember the words of the Lord Jesus,
that He said, "It is more blessed to give than to receive."

ACTS 20:35

Try this object lesson with a child. Have him hold out both hands, palms up, and put a nickel in each palm. Tell him to close his fists tight and keep them closed no matter what you say. Now tell him you're very poor and need some money. Ask if you can have his two coins. No—he's holding them tightly. Then tell him you're very rich and would like to give him two quarters to replace his two nickels. Ask if you can replace his nickels with quarters. No—he's still holding tight.

The illustration shows us what we sometimes fail to recognize: a closed hand misses two blessings in life. A closed hand cannot enjoy the blessing of giving to others who are in need, nor can a closed hand receive blessings God may want to bestow. He gives to us not only to meet our needs but also to teach us to give as Christ gave—fully, generously, and unconditionally.

Prayerfully hold out both open hands in front of you and present them to the Lord for His pleasure—to give or receive.

Our heavenly father never takes anything from His children
unless He means to give them something better.

GEORGE MÜLLER

WALKING BY FAITH

We walk by faith, not by sight.

2 CORINTHIANS 5:7

Imagine you've gone through a difficult experience in your life and you're fearful of what the future might hold. To encourage you, a friend says, "You can do it, one day at a time. Remember: just walk by religion, not by sight." Walk by religion? To a biblically literate Christian, the very sound of that phrase is off-putting, to say the least.

You probably know what Paul really said in 2 Corinthians 5:7: "We walk by faith, not by sight." But even the idea of walking by faith seems contrary to common sense. If we walked by religion, we would at least have a tangible structure—things that are seen—to pin our hopes on: buildings, traditions, schedules, liturgies, ministers, and the like. If we walk by faith, we have only the promises of God. But we also have "the evidence of things not seen" (Hebrews 11:1). We not only have God's promises but we also have the evidence from thousands of years of history that He has kept His promises to those who trust Him. And He will keep His promises for you.

If you are facing an uncertain future (and who isn't?), remember to walk by faith—faith in the God who promises He "will never leave you nor forsake you" (Hebrews 13:5).

Walking by faith means being prepared to trust
where we are not permitted to see.

JOHN BLANCHARD

THE RELIEF OF FORGIVENESS

Forgive us our debts, as we forgive our debtors.

MATTHEW 6:12

In this age of financial crisis, newspapers are full of articles about loans being "forgiven." The debt loads of entire nations are sometimes forgiven. There's talk about student loans being forgiven, or homeowners being forgiven for unpaid mortgages, or institutions being forgiven because they are "too big to fail." But one financial expert warned that there's no such thing as free forgiveness. Someone has to bear the burden of the debt.

Regarding our sins and souls, Jesus paid it all. We come to Him with a load of guilt and confess all our regrets. We tell Him about that moment of foolishness that causes shame. We admit the stupid thing we did or said. The tragedy we caused. The hurt we inflicted.

As we confess it, He forgives it. As we lay it before Him, He washes it away with the blood of Calvary. What God has forgiven should no longer have dominion over our minds. In the blood of Jesus, we have relief from our captivity of guilt and fear. As the hymn says, it's nailed to the cross, and we bear it no more.

There is unspeakable joy . . . for the person who knows release from guilt and the relief of forgiveness.*

STUART BRISCOE

---

*Stuart Briscoe, *The One Year Book of Devotions for Men* (Carol Stream, IL: Tyndale, 2000), 37.

FOR LOVE'S SAKE

Without your consent I wanted to do nothing,
that your good deed might not be by
compulsion, as it were, but voluntary.

PHILEMON 1:14

In Roman times, a wealthy man named Philemon lived in the Colosse region of Asia Minor. One day his slave Onesimus ran away after stealing some money. The fugitive trekked to Rome, where he met the apostle Paul and was converted to Christ. Paul sent him home with one of the shortest and most personal letters in our Bible—the epistle to Philemon. In it, the apostle exhorts Philemon to consider Onesimus "no longer as a slave but more than a slave—a beloved brother" (verse 16). Paul hints he would like to have Onesimus helping him in his ministry, but he stops short of using his authority to order Philemon to comply. "Though I might be very bold in Christ to command you . . . , yet for love's sake I rather appeal to you" (verses 8-9).

The Lord longs for us to obey because we *want* to, not because we *have* to. Some religions codify what must be done to others, but true charity comes from the heart. Let's serve God faithfully because we long to please Him each day.

We must constantly examine our own lives to insure
that proper actions are produced by proper motives.

JAMES A. BORLAND

FEBRUARY

AN ATTITUDE OF GRATITUDE

I thank my God always concerning you for the grace
of God which was given to you by Christ Jesus.
1 CORINTHIANS 1:4

How we love to hear words of appreciation! If you've ever felt taken for granted, you understand the importance of expressing appreciation to those around you. Whether it's the mom who hopes to hear, "Thanks for the great dinner, Mom" or a hardworking employee who wonders if his diligence is noticed, everyone needs to hear that he or she is appreciated.

The encouragement that comes from the expression of appreciation nurtures our souls. This attitude of gratitude is so important that Jesus told a special parable just to emphasize it.

Remember the ten lepers in Luke 17? Ten were healed, but only one returned to say thank you. The one who came back to Jesus to express his gratitude is the one Jesus commends as exemplary. As you look around, you will see people in your life who have gone out of their way to invest in you, to provide for you, or to be a blessing to you. Take a moment today to thank them.

Hem your blessings with thankfulness
so they don't unravel.

UNKNOWN

FIND A QUIET PLACE

When He had sent the multitudes away,
He went up on the mountain by Himself to pray.
Now when evening came, He was alone there.

MATTHEW 14:23

Are you addicted to Twitter, constantly describing your status in 280 characters or less and subscribing to others' updates? Even if you're not addicted, a lot of people apparently are. Plenty of websites describe signs of Twitter addiction and how to recover if you are so afflicted.

Social media sites, texting, email, the Internet, twenty-four-hour news cycles on radio and television—it's almost impossible to find a place to be alone with your own thoughts. And if you do find yourself in a silent place, it's only because you turned off or left behind those devices that are designed to keep you occupied with "critical" information around the clock.

The information you receive from God and His Word is more important than anything else you might hear. As your Creator and Heavenly Father, God wants to meet with you in a quiet place.

Turn off the distractions and meet alone with the Father who waits for you.

The time will come when winter will ask
what you were doing all summer.

HENRY CLAY

THE BEST DO REST

They ought always to pray and not lose heart.
LUKE 18:1, ESV

When we think of modern public health crises, insufficient sleep probably doesn't come to mind. But the lack of a good night's sleep is linked to astounding numbers of motor vehicle crashes, industrial disasters, and medical and occupational errors. Feeling sleepy? Can't get to sleep? Besides endangering yourself and others, you're also vulnerable to the disparaging influence of discouragement.

"Fatigue makes cowards of us all," quipped the great American football coach Vince Lombardi—and I can identify. How many times have you fallen vulnerable to discouragement when you're extremely tired? Even Jesus couldn't work 24-7. Withdrawing to a quiet place, He prayed. Minds and bodies dulled from lack of sleep and constant activity are hindered from radiating God's powerful love.

If you're discouraged today, set aside time from your busy schedule, and tell God how you feel. Spend time in the Word. Also, get a good night's sleep. When you awake, you'll be refreshed and energized to continue the work you're doing for God.

Rest time is not waste time. It is economy to gather
fresh strength. . . . It is wisdom to take occasional furlough.
In the long run, we shall do more by sometimes doing less.

CHARLES H. SPURGEON

FELLOWSHIP IN LONELINESS

I am with you always, even to the end of the age.
MATTHEW 28:20

Different types of loneliness invade our lives. Standing at the gravestone of a loved one, we feel the pang of separation. When there are no messages on our cell phones, we long to hear the voice of someone who cares.

Whether you're a pastor, ministry leader, spouse, parent, or child, you have likely experienced loneliness somewhere along life's journey. If you ache with loneliness, remember that you're in good company. The Bible gives abundant examples of lonely saints.

Even the apostle Paul, an incredibly gifted and blessed man, was not immune to loneliness. He was taken to heaven and shown things too wonderful to share with earthly beings. He authored much of the New Testament and founded all the missionary churches during New Testament times. But on occasion, he ached with loneliness: "At my first defense no one stood with me, but all forsook me" (2 Timothy 4:16).

Today you may encounter a lonely person hiding behind a smile. If you were that person, how would you hope to be greeted? Friendship is a sure antidote to a lonely soul. Be cheerful medicine to someone today.

The next time you find yourself alone . . . stand still,
whisper [God's] name, and listen. He is nearer than you think.

MAX LUCADO

DOING WHAT HE DID

Moreover it is required in stewards
that one be found faithful.

1 CORINTHIANS 4:2

Whether they realize it or not, children are stewards of things given by their parents: time, possessions, food, and more. It is the parents' responsibility to help their children make wise decisions about how to use these resources—in other words, how to be good stewards of the gifts that have been given to them.

All human beings were created to be stewards of the gifts of God: life, breath, talents, resources, relationships, and the creation in which we live (Genesis 1:28). Christians have been made stewards of even more: the grace of God, spiritual gifts, and the gospel, for example. As Christians we are to use our resources to accomplish what Jesus Christ would do in our place. And He said, "The Son of Man has come to seek and to save that which was lost" (Luke 19:10).

The question is: Are we being good stewards? We should be doing the same thing Christ would do in our place—seeking and saving the lost.

Stewardship is what a man does after he says, "I believe."

W. H. GREAVES

A CHANGE OF HEART

*I will give you a new heart and put a new spirit within
you; I will take the heart of stone out of your flesh
and give you a heart of flesh. I will put My Spirit
within you and cause you to walk in My statutes.*

EZEKIEL 36:26-27

A few years ago, a New York woman lost her chance for a heart transplant because of shoplifting. She had been freed from prison so she could go on the transplant waiting list, but before a donor became available, the woman stole $500 in toiletry items and ended up in jail again. She was no longer qualified for a transplant.

This woman is emblematic of the millions of people who forfeit the new heart God offers them. The Bible teaches that God wants to exchange our heart of stone for a new heart, a heart that is forgiven and tender and will beat forever in heaven. It's a gift of grace to be received through faith in God.

Having a change of heart doesn't just mean we've shifted our opinion or altered our attitude. It truly means that we have changed hearts. Don't forfeit your new heart. If you don't know Jesus as Savior and Lord, ask Him to give you a new heart today.

Give me a new, a perfect heart,
from doubt, and fear, and sorrow free.

CHARLES WESLEY

GET OFF THE BENCH!

*Be doers of the word, and not hearers only,
deceiving yourselves.*

JAMES 1:22

Imagine paying $1,000 or more for a ticket to the Super Bowl. You arrive at the stadium, brimming with excitement about the big game. Everywhere around you, the pieces are in place for the big showdown. Vendors hawk food of every kind, the crowd is enthusiastic, and the television crews are prepped and waiting for the kickoff. You anticipate victory for your favorite team, and you're even sporting their colors to show your loyalty.

The teams come out to the roar of wild cheers and complete their pregame rituals with boisterous confidence. Everything is ready for the contest to begin, but no one takes the field. Both teams remain on the sidelines. The crowd begins to jeer and taunt, but the players remain seated.

The teams have prepared for this day. The athletes have all they need to go out and play the biggest game of the year. But they are content to stay on the bench.

Think of your church as the Super Bowl. God wants to win a great victory in your community and in the world, but He needs you to become a dedicated and serious player first. Are you sitting on the bench? If so, it's time to stand up and get in the game!

The only thing necessary for the triumph
of evil is for good men to do nothing.

EDMUND BURKE

SOMEONE IS COMING

We should live . . . looking for the blessed hope and glorious appearing of our great God and Savior Jesus Christ.

TITUS 2:12-13

Christopher and Brandy, a couple from Seattle, were about four hundred miles from Hawaii in their thirty-eight-foot boat when high seas threatened to sink their vessel. They broke out their life rafts, put on survival suits, and used their radio to send a distress signal with their location—then huddled together with their two dogs to wait. The crew from the cruise ship *Golden Princess* heard the distress call and were able to rescue the couple and their dogs. Brandy said, "I knew someone would come out. I just didn't know how long it would take."

That's the perspective Christians should have when they find themselves in the middle of the storms of life: even if we don't know when, we know Someone is going to come. That Someone is Jesus Christ, of course—and His coming is called the "blessed hope and glorious appearing" in Titus 2. We persevere through the challenges of this life because our hope is built on the certainty of Christ's return. This world is not our home; we are just passing through.

When the waves get high, keep your eyes on the heavens for the One who has promised to come.

The only revelation from God which Christians still await is the revelation of Jesus Christ at His second coming.

GEOFFREY B. WILSON

READ ME

Seek first the kingdom of God and His righteousness,
and all these things shall be added to you.

MATTHEW 6:33

In the early days of software development, PC software would normally come with a text document titled "READ ME." This document explained anything the user needed to know about installation, late changes to the software that didn't make it into the manual, system requirements, or possible incompatibility issues. In other words, READ ME first—before installing the software—in order to avoid problems.

God's READ ME file is found in Matthew 6:33: "Seek first the kingdom of God." All who aspire to enter and dwell in the Kingdom of God need to know this: if you put God and His Kingdom first in your life's priorities, everything else necessary in life will be added to you. You will be able to trust that God will provide for you.

If you want to avoid worries with your software, look at the READ ME file first. If you want to avoid worries in your life, seek God's Kingdom first.

Worry is an indication that we think God cannot look after us.

OSWALD CHAMBERS

MAYONNAISE ON THE ROAD

You enlarged my path under me; so my feet did not slip.

2 SAMUEL 22:37

You may not consider mayonnaise to be a travel hazard, but when a load of mayo fell off a truck in the Hyogo prefecture of Japan, the spill caused an eight-car pileup, resulting in three injuries and a five-hour road closure. Because mayo contains eggs, vinegar, and oil, the shattered bottles created a slippery stretch of highway that police said was slicker than snow.

The highway of life can get slippery too. Sometimes we have to navigate tricky stretches, such as choosing to do what's right when those around us disagree; other times we encounter bends in the road with unexpected changes. But finding the right pathway is vital, and Jesus is the only Way. Proverbs 3:6 (NIV) says that God will lead us and make our ways straight. We can trust that God will direct our paths and help us get through the slick patches.

The most important thing about life's journey is being on the right road so our feet don't slide and our footsteps are secure.

Revival is just you and I walking along the Highway in complete oneness with the Lord Jesus and with one another, with cups continually cleansed and overflowing.*

ROY HESSION

---

*Roy Hession, *The Calvary Road* (Fort Washington, PA: CLC, 2000), 55–56.

ERASED

*As far as the east is from the west, so far has
He removed our transgressions from us.*

PSALM 103:12

"Guilty!" your subconscious whispers to you as you agonize over a past sin. Sometimes portrayed morbidly through paintings and music, guilt can be a devastating emotion. But for Christians, guilt should drive us to confession and forgiveness.

King David was a man after God's own heart, yet he succumbed to adultery. Whatever fleeting enjoyment he experienced with Bathsheba was annihilated by the agony of his guilt. And in his quest to cover up his sin, murder was committed. When David finally confessed his sin, God stepped in and offered His forgiveness.

Writing to the Colossian church, the apostle Paul portrayed God's forgiveness as "having wiped out the handwriting of requirements that was against us" (Colossians 2:14). The Greek word used for *handwriting* refers to the handwritten certificate of debt signed by a debtor. In Colossians Paul is saying that, just as wiping ink off a piece of parchment erases a debt, God's forgiveness permanently erases our sin.

Don't allow lingering sin to rob you of the blessings that are yours in Christ.

Your debt has been erased.

Sins are so remitted, as if they had never been committed.*

THOMAS ADAMS

---

*Thomas Adams, *A Puritan Golden Treasury* (compiled by I.D.E. Thomas by permission of Banner of Truth, Carlisle, PA, 2000), 110.

THE RIGHT WORDS

[The Lord said,] "My wrath is aroused against you
and your two friends, for you have not spoken of
Me what is right, as My servant Job has."

JOB 42:7

Imagine receiving directions to a friend's house in the form of a hand-drawn map. You trust in the hastily drawn lines, following them to what you believe is the right destination, only to end up dreadfully lost! Had you consulted an authentic road map, you might have seen that side road your friend forgot to draw. What he believed was correct sent you in the wrong direction.

When we encourage and comfort our friends, we want to be very sure that we use the best map—the Word of God! When Job was suffering, his friends started out well in their efforts to comfort him, but when they began to rely on their own wisdom, they took a wrong turn.

Our encouragement must include wise biblical counsel—the truth that comes straight from the heart and mind of God. When we rely on human truth, we offer our friends a false road map that will send them in the wrong direction. Encourage and comfort your friends today by using the truth found in God's Word.

God does not always provide explanations for your
difficulties, but He does provide the promises of His Word.

WARREN W. WIERSBE

CHANGING YOUR MIND

Do not be conformed to this world, but be transformed
by the renewing of your mind, that you may prove what
is that good and acceptable and perfect will of God.

ROMANS 12:2

The best way to change your life is to change your thinking. And the best way to change your thinking is to change your mental diet. What does a healthy mental diet include? Psalm 37:3 tells us to "feed on His faithfulness." Jeremiah 15:16 says, "Your words were found, and I ate them, and Your word was to me the joy and rejoicing of my heart." We can always ask Jesus to give us good nutrition. In John, He promises to lead us to find pasture (10:9).

If a spiritual dietitian analyzed what goes into your mind each day, what would the report say? What proportion of your mental food is godly and scriptural? While it's sometimes very hard to control our thoughts, it's not so hard to control what we're allowing into our minds. Improving our mental diet enriches our thinking, elevates our attitudes, and renews our spirits. Cut out the junk and fill your mind with whatever is true, noble, just, pure, lovely, and of good report (Philippians 4:8).

The remarkable thing is, we have a choice every day
regarding the attitude we will embrace for that day.

CHUCK SWINDOLL

THE NATURE OF GOD'S LOVE

Greater love has no one than this,
than to lay down one's life for his friends.

JOHN 15:13

The 1970 film *Love Story* became famous for the words "Love means never having to say you're sorry." That line is just one of many ways people have described love through the years. But Jesus Christ gave us the best example of true love. That kind of love is manifested by one person being willing to lay down his or her life for a friend. Although ultimately, "to lay down one's life" means "to die," we can also show true love by laying down our own desires, time, or opinions. True love is giving of oneself for a friend.

John 3:16 says that God loved the whole world. But John 15:13 says that Jesus loves *you* personally, because as His follower, you are His friend (John 15:14-15). If you ever feel small in light of the entire world, you can erase that feeling by taking Jesus' words to heart. You are His friend if you are His follower, and He laid down His life for you.

Our love to God is measured by our everyday
fellowship with others and the love it displays.

ANDREW MURRAY

WATCH AND PRAY

When He came to the place, [Jesus] said to them,
"Pray that you may not enter into temptation."
LUKE 22:40

In his letter to the Ephesians, the apostle Paul uses the armor of a Roman soldier as a metaphor for the believer's spiritual armor: belt, helmet, breastplate, sword, shoes, and shield. But Paul includes something in the Christian's preparation for spiritual battle that he did not draw from the Roman military: prayer. After describing the armor, Paul adds, "Praying always with all prayer and supplication in the Spirit, being watchful to this end with all perseverance and supplication for all the saints" (Ephesians 6:18).

That prayer language mirrors what Jesus said to His disciples in the garden of Gethsemane on the night of His arrest and trial. Jesus had just warned Peter about the coming temptation to deny Him (Luke 22:31-34) and the disciples about the opposition they would face (verses 35-38). As the hour of His trial grew near, Jesus admonished the disciples—twice—to pray lest they succumb to the temptations to deny Him and flee from persecution.

Waiting until the battle is underway is waiting too late to fight. Fighting begins on our knees as we call upon God for victory over temptation.

Christian, seek not yet repose; cast thy dreams of ease away; thou art in the midst of foes: watch and pray.

CHARLOTTE ELLIOTT

THE SURPRISE OF GOD'S LOVE

God demonstrates His own love toward us, in that while we were still sinners, Christ died for us.

ROMANS 5:8

Jesus shocked His Jewish audience when He replaced the non-biblical idea of hating one's enemies with the idea of loving them (Matthew 5:43-44). The Jewish tradition of hating one's enemies had achieved Scripture-like status among the Jews—a status Jesus debunked.

The apostle Paul takes that teaching a step further when he points out that it would be a rare occasion when someone might die for another person—even a righteous person (Romans 5:7), much less an enemy. Who would die for an enemy? God did, Paul says. God demonstrated His love for us—His enemies (Romans 5:10; Colossians 1:21)—by dying for us. So when God says, "I love *you*," He is saying He chose to love someone who, before being reconciled to Him through faith in Christ, was His enemy. What a shock to the world's system! The world thinks it's normal to love our friends but not to love our enemies. Yet God's love is countercultural again.

God loves both His friends and enemies, as should we. If there is someone unlovely in your life today, surprise him or her with your love.

You never so touch the ocean of God's love as when you forgive and love your enemies.

CORRIE TEN BOOM

ECONOMY OF THE HEART

*Bearing with one another, and forgiving one
another, if anyone has a complaint against another;
even as Christ forgave you, so you also must do.*

COLOSSIANS 3:13

In his book *The Gift of Forgiveness*, Charles Stanley writes, "Forgiveness is something each of us has had to deal with one way or another. What might take you just a short time to work through might be a process that takes someone else time, prayer, and godly counsel. But it is a process we cannot ignore, not if we want to be free to become the persons God created us to be."*

Stanley goes on to say that if we refuse to deal with the bitterness and resentments that put us in bondage, we cannot have the fellowship with our Father we are supposed to have.

It's not easy to forgive another person. Some wounds are deep and last for decades. But hatred and bitterness are bars that imprison us. When we place the other person in God's hands and release the bitterness to Him, we're set free, just as truly as if we were released from jail.

Forgiveness is the economy of the heart. A Christian will
find it cheaper to pardon than to resent. Forgiveness saves
the expense of anger, the cost of hatred, the waste of spirits.

HANNAH MORE

*Charles Stanley, *The Gift of Forgiveness* (Nashville: Thomas Nelson, 1991), 105.

WHOSE IMAGE?

Whose image and inscription is this?

MATTHEW 22:20

More than 40 percent of Americans between the ages of twenty-six and forty have a tattoo. However, many people come to regret their tattoos, and that has spawned a new and thriving business—tattoo removal.

But some things cannot be reversed. One day, the dreaded "mark of the beast" will be stamped on the foreheads or hands of those worshiping the Antichrist, and no laser will be able to remove it. How much better to have the image of Christ stamped on our hearts.

As Christians, we're to be conformed to the image of God's Son (Romans 8:29). We're to bear the image of Christ (1 Corinthians 15:49). As we behold the glory of the Lord, we're transformed into His image from glory to glory by the Spirit (2 Corinthians 3:18).

Jesus once taught a lesson by observing the image on a coin (Matthew 22:19-22). In the same way, our worth is determined by whose image is stamped on our lives. The hymn "O to Be Like Thee" has a prayer for us: "Come in Thy sweetness, come in Thy fullness; stamp Thine own image deep on my heart."

Adam's likeness now efface; stamp Thine image in its place.

CHARLES WESLEY

HAVING EARS TO HEAR

*News of these things came to the ears of the church
in Jerusalem, and they sent out Barnabas to go as far
as Antioch. When he came and had seen the grace
of God, he was glad, and encouraged them all.*

ACTS 11:22-23

Have you ever noticed that sometimes children seem to have selective hearing? Their parents can ask them to pick up their toys, brush their teeth, or finish their homework, but there is no response. Either they aren't listening or they don't want to do what is being asked of them.

Fortunately, the congregation in Jerusalem didn't have the same hearing problem. When the church members found out about the wonderful work happening in Antioch, they didn't turn a deaf ear. They acted promptly and sent Barnabas there to build up the believers and encourage them to remain true to God. This kind of support spurred on the believers in Antioch to carry on their mission.

Our churches can be like the one in Jerusalem by listening to what God is doing locally and around the world. We can then discern how we can be involved—in finances, prayer, or support— with those He's sending out. Let's listen to what God is asking us to do.

Unity is necessary among the children of God if we are going
to know the flow of power . . . to see God do His wonders.

A. W. TOZER

CHANGING DIRECTIONS

Jonah arose to flee to Tarshish from the presence of the LORD.

JONAH 1:3

Nothing's more terrifying than seeing a car racing toward you going the wrong way on the freeway. At that moment, many lives are in danger. According to the most recent figures, over 1,700 people die annually in the United States from crashes caused by drivers traveling the wrong way on a highway. Statistics indicate that two-thirds of those wrong-way drivers are drunk. Others take the wrong ramp onto the highway. Maybe some are fleeing the police.

It's always dangerous to go the wrong way. It didn't work out very well for Jonah, and it won't work out for us. Is your life headed in the wrong direction? Has Satan gotten the better of your judgment? Do you need to make some changes?

Don't be like the man who said he was making a 360-degree change. Turn exactly 180 degrees. Repent of any and all sin. Rededicate yourself to Jesus Christ in body, mind, and soul. As Ezekiel 33:11 says, "Turn, turn from your evil ways! For why should you die, O house of Israel?"

Let the Lord help you get out of the wrong lane today.

Repentance is one of the most positive words in
any language. It tells us we can change direction.
It assures us God will help us improve.

ROBERT J. MORGAN

THE PERMANENCE OF GOD'S LOVE

Who shall separate us from the love of Christ?
ROMANS 8:35

Separation anxiety" is defined as the fear or dread felt by a person at the prospect of being separated from a beneficial relationship or environment. It becomes a disorder when such anxiety impairs one's ability to function normally. The great reformer Martin Luther might have suffered from such anxiety at the prospect of being separated from God due to his own sinfulness. Only his discovery that a relationship with God is sustained by faith, not works (Romans 1:17), set Martin Luther free from his anxiety.

No Christian should ever fear being separated from the love of God. That is the clear testimony of God Himself written in His inspired Word. Living in a world of imperfect love and failing relationships, we may find it challenging to rest in a love so pure and so permanent. But God's love is indeed pure and permanent. Paul exhausted his creativity trying to think of something that could come between us and God's love—and he failed (Romans 8:38-39)!

"Be anxious for nothing," Paul writes in Philippians 4:6—and that includes the permanence of God's love.

The true measure of God's love is that
He loves without measure.

UNKNOWN

GOOD QUESTIONS

So [Thomas] said to them, "Unless I see in His
hands the print of the nails . . . and put my
hand into His side, I will not believe."

JOHN 20:25

The disciple named Thomas is usually referred to as "doubting Thomas" because of his insistence on walking by sight, not by faith, regarding the resurrection of Jesus. But let's not be too hard on Thomas. There are many aspects of biblical experience that stretch the rational mind. The Bible is not *irr*ational, but it can be *trans*rational—asking us to believe things that transcend our understanding (the Virgin Birth, miracles, the resurrection of Christ, and so on).

Let's give Thomas credit for being honest enough to articulate his doubts in precise language. He wanted to see the resurrected Christ—and evidence that it was really Him—before he committed himself to such a revolutionary event. Thomas would have had a problem if, after seeing Christ (John 20:26-27), he still refused to believe. It's one thing to ask for evidence or understanding; it's another to reject the evidence or understanding.

God is not threatened by our doubts. He is the One who says, "Come now, and let us reason together" (Isaiah 1:18).

Turn your doubts to questions; turn your questions
to prayers; turn your prayers to God.

MARK LITTLETON

LEARNING TO FORGIVE

You shall know the truth,
and the truth shall make you free.

JOHN 8:32

When we forgive someone, we're not minimizing the harm the person caused nor condoning the sin that was committed. We're simply choosing to place the offense in the nail-scarred hands of Christ.

In his book *Forgiveness . . . The Ultimate Miracle*, Paul J. Meyer shares a story about a woman named Renee who hated her father because of long-term abuse. When Renee became a Christian at the age of forty-one, she faced a dilemma. She knew she'd been forgiven of all her sins through Christ, but she had no desire to forgive her father. As she studied the Bible, however, she began to realize that forgiveness isn't a feeling but a requirement. One day she prayed to God: "I, Renee, release my father into your loving arms. Please release me from the bondage of unforgiveness." Her attitude toward her dad began to change, and so did his own heart. He eventually confessed Christ as his Savior and was baptized at the age of eighty-four.

Learning to forgive others helps both the forgiven and the forgiver.

Forgiveness does not mean we have to allow
ourselves to be mistreated. . . . [It] does mean that
we allow God to work in our lives and in the lives of
the people against whom we hold bitterness.*

PAUL J. MEYER

---

*Paul J. Meyer, *Forgiveness . . . The Ultimate Miracle* (Orlando: Bridge-Logos, 2006), 43–45.

COULD WE WITH INK
THE OCEANS FILL

You are an epistle of Christ . . . written not with
ink but by the Spirit of the living God.

2 CORINTHIANS 3:3

This may be a far-fetched illustration, but let's give it a try. According to the *British Medical Journal*, a seventy-six-year-old woman visited her doctor complaining of stomach problems. When the scans came back, doctors were amazed to see a long object in her stomach. It was a pen! The woman remembered having put a pen in her mouth, losing her balance, falling, and swallowing the pen—twenty-five years earlier. Her doctor at the time didn't believe her, and the X-ray equipment didn't detect a pen, so nothing was ever done.

Now here's the remarkable thing: when surgeons removed the pen, it still worked.

Sometimes we feel like we're being swallowed up in troubles, trials, pressures, and problems. But our God watches over us just as He watched over Jonah in the belly of the fish (Jonah 2). Trials produce testings, but from testings come testimonies. No matter what trials come our way, we never lose our message of salvation. We never run out of ink to share the Good News. Because of Christ, we can always write these words from the classic hymn: "Great is Thy faithfulness!"

Most of the world around you doesn't read the Bible.
So . . . God gives the world a living epistle—you.*

KAY ARTHUR

---

*Kay Arthur, *As Silver Refined* (Colorado Springs: WaterBrook Press, 1997), 46.

TODAY IS THE DAY

[God] says: "In an acceptable time I have heard you,
and in the day of salvation I have helped you." Behold, now
is the accepted time; behold, now is the day of salvation.

2 CORINTHIANS 6:2

The word *procrastinate* comes from a Latin compound word: *pro,* which means "forward," and *crastinus,* which means "of tomorrow." So procrastinating is moving or pushing something from today to tomorrow (or the day after tomorrow, *ad infinitum*).

Most things in life that need to be done—paying the bills, painting the house, changing the oil in the car—allow for a few "tomorrows" before they absolutely have to be done. Why? Because if you die before you get the house painted, it might be an inconvenience for someone else, but not the end of the world. There are, however, other things in life that don't allow for such putting off because they have eternal ramifications. Most important is one's decision regarding Christ. Hebrews 9:27 says we die and then comes the judgment—there are no tomorrows or do-overs when it comes to salvation.

You can survive if you procrastinate about some things. But a decision about surrendering your life to Christ is not one of them.

Pride is the devil's dragnet, in which he takes more
fish than in any other, except procrastination.

CHARLES H. SPURGEON

SEEING THE UNSEEN

We do not look at the things which are seen, but at the things which are not seen. For the things which are seen are temporary, but the things which are not seen are eternal.

2 CORINTHIANS 4:18

The cofounder of Apple, the late Steve Jobs, was actually fired from his position as CEO of the company before he came back to lead its renaissance. In a commencement address at Stanford University in 2005, Jobs said, "I didn't see it then, but it turned out that getting fired from Apple was the best thing that could have happened to me."

Many people, Christians and non-Christians alike, testify that failure has been a back door to success. But even when failure doesn't lead to outward success, Christians can trust that God is working in the midst of their failure. When anyone experiences failure—or any kind of affliction—he or she tends to focus on what is seen and what is happening at that moment. But for Christians experiencing failure, God is at work in the unseen—shaping our character into the image of Jesus Christ (Romans 8:28-29). Only Christians can be confident that God is going to use their failure for a deep purpose in their lives.

If you regret a failure in your life, thank God for the unseen work He is doing in you today.

The Christian message is for those who
have done their best and failed!

UNKNOWN

MAKING CHANGE

Because they do not change,
therefore they do not fear God.

PSALM 55:19

Remember this number: 318. That's the number for change, and people who fear God are changing every day.

Second Corinthians 3:18 says, "We all, with unveiled face, beholding as in a mirror the glory of the Lord, are being transformed into the same image from glory to glory."

Second Peter 3:18 says, "Grow in the grace and knowledge of our Lord and Savior Jesus Christ."

You can change. None of us is the same person we were a year or a decade ago. Our bodies are changing—there's no denying that. But our minds, hearts, habits, personalities, and relationships are changing too. We just need to make sure we are changing for the better, that we're being transformed from glory to glory, that we're growing in the grace and knowledge of Christ. Those who refuse to change are not God fearers, because those who love Him are changing every day. Don't be afraid to make some changes in your life, and don't be afraid to let Christ change you from within.

I'll go anywhere as long as it's forward.

DAVID LIVINGSTONE

REST AND REFRESH

Jesus stood and cried out, saying, "If anyone thirsts, let him come to Me and drink."

JOHN 7:37

They were nuns, monks, hermits, and ascetics and were known as the Desert Fathers and Desert Mothers. The movement began with Anthony the Great, who moved to the Middle Eastern desert around AD 270, and thousands of others followed in his footsteps seeking spiritual purity, enlightenment, solitude, and perfection.

Their pattern of "retreating" contributed to today's practice of taking a "retreat" to refresh oneself spiritually. Fortunately, it's not necessary to retreat to the desert or a mountaintop, either temporarily or permanently, to find spiritual refreshment. Jesus said that if we would come to Him—for living water (John 4:10) or for rest (Matthew 11:28-30)—we would find it in abundance. We can create that place of rest in a place of prayer or Bible study or meditation or worship—anywhere we can retreat from the cares and busyness of life. When we turn over those cares to God in prayer through Christ, His peace will guard our heart and mind (Philippians 4:6-7).

If you can retreat to a serene spot in nature—wonderful! If that's not possible, retreat with Jesus wherever you can. He will meet you there.

You made us for yourself, O Lord, and our hearts are restless till they rest in you.

AUGUSTINE

MARCH

BY ADOPTION

You received the Spirit of adoption by
whom we cry out, "Abba, Father."

ROMANS 8:15

Every now and then, we see these encouraging headlines: "Couple Adopts Abandoned Baby." "Family Takes in Handicapped Youth." "Needy Child Finds Loving Home." Such stories are heartwarming reminders that some children who have no family can find a place to belong.

The apostle Paul uses the illustration of adoption to explain how we are drawn into the family of God. We are alone, bound in sin, until we are found by God and welcomed into His family. Because of His love and grace, we are adopted as His own children (Ephesians 1:5).

In the first century, an adopted son was chosen by his father to carry on the family name and inherit his estate. There was nothing inferior about this son. In fact, Bible scholar F. F. Bruce suggests that because of the father's intentional choice, the adopted son "might well enjoy the father's affection more fully and reproduce the father's character more worthily."

Our place in God's family gives us great rights and privileges, but it also gives us responsibilities. Since your Heavenly Father chose you to be a part of His eternal family, live up to that calling today by asking Him to reproduce His character in your life.

All are equally welcome to Christ,
and all have an equal need of Him.

ADAM CLARKE

MERCY

*Let the wicked forsake his way, and the unrighteous man his
thoughts; let him return to the LORD, and He will have mercy
on him; and to our God, for He will abundantly pardon.*

ISAIAH 55:7

God's mercy extends to both our lesser shortcomings and our greatest sins. As theologian Jonathan Edwards put it, "The mercy of God is as sufficient for the pardon of the greatest sins, as for the least; and that because his mercy is infinite. That which is infinite is as much above what is great, as it is above what is small. . . . So the mercy of God being infinite, it must be as sufficient for the pardon of all sin, as of one."

If you fear you've sinned so greatly that God can't forgive, you're forgetting His limitless mercy. If you worry that you've outrun the boundaries of God's grace, you've forgotten that all His attributes are as infinite and eternal as He is.

As we share the gospel with others, we'll find some people so mired in guilt that they've decided God cannot forgive them. Mercy is God's compassion for us, especially in His provision of Christ's blood for our sins. Because of Jesus, He will abundantly pardon.

When the Law discloses our guilt, we should not
despond, but flee to the mercy of God.

JOHN CALVIN

PROPHETIC MILEPOSTS

When you see these things happening,
know that the kingdom of God is near.

LUKE 21:31

As early as Roman times, *stone* columns were set by the side of roads to indicate the number of *miles* to a particular destination. Thus, the term *milestone* was born and is still used today. Called mileposts in America, they occur at regular intervals along the interstate highway system, indicating miles traveled from a state line. In 1920, a Zero Milestone was erected just south of the White House in Washington, DC. Distances from the nation's capital were to be measured from that point.

Just as a highway milestone, or milepost, serves to keep one oriented on a geographical journey, so God's prophetic markers keep people oriented on humankind's journey through time. We could say that the Zero Prophetic Milestone is Genesis 3:15, where the prophetic promise of Satan's defeat is found. The destination is the eternal city, the new Jerusalem (Revelation 21–22). In between, prophetic markers are found in Scripture—especially related to the past, present, and future of God's chosen people, Israel.

The greater your knowledge of God's prophetic markers, the greater your security in an insecure world.

In Him history and prophecy are one and the same.

A. W. TOZER

MARCHING INTO THE SEA

*The children of Israel went into the midst of the
sea on the dry ground, and the waters were a wall
to them on their right hand and on their left.*

EXODUS 14:22

Hebrews 11:1 in the New Living Translation says that faith "gives us assurance about things we cannot see." We may find ourselves in places where we cannot see the outcome. Faith says, in those places, "Trust God's promises."

Moses and the Israelites found themselves in such a place when they marched out of Egypt. They were on the banks of the Red Sea, and the Egyptian army was closing in. The Israelites couldn't see a way out; only faith in God's ability to keep them safe would help. It seemed like madness to march through the water—who had ever seen such a thing before? But that's what God instructed. They had to believe not only that the waters would part but that the waters wouldn't crash back upon them as they walked across the floor of the sea. By faith, the Israelites marched into the place where the Red Sea had been, and they were saved.

The purpose of places in which we lose our vision is to strengthen our faith. If that's where you are today, let God's promises give you assurance about the things you cannot see.

It's always too early to quit.

NORMAN VINCENT PEALE

GRACE

Where sin abounded, grace abounded much more.
ROMANS 5:20

Preacher and writer John Bunyan surrendered to Christ after living what he called a "morally reprehensible life" without God. In 1653 he was received into the Congregational Church and began preaching about his new life in Christ. He was able to preach for several years without imprisonment, but when he began preaching in Bedford, England, in 1660, he was arrested and imprisoned for preaching without a license from the Anglican Church. Bunyan was given the opportunity to be released if he would promise not to preach in private gatherings, but he refused to follow the mandatory dictates of the state church. Though Bunyan was confined to prison for more than twelve years, his voice was never silenced. During his imprisonment, he wrote his great classic *The Pilgrim's Progress* and his autobiography, *Grace Abounding to the Chief of Sinners*. According to Bunyan, his conversion was "a miracle of precious grace" without which he would have perished by the stroke of eternal justice.

The grace that John Bunyan experienced is God's favor freely bestowed on us in Christ—God's Riches At Christ's Expense (GRACE). As we share the gospel with others, *grace* should be among the first words on our lips.

Abounding, amazing grace—how sweet the sound!

His whole gospel is a gospel of grace,
words of peace, and salvation.

JOHN BUNYAN

HEAVENLY TRANSLATOR

We do not know what we should pray for as we ought,
but the Spirit Himself makes intercession for us.

ROMANS 8:26

Have you ever been at a loss for words? Perhaps a comment took you off guard or bad news shocked you into stunned silence. There are times when we don't know what to say.

The same thing can happen to us when we pray, especially when we are facing challenging circumstances. We turn to God in prayer, and yet we may not have the words to convey our deepest yearnings—giving voice to our longings, our needs, our sincerest concerns.

In those moments, we need to remember that when we can't find the words to express ourselves, the Holy Spirit comes to our aid. He speaks to God on our behalf—translating the concerns of our hearts—in ways we cannot comprehend. He is there as our Advocate, representing our concerns to God the Father.

When we can't find the words to express ourselves to God, our hearts' desires will be translated to our loving Heavenly Father by our Comforter, the Holy Spirit.

The Spirit-filled, prayerful Christian actually
possesses the mind of Christ, so that his reactions
to the external world are the same as Christ's.

A. W. TOZER

A DEEP, SETTLED PEACE

*Peace I leave with you, My peace I give
to you; not as the world gives.*

JOHN 14:27

In his devotional book *By the Still Waters,* Vance Havner tells of attending a small service in a little church on a cold February night. The people in the congregation were local farming folk, and a time was given for sharing testimonies. The last to speak was a humble woman plainly dressed. She rose and simply said, "I praise the Lord for a deep, settled peace. The world did not give it to me, and the world can't take it away."

"That testimony lingers with me," shares Havner. "I think of scholars and sages ransacking libraries and perusing heavy philosophies, searching for the secret of peace, while the plain, farm-woman had been enjoying it through the years."

There's much we don't comprehend. The plans that God has foreordained for us are beyond our understanding, but we know that when we are with Him, there will be a peace we have never imagined.

The world didn't give it, and the world cannot take it away.

There are thousands of earth's rich and renowned
who would give it all for the childish confidence
of the soul that on Jesus hath leaned for repose.*

VANCE HAVNER

---

*Vance Havner, *By the Still Waters* (New Tappan, NJ: Revell, 1934), 84–85.

WE KNOW!

We know that all things work together for good.

ROMANS 8:28

When seemingly bad things happen to good people, it is a normal, human response to ask why. We long to understand the apparent senselessness of accidents, suffering, failure, or persecution. Our faith can be shaken as we struggle to understand how a loving God could allow bad things to happen.

In difficult times, we are privileged to have the blessed promise penned by the apostle Paul but authored in the heart of God. There is no hesitancy in Paul's assertion. His conviction is firm, born out of a lifetime of suffering and persecution. He declares that we know! We know, deep in our hearts, that bad things do not need to be feared.

We know this because our omnipotent God is at work behind the scenes, bringing good out of what seems bad for every person who claims allegiance to Him.

Because of the love of God for us, we can be certain that God is at work for the good of His people. Since God is good, the work He is doing for His people is good. The ultimate good toward which He is working is His glorification and the salvation of His children.

Life is a grindstone, and whether it grinds a man down or polishes him up depends on the stuff he's made of.

JOSH BILLINGS

KEEP THE END IN MIND

*When these things begin to happen, look up and lift up
your heads, because your redemption draws near.*

LUKE 21:28

Your doctor tells you, "You're going to feel worse before you feel better." Those aren't encouraging words when you want to recover quickly from an ailment, yet the hope of wellness spurs you on through the recovery process.

The "happy ending" prognosis can also be applied as we look at the signs of the end times. Negative financial overtones are predicted as we transition to a new world order. But for the believer, a downturn in the economy doesn't instill gloom. It's good news: our redemption draws near!

The final stage of our redemption—initiated at the Cross—is inaugurated by the end times, when the church will be ushered into the safety of the Kingdom. Unveiling the signs that would signal His coming, Jesus used a joyful image, "lift up your heads," to describe how believers should await His return. Should our heads be downcast in gloom? No! Luke 21 tells us, "Look up and lift up your heads, because your redemption draws near" (verse 28).

Signs of the times are everywhere.
There's a brand new feeling in the air.
Keep your eyes upon the eastern sky,
Lift up your head, redemption draweth nigh.

GORDON JENSEN

LIGHTNING STRIKE

As the lightning comes from the east and flashes
to the west, so also will the coming of the Son of Man be.

MATTHEW 24:27

More than a hundred lightning bolts strike the earth each second. That's nearly ten million lightning strikes a day. Lightning is a river of electricity rushing through the air, traveling at the speed of 60,000 miles per second. A lightning bolt can be ten miles long and brighter than 10 million 100-watt lightbulbs. In that split second, a single flash can generate as much voltage as all the electrical generating plants in the United States.*

Jesus said that we don't have to be worried about the exact time of His coming, and we shouldn't be deceived by those making false predictions. When He comes, there will be no doubt. As lightning flashing from the east to the west, splitting the sky in a millisecond, so will His coming be.

The next time you see a bolt of lightning cleave the sky, think of it as a reminder that His coming is near.

Light in the eastern sky, Jesus returning!
Light in the western sky, Jesus is near!

DANIEL B. TOWNER

---

*Seymour Simon, *Lightning* (New York: HarperCollins, 1997), 5–6.

GOD KNOWS YOU!

For whom He foreknew, He also predestined to
be conformed to the image of His Son, that He
might be the firstborn among many brethren.

ROMANS 8:29

Imagine a couple that has just learned they are expecting a child. They don't know the baby's gender, personality, or future. All they know is that, within nine months, they will give birth to a baby. Then they will resolve to guide their child's development and shape his or her future as best they can.

While parents prepare to meet their child's every need, their efforts are limited because they are still discovering how to best care for this new life. How different that is from our heavenly Father! God the Father knew you intimately before you were born. Even before you were conceived, He knew the details of your life, the good and bad, and the spiritual response of your heart.

But God's foreknowledge isn't passive information. It led Him to fix His love on you and to delight in you as His child even before you knew Him. When you decided for Him, He had already decided for you. The purpose of this decision is that you may be conformed to the image of Jesus. Let the loving Father shape you to look like His Son today.

You know what you ought to do,
then do it, not halfway, but out and out.

EMMA MOODY

NOTHING ELSE MATTERS

What then shall we say to these things?
If God is for us, who can be against us?

ROMANS 8:31

March Madness is here! How we love to fill the stands and shout cheers for our team and jeers against our opponent. Everyone knows which team fans are for and who they are against by the colors they wear and the cheers they chant.

Today, Paul asks us to consider the fact that God is our greatest fan! The question is, "If God is for us, who can be against us?" In other words, because God is for us, it doesn't matter who or what is against us.

No one can take away your salvation. No one can shut off God's love for you or foil God's plan for you. If anyone were able to do any of those things, he or she would have to be greater than God Himself. Even the powers of hell may set themselves against you, but they will not prevail. Why? Because God is greater, and He is on your side!

In his question, Paul is assuming a positive answer. If God be for us, no one can be against us. If God be for us, nothing else matters.

Is it not wonderful news to believe that
salvation lies outside ourselves?

MARTIN LUTHER

NOW I UNDERSTAND

Be watchful in all things,
endure afflictions . . . fulfill your ministry.
2 TIMOTHY 4:5

Clayton Christensen is a professor at Harvard Business School and is well known for articulating his theory of disruptive technology—an unexpected product or service that disrupts an existing market and helps create a new category of customers. Examples of disruptive technologies include desktop publishing, CD-ROMs, DVDs, personal computers, steamships, telephones, and automobiles. Disruptive technologies are usually resisted at first and then accepted because of their benefits and efficiencies.

God allows disruptive moments in our lives that we almost always question or resist because they are painful, unanticipated, misunderstood, and often not optional. Yet in hindsight, they are always embraced for the good or blessing that results. In the Old Testament, Job is the classic example of a life being disrupted, while Paul's thorn in the flesh (2 Corinthians 12:7-10) is an obvious New Testament example.

If God has allowed a disruptive moment in your life, walk through it by faith rather than by sight (2 Corinthians 5:7).

We all face a series of great opportunities
brilliantly disguised as impossible situations.
CHUCK SWINDOLL

DARK NIGHTS

*You have tested my heart; You have visited me in the
night; You have tried me and have found nothing;
I have purposed that my mouth shall not transgress.*

PSALM 17:3

L*a noche oscura del alma"—"The Dark Night of the Soul."*
That's the name of the poem written by St. John of the Cross,
a sixteenth-century Spanish poet, while he was in prison for trying to reform his monastic order. The dark night represents the
difficulties and trials we experience on the road to heaven.

"Dark night" also pictures the isolation we feel during times
of spiritual tests. We sometimes lie in bed at night, surrounded
by darkness, longing for sleep but consumed with our thoughts
and questions. The psalmists, especially David, were candidly
honest about their literal and spiritual dark nights. David made
good use of his sleepless nights, crying out to God for relief and
answers (Psalm 22:2; 42:8). And he relied on the natural order
of things to remind him that "weeping may endure for a night,
but joy comes in the morning" (Psalm 30:5).

If you are in the midst of your own dark night, use the time
wisely. If there are tears, let them water the words you pour out
to God, remembering that joy comes in the morning.

Faith is a plant that can grow in the shade, a grace
that can find the way to heaven in a dark night.

WILLIAM GURNALL

FUTURE VACANCY

If we believe that Jesus died and rose again, even so
God will bring with Him those who sleep in Jesus.
1 THESSALONIANS 4:14

If you're looking for a new vacation destination, Reuters reports that a Russian company wants to launch a hotel 217 miles above the earth. A five-day stay in the space hotel, including the exciting ride to get there, is estimated at a cool $1 million.*

Temporary lodging, a billion-dollar industry today, has been around for centuries. It's the way that New Testament Christians described the temporary place where they buried their loved ones. The believer's body was placed into a *koimateriam,* Greek for "hotel" or "inn." The word choice reflected the believers' firm expectation in the Resurrection. If a believer dies before the Rapture, Christ will come to the "hotel" where the body is and reunite it with the person's spirit, which has been with Him.

The Rapture assures us the cemetery is only a motel for the body of the believer. Our hope is in the Resurrection—that glorious moment when all believers are suddenly caught up into glory and hope bursts into reality. If you're missing a loved one whose spirit is with Jesus, fix your hope on the Resurrection (John 11:25).

Our Lord has written the promise of resurrection,
not in books alone, but in every leaf of springtime.

MARTIN LUTHER

---

*Alissa de Carbonnel, "Russia Plans Orbiting Hotel in Space," Reuters, August 19, 2011, http://www.reuters.com/article/2011/08/19/us-russia-space-tourism-idUSTRE77121720110819

SPIRITUAL SOLSTICE

When I remember You on my bed,
I meditate on You in the night watches.

PSALM 63:6

Depending on how one views the calendar, the winter solstice takes place between December 21 and 22 each year. It occurs when the earth's axis is tilted farthest away from the sun in its annual orbital path. Practically speaking, it marks the end of long nights and short days and is the beginning of short nights and long days.

Spiritually speaking, we long for a winter solstice type of moment in our lives when we are going through times of trouble. We want to reach a point when we see more light than darkness each day, when the darkness of discouragement gives way to the light of joy in our lives. Until that light appears, we can use the darkness as a time to meditate and reflect on the unchanging character and nature of God. While darkness may affect how we see Him, darkness does not change Him. The psalmist David says he thinks about God as he lies on his bed at night, meditating on Him through the "watches"—the progression—of the night.

Ask God to walk with you through the stages of your dark night. Remember who He is and what He has done for you.

Over every mountain there is a path,
although it may not be seen from the valley.

THEODORE ROETHKE

FEAR IS THROWN AWAY

*There is no fear in love; but perfect love casts
out fear, because fear involves torment.*

1 JOHN 4:18

When children are frightened, they need comfort more than courage, consolation more than logic, and compassion more than proof. Frightened children need to be wrapped in the caring arms of a loving adult until the fear melts away—finding consolation in the presence of someone who cares.

That's exactly what God does when we are afraid. He longs to wrap us in His loving arms. He wants us to know Him intimately as our wonderful, protective Father. The closer we draw to Him, the more we can trust in His perfect love. We can't really fathom what perfect love means, because our best attempts at understanding God's flawless love are marred by our sinful nature!

The apostle Paul reminds us that God's perfect love is indeed difficult to understand. He writes in Ephesians 3:17-19, "That you may be able to comprehend with all the saints what is the width and length and depth and height—to know the love of Christ which passes knowledge; that you may be filled with all the fullness of God."

Today let His perfect love throw away your fears. As you do, you will feel His loving arms wrapping around you with comfort, consolation, and compassion.

Fear knocked on the door. Faith answered. No one was there.

ANONYMOUS

GOOD MORNING AFTER GOOD NIGHT

Then we who are alive and remain shall be caught up
together with them in the clouds to meet the Lord in
the air. And thus we shall always be with the Lord.

1 THESSALONIANS 4:17

The death of a loved one through prolonged illness, serious memory impairment, or unexpected trauma is a life-changing experience. How comforting to know that God sees each tear and hears each cry. He also sees the joyful reunion that awaits believers.

"In a moment, in the twinkling of an eye, at the last trumpet . . . the dead will be raised incorruptible" (1 Corinthians 15:52). The imagery describing the Rapture is noteworthy: in biblical times ambassadors were sent to usher a visiting king into a city. That's what Almighty God has planned for us. He's sending Jesus, the King, to escort the living and those who have died into heaven— never to be separated again.

We do sorrow when death parts us from loved ones—but not without hope. The Cross removed the sting of death that permanently separates. If you are grieving a loss today, meditate on the destiny that awaits believers—that most blessed reunion in the sky!

It is but a good night to those we hope
to see with joy in the morning.

MATTHEW HENRY

MARCHING AROUND JERICHO

You shall march around the city, all you men of war;
you shall go all around the city once.
This you shall do six days.

JOSHUA 6:3

God told Moses to part the Red Sea. God told Gideon to defeat a large army with only three hundred soldiers. Jesus told Peter to walk on the water. Jesus told His disciples to feed thousands of people with some bread and fish. Jesus told a blind man to go wash the mud off his eyes to regain his sight. Jesus told a paralyzed man to stand up and walk home.

God has issued some impossible-sounding directions to people, but perhaps none as impossible as those issued to Joshua: march around Jericho with the Ark of the Covenant once a day for six days. On the seventh day march around Jericho seven times. Blow the trumpets and shout, and the walls will come tumbling down. Marching around the city must have sounded like madness to Joshua, but there is no indication he hesitated. He did exactly as God directed, and God's words were fulfilled. On the seventh day, the walls fell down and Jericho was captured.

God may ask you to do something impossible sounding: forgive an enemy, give generously to an ungrateful person, or serve at an incredibly inconvenient time. Calling Him "Lord" carries the expectation of obedience.

Faith is the starting-post of obedience.

THOMAS CHALMERS

EXPERIENCE PATIENCE

By your patience possess your souls.

LUKE 21:19

Missionary J. O. Fraser, who worked among the Lisu people of China, once commented about the necessity of waiting on the Lord to do His work without the frantic, panicked rushing about that characterizes much of our labor.

He said, "In the biography of our Lord nothing is more noticeable than the quiet, even poise of His life. Never flustered whatever happened, never taken off His guard, however assailed by men or demons in the midst of fickle people, hostile rulers, faithless disciples—always calm, always collected. Christ the hard worker indeed—but doing no more, and no less, than God had appointed Him, and with no restlessness, no hurry, no worry. Was ever such a peaceful life lived, under conditions so perturbing?"*

The Bible teaches that the fruit of the Spirit is patience. We should do things as efficiently as we can, but in the end so much of life requires waiting on our Lord's timing. What situation demands your patience today? Remember—He is called the "God of patience" (Romans 15:5).

Patience is passion tamed.

LYMAN ABBOTT

---

*Geraldine Taylor, *Behind the Rangers: The Life-Changing Story of J. O. Fraser* (Singapore: OMF International, 1998), 191.

THE ONE YOU FEED

Walk in the Spirit, and you shall not fulfill the lust of the flesh.

GALATIANS 5:16

A poem by an unknown author says, "Two passions beat within my chest, the one is foul, the other blessed. The one I love, the other I hate; the one I feed will dominate." This is similar to the message of Galatians 5:17, which says, "The flesh lusts against the Spirit, and the Spirit against the flesh; and these are contrary to one another." While God's children are on earth, we're subject to the temptations of the world, the flesh, and the devil. We need to make sure we're feeding the right passions, impulses, and attitudes.

As it relates to the future, that means keeping our eyes on Christ in faith, not on the world in fear. While being aware of the events of the last days and the coming of the Antichrist, we mustn't overly focus on them, but instead we should focus on our Lord and His glorious return.

Keep your eyes on the Lord, feed on His faithfulness, resist the devil, and draw near to God. Feed your faith and starve your fears.

Don't give your fears any of your time or energy.
Don't feed them with gossip or negative news shows
or frightening movies. Focus on your faith and feed it.*

JOHN MAXWELL

*John Maxwell, *The Maxwell Daily Reader* (Nashville: Thomas Nelson, 2007), 344.

HE WILL LIFT YOU UP

*[Judah said,] "There is so much rubbish that
we are not able to build the wall."*

NEHEMIAH 4:10

Nehemiah is known as the great builder and rebuilder. Under his guidance, the people of Israel cleared the rubble and constructed walls nonstop.

A month into their unending work, Judah told Nehemiah, "The strength of the laborers is failing, and there is so much rubbish that we are not able to build the wall" (Nehemiah 4:10). Nehemiah was dealing with a group of discouraged builders. Longing to see progress, they could only see rubbish in need of removal.

Nehemiah's remedy was to organize and encourage the Israelites. He first reminded them that God was with them. Then he assigned them to work in shifts so they could rest regularly. Each family was given their own section of the wall to complete. With these changes came a renewed sense of community and focus.

It's easy to become discouraged when you are isolated and tired. Perhaps you have worked late too often, or things have happened in your family to make it impossible for you to rest. Follow Nehemiah's example today, and work with your church family to be restored and to defeat discouragement.

Teamwork . . . is the fuel that allows common
people to attain uncommon results.

ANDREW CARNEGIE

CAUSE FOR CELEBRATION

Let us be glad and rejoice and give Him glory,
for the marriage of the Lamb has come,
and His wife has made herself ready.

REVELATION 19:7

If you look closely at the word *celebrate*, you will see within it the root of another familiar word: *celebrity*. Both have their origins in the Latin word for "famous." Not every celebrity is famous for the best of reasons, but there is a Person who is—and He will be celebrated for all eternity.

Revelation 19 describes the vision seen by the apostle John: the marriage supper of the Lamb and the return of Jesus Christ to earth as King of kings and Lord of lords. And the celebration of praise John heard for the Lamb was like "the voice of a great multitude, as the sound of many waters and as the sound of mighty thunderings" (verse 6). There will be no paparazzi in heaven with their cameras, only the bride of Christ, the church, "arrayed in fine linen, clean and bright," praising the Lamb of God for making her righteous, washed clean by His shed blood (verse 8).

If you want to be part of that celebration, you must be ready for the Rapture—when Christ gathers His bride to Himself and takes her to heaven. It's a celebration you don't want to miss.

Faith is the marriage of the soul to Christ.

RICHARD SIBBES

NEVER DEFEATED

Do not grow weary in doing good.

2 THESSALONIANS 3:13

Discouragement can be difficult to identify because it often masquerades as something else. It can wear the disguise of frustration, leading us to believe that our best efforts will never result in anything useful. It can cloak itself in fear of failure, making us think that we might try but won't ever accomplish the things we dream of. Or it may wear the costume of self-pity, causing us to think that no one has it as tough as we do.

How do we deal with such a destructive enemy that hides behind these false fronts? Nehemiah fought off discouragement by focusing on the big picture in the face of difficulty.

If you are discouraged today, remember that God is always in control, and He is with you. Nehemiah 4:14 says, "Remember the Lord, great and awesome, and fight for your brethren, your sons, your daughters, your wives, and your houses."

Our God is truly an awesome God, and when we get the big picture, acknowledging Him in all His power and glory, we will not be discouraged. We will be able to uncloak discouragement in all its disguises and take heart in God's power and might.

The trick is to put it all in perspective . . .
and that's what I do for a living.

ERMA BOMBECK

HOW LONG?

How long, O LORD? Will You forget me forever?
How long will You hide Your face from me?

PSALM 13:1

On November 15, 2010, the CEO of Facebook announced that his service's 500 million users would get a new way to communicate even more quickly: a Facebook email account. Traditional email suffers from a time delay, but incorporating email into Facebook's messaging system would be yet another way to remove delays in communication.

The digital age—specifically the Internet and various messaging methods—has already helped shrink the world and eliminate time delays. But when it comes to communicating with God, the digital age hasn't changed anything except perhaps to make us more impatient with God. We are used to getting answers and replies to questions immediately, and we forget that God works on His timetable, not ours. But when an answer or response from God takes time, we are forced to stop, think, consider, evaluate, meditate, contemplate, revise, repent—and most of all, let God be God. God is not impulsive, nor should we be. Not getting immediate answers, if that's how God responds, forces us to be more thoughtful.

If you are waiting for an answer from God, know there is a reason for His (seeming) delay. What seems like a delay on earth is a sign of a purpose or reason in heaven.

The only preparation for tomorrow
is the right use of today.

UNKNOWN

MARCHING LITE

*Then the LORD said to Gideon, "By the three
hundred men who lapped I will save you,
and deliver the Midianites into your hand."*

JUDGES 7:7

Jesus lived a Spartan life—at least during His three years of ministry. Yes, He came from a home in Nazareth, but His ministry years are best characterized by Matthew 8:20: "The Son of Man has nowhere to lay His head." His was a life of dependence on His Father—we never see that He packed a bag when He left to journey from one place to another. In the purely human realm, an example of dependence we might more easily identify with is Gideon.

Gideon was a simple farmer called by God to drive the Midianites out of Israel. When Gideon rallied an army of 32,000 men, God first reduced it down to 10,000, then to 300—and equipped them only with torches and trumpets. Marching against the innumerable Midianites with 300 men would have seemed like madness to Gideon—and to us. But Gideon learned that victory comes from the Lord, not from human strength or resources.

As the saying goes, God plus one equals a majority. If you are facing a formidable challenge, don't be discouraged by a lack of resources. Be encouraged by the presence and promises of God.

We never test the resources of God until
we attempt the impossible.

F. B. MEYER

NO MORE FEAR

Behold, God is my salvation, I will trust and not be afraid.

ISAIAH 12:2

The word *Armageddon* often shows up in the news as journalists discuss the fears facing our world. But perhaps the thing bothering you today isn't Armageddon. It's the deficit in your bank account, a problem in your family, or a rift in your church.

One of the great phrases in the book of Revelation is "no more." We're told of a day for God's children when there will be no more tears, no more death, no more sorrow, no more pain.

Clarence Macartney said, "When I read those great 'no mores' in the Book of Revelation where the heavenly life is described . . . I feel I would like to add another great 'no more'—'There shall be no more fear.' When Christ was born at Bethlehem, that was what the angels said to the shepherds, 'Fear not.' Christ came to banish fear. . . . Over the portals of heaven are written these words, greeting man as he enters the heavenly city, 'Fear not!'"

Whether you're worried about Armageddon in the future or aggravations today, trust Him and don't be afraid.

The Psalmist said, "What time I am afraid, I will trust
in Thee." That is good, very good. But still better is
what Isaiah said, "I will trust, and not be afraid."*

CLARENCE MACARTNEY

---

*Quoted in Warren W. Wiersbe, *Classic Sermons on Overcoming Fear* (Grand Rapids: Kregel, 1991), 49–50.

GOD NEVER FAILS

Has His mercy ceased forever?
Has His promise failed forevermore?

PSALM 77:8

Sir Winston Churchill, the legendary politician and statesman known for his leadership of the United Kingdom during the Second World War, once said, "Continuous effort—not strength or intelligence—is the key to unlocking our potential." We can't rest on our victories; neither can we wallow in our defeats. We all fail, and sometimes our failures can demoralize us. But even in failure there are benefits to be gained and progress to be made.

Some lessons can only be learned in failure, and a day is never lost if a lesson is learned. Failure is often a path to success if we persevere. Basketball great Michael Jordan understood this. He once said, "Failure always made me try harder next time."

As we encounter our ups and downs, it's helpful to remember that God never fails and that His mercy never ceases. As we read in Lamentations 3:22-23, "His compassions fail not. They are new every morning." If your own failure has you questioning God's faithfulness today, place your worries in His hands. He will never fail you, no matter how many times you may fail.

Success consists of going from failure to
failure without loss of enthusiasm.

WINSTON CHURCHILL

STEADFAST AND SURE

This hope we have as an anchor of the soul,
both sure and steadfast.

HEBREWS 6:19

Priscilla Owens was a schoolteacher in Baltimore, Maryland, and a faithful church worker. As time allowed, she also composed Christian hymns. We know her as the author of the song "Will Your Anchor Hold?" The chorus says, "We have an anchor that keeps the soul steadfast and sure while the billows roll." Owens also wrote the popular hymn that says, "We have heard the joyful sound: Jesus saves! Jesus saves!"

Jesus Himself is the only hope for the future of the world, for the future of the nation of Israel, and for those who comprise the final generations of history. He's also our only hope today. The Bible says, "Nor is there salvation in any other, for there is no other name under heaven given among men by which we must be saved" (Acts 4:12).

Here's the great thing. When we hear the joyful sound of Jesus calling to us, we discover we have an anchor that keeps the soul steadfast and sure while the billows roll.

Don't fear the billows today; rejoice in the blessings.

Fastened to the Rock that cannot move,
grounded firm and deep in the Savior's love.

PRISCILLA OWENS

EXPERIENCE HOPE

*May the God of hope fill you with all joy
and peace in believing, that you may abound
in hope by the power of the Holy Spirit.*
ROMANS 15:13

Linguists tell us that the English words *hope* and *hop* appear to be related. It's the idea of leaping in expectation. *Hope* is defined as the attitude of anticipation. It's looking forward to those things we know will happen. Hope is related to optimism and a positive view of the future. That's a reality that only Christians can truly experience. One of the blessings given to us in Christ is an unassailable positive anticipation toward a certain future. It's such an exclusive attitude that the Bible tells us to always be ready to explain to others the reason for the hope that is within us.

The word *hope* appears 154 times in the Bible. There are 153 more references for you to investigate. So hop to it—and be hopeful today!

He is not only called the God of hope because He is
the object of hope, but because He is the author
of it; and all the Scripture is written to work hope
in us, so saith v. 4 of the same chapter.*

THOMAS GOODWIN, PURITAN, ON ROMANS 15:13

* *The Works of Thomas Goodwin,* vol. 1 (Edinburgh: James Nichol, 1861), 307.

LOOKING BACK, LOOKING FORWARD

*The Son of Man must be delivered into the hands of
sinful men, and be crucified, and the third day rise again.*

LUKE 24:7

Suppose someone told you of two unlikely events that would happen in the future—one in a few days, the other at an undetermined time in the future. In spite of the details he gave about each event, you found it hard to believe that he could predict the future with that kind of accuracy. Within a few days you learn that the first predicted event took place exactly as the man said. How would that change your thinking about the likelihood of the second event?

It would probably change your thinking radically. Strangely enough, even though Jesus Christ predicted His own death and resurrection on the third day—both of which were fulfilled in detail—many people don't take seriously His promise to return to earth. On the same occasion on which Jesus told His disciples of His impending death and resurrection, He said, "The Son of Man will come in the glory of His Father with His angels, and then He will reward each according to his works" (Matthew 16:27).

It would be unwise to look back at Christ's death and resurrection in belief, but not look forward to His second coming with expectation.

The ambition of my life is to be as holy
as a saved sinner can be.

ROBERT MURRAY MCCHEYNE

APRIL

FROM LAMB TO LION

He who testifies to these things says,
"Surely I am coming quickly."
REVELATION 22:20

The first time Jesus came to earth, He arrived quietly. The Lamb of God who would take away the sins of the world through His own death and resurrection came as a babe in a manger. But the second time Jesus comes to earth, He will appear magnificently in the sky—the Lion of Judah bringing judgment.

It might surprise you that in the Bible, references to the Second Coming outnumber references to the first by a ratio of eight to one. Scholars count 1,845 biblical references to the Second Coming, including 318 in the New Testament. Second only to faith, the Second Coming is one of the most dominant subjects in the New Testament. The Lord Himself referred to His return twenty-one times.

Are we anticipating His second coming as ardently as we celebrate the baby in the manger? Final victory and the eternal reign of Christ are in our future. As you live in expectation of that day, radiate His love to others by showing a sincere interest in their lives. Don't waste a minute. Go share the hope that is in you.

As the bells ring out the joys of Christmas, may we
also be alert for the final trumpet that will announce
His return, when we shall always be with Him.

ALAN REDPATH

CONFESSION SESSION

Wash me thoroughly from my iniquity,
and cleanse me from my sin. For I acknowledge
my transgressions, and my sin is always before me.

PSALM 51:2-3

Guilt is a powerful emotion. Guilt can be painful when it is gnawing away at our cowardly consciences, pressing us toward the freeing act of confession.

When King David wrote this psalm, he was experiencing guilt at its worst. His sin with Bathsheba was on his mind constantly. He was confronted by the prophet Nathan and finally saw what a horrible thing he had done. David needed to have a confession session!

When we sin, it's never in a vacuum; we hurt both ourselves and others. But the greatest offense of our sin is against God. When we go against His loving will for us, disobeying His commands, it grieves His loving heart.

To deal with guilt in a way that pleases God, we need our own confession session—a time of agreeing with Him that we have sinned and that we need His forgiveness. Next we must confess to the person whom we have sinned against. Only then will our confession session result in the freedom of a clear conscience.

Biblical forgiveness . . . is the beginning
of restored freedom and renewed health.

KEN NICHOLS

NEVER TOO LATE

Jesus said to him, "Assuredly, I say to you,
today you will be with Me in Paradise."

LUKE 23:43

You may be familiar with the story of the pastor who asked a group of children in Sunday school how many of them wanted to go to heaven. All but one little boy raised a hand. When the pastor asked him why he didn't want to go, the little boy said, "Oh, I do want to go to heaven. But if you're getting up a load right now, I can't go. Mama said to come home for lunch right after church."

Rarely do we talk about going to heaven *today*. And Jesus only used that word to describe going there with one person: the thief on the cross. There were two thieves crucified with Jesus—one mocked Jesus while the other one asked Jesus to remember him in His Kingdom. Then Jesus said, "Today you will be with Me in Paradise." Jesus affirmed what they both knew—that within hours their physical bodies would die—but He assured the thief that they would enter Paradise together.

It's never too late to place your faith in Jesus—He awaits the cry of a repentant heart. Don't make the eternal mistake of thinking you've waited until it's too late to believe.

Death to a saint is nothing but the taking of a
sweet flower out of this wilderness, and
planting of it in the garden of paradise.

THOMAS BROOKS

DEFENDING THE TREASURE

*We have this treasure in earthen vessels, that the
excellence of the power may be of God and not of us.*

2 CORINTHIANS 4:7

Depending on where you live, this past winter you may have joined a growing number of homeowners who have installed an insulating "jacket" around their home's hot-water heater—especially if the unit is located in a garage, attic, or crawl space. The goal is to help the water fend off the relentless freezing-cold air. The more the water is protected, the less energy the heater must use to keep the water hot.

There is something more important we have to protect: the gospel of the grace of God. That is the treasure Paul spoke about in 2 Corinthians 4:7. Amazingly, God deposited His treasure in us, fragile "earthen vessels" that are subject to the relentless ways of the world and attacks of the devil. But Paul says the treasure is protected so "that the life of Jesus also may be manifested in our mortal flesh" (verse 11).

Whenever you are feeling the pressures of life, remember that if you are God's child by faith in Christ, God is committed to protecting the treasure He has deposited in you.

A sov'reign Protector I have . . . and walls of salvation
surround the soul He delights to defend.

AUGUSTUS M. TOPLADY

THE BIGGER, THE BETTER

*For David, after he had served his own generation
by the will of God, fell asleep, was buried
with his fathers, and saw corruption.*

ACTS 13:36

The phrase *carbon footprint* has entered the cultural conversation as a sign of the times. It's not a path left by the boots of coal miners but a measure of the emission of greenhouse gases into the atmosphere. The carbon footprint measurement of cars, factories, animals, cities—any physical entity at all—has become a relevant variable in the analysis of changing climate conditions.

In addition to their carbon footprint, Christians can also measure their spiritual footprint. Our spiritual footprint is the measurement of all we are doing to change the spiritual climate in our world. Although smaller is better for carbon footprints, spiritual footprints are the opposite: the bigger, the better. We can leave a spiritual footprint both while we are here and after we are gone through our actions, prayers, and investments of time, talent, and treasure.

Every Christian can serve God faithfully in his or her generation. By wise planning and stewardship, we can expand our spiritual footprint even after entering glory.

The use of our possessions shows us
up for what we actually are.

CHARLES C. RYRIE

FAITH AND FUNDS

*Yours, O LORD, is the greatness, the power and
the glory, the victory and the majesty; for all
that is in heaven and in earth is Yours.*

1 CHRONICLES 29:11

During the Great Recession that began in 2008, the government injected massive amounts of money (or credit) into the economy in hopes of jump-starting a recovery. The average citizen wondered, "If the government is in debt, where does it get all this new stimulus money?" Since ordinary citizens could not create "new money," the government stimulus packages were confusing to many. Where did this "new money" come from?

While the technical answer to that question involves the Federal Reserve extending new lines of credit to member banks, there is a spiritual application to be gleaned: however the money was created, measured, or accounted for, God owned it all. The Christian's hope should never ultimately be in the government's ability to change the money supply. Our hope is in the One who accomplishes His purposes on the earth through establishing and removing kings (and their policies). After all, Jesus said we cannot serve both God and money (Matthew 6:24, NIV).

When we serve God, we put our trust for everything—including the money needed to live—in Him alone.

In the battle of faith, money is usually
the last stronghold to fall.

RON DUNN

HOLY ANGER

Be angry, and do not sin.

EPHESIANS 4:26

When the Bible commands us to "be angry," it is not commanding us to lose control. Fits of rage are clearly condemned as sin. But an honest, deep sense of right is sometimes best expressed with an appropriate show of anger.

Parents who discovered their neighborhood grocer selling cigarettes to their teenage son started a campaign that resulted in a law that holds merchants liable if they sell cigarettes to underage buyers. These parents expressed their anger in an appropriate way.

Jesus expressed anger at the extortion and racketeering going on at the Temple in Jerusalem. He didn't throw a fit of rage. He deliberately overturned their tables and drove the money changers out.

Misdirected anger, described as anger that results in violence or vengeful activity against others, grieves the Holy Spirit. Road rage is a prime example of misdirected anger. Abuse falls under the same heading.

How can you avoid grieving the Holy Spirit? Give God first place. Recognize the importance of prayer and Bible reading. As you pray and study the character of God, you will learn to deal with your anger. Express your anger by righting wrongs. Let go of misdirected anger. Give it to God.

A grudge is like a baby; it has to be
nursed if it's going to survive.

JOHN ORTBERG

ANTICIPATION

[Let us] lay hold of the hope set before us.

HEBREWS 6:18

Psychologists tell us that anticipation is an emotion with marvelous healing powers. People who are snowbound sustain their spirits by anticipating the longer days of spring and summer. Couples who are separated by military deployment stay sane by anticipating their reunion. Students anticipate the end of the semester. Employees look forward to their vacations. Brides and grooms are eager for their wedding day.

Can you imagine a world without anticipation? How would we feel with nothing to look forward to? Welcome to non-Christianity. Without Christ, there's no ultimate anticipation. There may be momentary excitement, but lasting expectancy is missing. The future has no promise; it holds no hope. Everything will perish. For a non-Christian, death is the termination of any happiness that may be found on the earth. But for Christians, death brings us to the beginning of an eternity spent in heaven.

Thank God we have a message of hope! Our joy is complete as we look to the future return of our Lord and to the mansions He is preparing for us. Let's live in anticipation today!

On every page of the Bible there are words of
God that give reason to hope. . . . In the promises
of God I find inspiration and new hope.*

CHARLES L. ALLEN

---

*Charles L. Allen, *The Miracle of Hope* (Old Tappan, NJ: Revell, 1973), 48.

NOTHING NEW

That which has been is what will be,
that which is done is what will be done,
and there is nothing new under the sun.

ECCLESIASTES 1:9

You no doubt heard that the economic recession of 2008 was the "worst since the Great Depression"—emphasis on "worst." While experts may disagree about that description, the Great Recession certainly wasn't the *only* recession since the Great Depression—there have actually been twelve recessions since the Great Depression (not counting the most recent one). And according to some economists, there have been forty-seven recessions since 1790, including the latest one.

What does that tell you about humans' ability to manage the economy? At the very least it proves that what Solomon said is true—there's nothing new under the sun. And it also proves that humans are not smart enough to keep things in this world stable. Those who depend on their finances for hope and stability will, at least a few times in their lives, be sorely disappointed when the economy turns sour.

Rather than putting our trust in our understanding, or that of human leaders, we should trust in the Lord with our whole heart (Proverbs 3:5-6). He is the only One who can provide stability in an unstable world.

I have held many things in my hands and I have lost them all;
but whatever I have placed in God's hands, that I still possess.

MARTIN LUTHER

THAT'S AN ORDER

The steps of a good man are ordered by
the LORD, and He delights in his way.

PSALM 37:23

Have you ever thought about the word *order*? What a variety of applications! A fast-food worker takes our *order* for French fries. Soldiers line up in alphabetical *order* to receive their *orders*. Our business meeting is called to *order* at a certain time, but the moderator rules our motion "out of *order*." We work hard in *order* to make money; we spend it by filling out *order* forms for purchases; then we sit on the sofa and watch an old episode of *Law and Order*.

The root idea of the term is conforming to an authoritative standard, a command, an arrangement, a proper direction, or a regulation.

When the psalmist says that God orders our steps, he means that God decrees the path we should take. We live a God-ordered life—under His orders, ordered and arranged by His omniscience, and all in order to please Him.

The word *order* implies control. Our source of guidance must remain the One who understands us from the first to the last. Are you under His orders today?

Order my footsteps by Thy Word and make my heart sincere;
let sin have no dominion, Lord, but keep my conscience clear.

ISAAC WATTS

OVERFLOW OR RUNOFF

*My people have committed two evils: They have forsaken
Me, the fountain of living waters, and hewn themselves
cisterns—broken cisterns that can hold no water.*

JEREMIAH 2:13

Imagine an ever-flowing fountain, accessible and attractive, the waters fresh and pure. The copious flow of water splashes from rock to rock as if dancing down stair steps. At the fountain a man finds the resources to quench his thirst, irrigate his crops, and water his flocks. The fountain is never diminished in drought, so the man is never lacking water.

Now imagine this man deliberately ignoring the fountain. With illogical obstinacy he prefers to dig a hole in the ground for runoff water, which quickly seeps out of his broken cistern, leaving him nothing but mud.

That's the Bible's picture for those looking for happiness in the wrong places. The world is filled with broken cisterns, but only Jesus can give satisfying joy. He said, "Whoever drinks of this water will thirst again, but whoever drinks of the water that I shall give him will never thirst. But the water that I shall give him will become in him a fountain of water springing up into everlasting life" (John 4:13-14).

True happiness can be found only in Christ, the living water.

I came to Jesus, and I drank of that life-giving stream; my thirst was quenched, my soul revived, and now I live in Him.

HORATIUS BONAR

THERE IS A RIVER

There is a river whose streams
shall make glad the city of God.

PSALM 46:4

Ralph Erskine, a Scottish preacher in the 1700s, reckoned that the river in Psalm 46:4 is a picture of God Himself, for it is God alone who makes His people glad.

God the Father is a river. In Jeremiah 2:13, He is called the fountain of living waters who quenches the spiritual longings of our hearts.

God the Son is a river, for Zechariah 13 talks about the fountain that cleanses from sin, and Jesus Himself is the water of life. He promised the Samaritan woman the living water of eternal life (John 4:10).

God the Spirit is a river, for Jesus said, "He who believes in Me, as the Scripture has said, out of his heart will flow rivers of living water" (John 7:38).

We can't find happiness in life by looking for it apart from God. Happiness sought for its own sake is self-defeating. It's ultimately a by-product of knowing our Lord, for He is a river whose streams make glad the city of God.

Take heed of forming plans for happiness, as though it
lay in the things of this world, which soon pass away.

MATTHEW HENRY

A MATTER OF PERSPECTIVE

[Moses considered] the reproach of Christ greater riches than the treasures in Egypt; for he looked to the reward.

HEBREWS 11:26

Most of the anxiety we experience in life has to do with the future—the unknown. Even if we are going through something difficult *right now*, we still think of the future. We wonder, *How long is this going to last? How is this going to change my life? How can I keep this from happening again?*

When it comes to the future, there are only two ways to approach it: with faith or with fear. When Moses grew up in the lap of luxury in Egypt, every day he watched his Hebrew brethren suffer as slaves. He had to make decisions about his future. *"By faith* he forsook Egypt, *not fearing* the wrath of the king" (Hebrews 11:27, emphasis added). Why? Because "he looked to the reward" (Hebrews 11:26). Moses faced his future with faith, not with fear, because his perspective was heavenly, not earthly. He gave up the riches of Egypt to gain the rewards of eternity, knowing there was no comparison.

If you are tempted to fear something in your future, let a heavenly perspective give you faith instead. A heavenly perspective means seeing life—including the future—the way God sees it.

Expect great things from God; attempt great things for God.

WILLIAM CAREY

NOW IS THE TIME

*As [Paul] reasoned about righteousness, self-control,
and the judgment to come, Felix . . . answered, "Go away
for now; when I have a convenient time I will call for you."*

ACTS 24:25

Felix, the procurator of Judea, kept Paul in prison for two years even though all the evidence pointed to Paul's innocence. Again and again, he would send for Paul and listen as Paul talked about "righteousness, self-control, and the judgment to come." For two years, Felix procrastinated about a decision. Finally, he sent Paul away saying he would call him at a more convenient time. But for Felix, a more convenient time never came.

You may have heard of the Procrastinators Anonymous Club. Meetings were infrequent because no one got around to sending out notices. Breakfast meetings never started before noon, and they had their Christmas party in July. Some things about procrastination are funny. Some are not.

Setting aside a more convenient time to receive Jesus may not be an option. Every day, people face uncertainties. An accident may snuff out a life before that person has made a decision about Christ. Don't let that happen to you. Today is the day of salvation. A more convenient time to accept the gospel may never come.

There is no way that you can keep from
being conformed to the world unless you are
being transformed by the renewing of your mind.

RAY STEDMAN

HOW BLESSED IS THE MAN

Let every soul be subject to the governing authorities.
For there is no authority except from God, and the
authorities that exist are appointed by God.

ROMANS 13:1

Most people in the United States don't look forward to April 15. It is the most dreaded day of the year: Tax Day. Not only do we have to labor through the tax forms (or pay someone else to do it for us), but we have to bid farewell to a portion of our hard-earned money. And yet it would pay us well to be cheerful givers on this day since God's will for every Christian is to "be subject to the governing authorities" (Romans 13:1).

There is always a blessing, directly or indirectly, in submitting to the will of God even when it seems undesirable—like paying taxes. Blessed are those, Jesus said, who manifest a submissive spirit toward God as Lord in their lives: humble in spirit, mourning over sin, meek, hungering and thirsting after righteousness, merciful, pure in heart, making peace (Matthew 5:3-9). To obey the governing authorities is just one more way of submitting to the will of God and living a blessed, or happy, life.

On Tax Day or any day, find ultimate happiness by submitting to the will of God in all things.

Worship is the submission of all of our nature to God.

WILLIAM TEMPLE

BRICK BY BRICK

We do not lose heart. . . . Inwardly we
are being renewed day by day.
2 CORINTHIANS 4:16, NIV

Thomas Carlyle labored with intensity on his first volume about the French Revolution, and he felt it could be his greatest work. He gave the manuscript to his friend John Stuart Mill, and Mill read it by the fire. One morning Mill's maid, cleaning the room and seeing the scattered pages on the floor, threw the manuscript into the fire. When Carlyle learned his work had been burned to ash, he sank into an abysmal depression. Some time later, still desolate, he saw a brick mason through the window. The man was standing on a scaffold, singing and whistling to himself as he built the wall of a house one brick at a time. Carlyle decided he would write his book again, one page at a time. His three-part history of the French Revolution became famous, and he is remembered as one of Scotland's literary giants.

Perhaps you've lost something very valuable to you. Don't give up. Tomorrow still holds a bright promise, and the Lord blesses faithful, plodding work. Let's take it step by step, day by day, and moment by moment.

Looking to Jesus till glory doth shine,
moment by moment, O Lord, I am Thine.

DANIEL WHITTLE

COMFORTED TO COMFORT OTHERS

Rejoice with those who rejoice,
and weep with those who weep.

ROMANS 12:15

When Mitch Albom heard that his favorite college professor, Morrie Schwartz, was dying of Lou Gehrig's disease, he visited him for the first time in over twenty years. He asked Morrie why he bothered to follow the news each day since he was not going to be around to see how things turned out. "It's hard to explain, Mitch," Morrie said. "Now that I'm suffering, I feel closer to people who suffer than I ever did before. . . . I feel their anguish as if it were my own."[*]

In his letter to the Corinthians, Paul lays out the progression of comfort in suffering by saying that God comforts us when we are hurting so we can comfort others with that same comfort (2 Corinthians 1:3-4). When we suffer, we receive the comfort of God so we can replicate that comfort for others.

We don't have to pray for suffering—it will find us easily enough. But we should pray for an empathetic heart to feel the anguish of others and be prepared to comfort them as we ourselves would want to be comforted.

Learn to write your hurts in the sand and
to carve your blessings in stone.

UNKNOWN

---

[*] Mitch Albom, *Tuesdays with Morrie: An Old Man, a Young Man, and Life's Greatest Lesson* (New York: Broadway, 2002), 50.

GOOD-BYE, WORRY!

Cast all your anxiety on him because he cares for you.

1 PETER 5:7, NIV

In C. S. Lewis's *The Screwtape Letters*, the senior devil, Screwtape, explains to the junior devil, Wormwood, why they must tempt humans to worry and not trust God: "There is nothing like suspense and anxiety for barricading a human's mind against the Enemy [God]. He wants men to be concerned with what they do; our business is to keep them thinking about what will happen to them."*

But as we wrestle with the daily burdens of life, how do we not worry about our tomorrows? The apostle Peter explains the simple but profound solution to worry: "Humble yourselves . . . casting all your care upon Him" (1 Peter 5:6-7). Entrusting ourselves and our troubles to God is our singular defense against worry.

Are you submitting with patience to God's will? What will you gain from worrying about your tomorrows? Humble yourself before Him. God is your all-sufficient provider. He cares for you!

Worry is an old man with bended head,
carrying a load of feathers which he thinks are lead.

CORRIE TEN BOOM

---

*C. S. Lewis, *The Screwtape Letters* (New York: HarperCollins, 2001), 28–29.

THIS I KNOW

The very hairs of your head are all numbered.

MATTHEW 10:30

Some have far more hair on their heads than others. But God wants us to know He's counted every hair. Theologically, you may accept the doctrine of God's sovereignty as biblical and true. Yet when your life seems derailed by the loss of a job, a home, or a loved one, do you question God's plans?

Abraham laughed, wondering how God could ever fulfill His promise of birthing a nation through his seed (Genesis 17:17). God came through. Moses thought he'd hit a dead end at the Red Sea with more than two million people following his directions (Exodus 14:16). God came through. Joseph was locked up in a prison, rejected by his brothers and falsely accused by his employer's wife (Genesis 50:20). God came through.

The One who knows the number of hairs on your head, who hears your cries during the night, who understands your confusion amid heartbreaking loss, is able to use your circumstances to accomplish His ultimate purposes. Have you been feeling that God's plans for you are thwarted by misfortune? Not so! Rejoice that a loving God holds you in His grip.

Nothing is a surprise to God; nothing is a setback
to His plans; nothing can thwart His purposes;
and nothing is beyond His control.

JONI EARECKSON TADA

CRUSH-PROOF FAITH

We are hard-pressed on every side, yet not crushed;
we are perplexed, but not in despair.

2 CORINTHIANS 4:8

Are you afraid you will fail?

Gabrielle "Coco" Chanel was born in 1883, orphaned early in life, and raised by nuns. She set out to become a singer, but after only a couple of opportunities, her singing career ended, and she took a job as a hatmaker. Later, she began designing women's fashions, and in 1921 she introduced her first fragrance, Chanel No. 5. Coco Chanel might never have created her beautiful perfume or become an icon in the fashion industry if her singing career had been successful.

Failure is part of everyone's life. Today's verse indicates that as human beings, we can expect discouragement and failure. Yet, we are "not crushed" and "not in despair" as a result.

When we fail, we can ask God to help us learn from that failure and to bring about positive changes in our lives.

Are you afraid to fail? You need not be crushed. You need not be in despair. God is with you. As someone once said, "Yes, I stumble, but I know I'm stumbling in the right direction."

In all my perplexities and distresses, the Bible has never failed to give me light and strength.

ROBERT E. LEE

A CHANGELESS GOD
IN A SENSELESS WORLD

Every good gift and every perfect gift is from
above, and comes down from the Father of lights,
with whom there is no variation or shadow of turning.

JAMES 1:17

No matter how dear your friends are, they can fail you. No matter how much money you have, you can go broke. No matter how diligently you exercise, you can get sick. Your most trusted walking stick can break. Your dearest dream can die. Life is as uncertain as the clouds that gather and scatter. It's as fickle as the waves of the ocean.

How sad to be in a senseless world without a changeless God. We have a God with whom there is no variation nor shadow of turning. He doesn't have shifting moods, bad days, "oops" moments, momentary breakdowns, or changes of heart. He's as consistent as a plumb line, as steady as a rock, and as unchanging as eternity. He is as He has always been and will always be. Forever He is enthroned in the highest, and forever His Word is fixed in the heavens.

Our forefathers walked with God, and so can we. So can our children and grandchildren. He's the same in every generation. His promises cannot fail, His presence cannot dim, His power cannot wane. We can trust Him completely.

Culture changes. Churches change.
Life changes. God doesn't.

JIM L. WILSON

MEEK, NOT WEAK

*Sanctify the Lord God in your hearts, and always be ready
to give a defense to everyone who asks you a reason
for the hope that is in you, with meekness and fear.*

1 PETER 3:15

It is ironic that a word that rhymes with *meekness*, the word *weakness*, is actually so different in meaning. Perhaps because the two words sound alike, many confuse meekness with weakness. But the two are in no way similar.

One of the best places to find proof that meekness is not weakness is in the life of Moses. The King James Version of Numbers 12:3 says, "The man Moses was very meek, above all the men which were upon the face of the earth." Scripture tells us that Moses was meek. But his biography from Exodus through Deuteronomy dispels the notion that meek equals weak. Moses killed an Egyptian guard who was abusing a Hebrew slave. He demanded that Pharaoh let the Hebrews go. And he called down judgment on the Hebrews when they sinned against God in the wilderness. Moses was meek (meaning humble and submissive to God), but he was not weak.

Don't confuse meekness with weakness. Instead, "be strong in the Lord and in the power of His might" (Ephesians 6:10).

To be truly meek means we no longer protect ourselves,
because we see there is nothing worth defending.

D. MARTYN LLOYD-JONES

CLEAN HANDS

When Pilate saw that he could not prevail at all, but
rather that a tumult was rising, he took water and washed
his hands before the multitude, saying, "I am innocent
of the blood of this just Person. You see to it."

MATTHEW 27:24

Harry Truman coined the phrase "The buck stops here" with a sign bearing this inscription conspicuously placed on his desk in the Oval Office. President Truman made it clear that he understood his responsibility as chief executive—he alone was morally and legally accountable for the actions of his office and his nation.

Pontius Pilate would never have had a similar motto. Pushed and pressured by the many influences that played on his weak mind, Pilate chose the most expedient route, siding with the agitated crowd.

Pilate hoped he could somehow avert the responsibility for his bad choice by symbolically washing his hands of the blood of Christ. Instead, he is remembered for sending Jesus to the cross.

When Christians accept responsibility for all we say and do, God is pleased. We may have a majority going against us, as Pilate did, but God rewards those who accept responsibility for their choices.

God pays in joy that is fire-proof, famine-proof and devil-proof.

BILLY SUNDAY

EATING SCRIPTURE

Man shall not live by bread alone, but by every
word that proceeds from the mouth of God.

MATTHEW 4:4

It's amazing what companies try to sell us to eat. A Scottish company offers a potato chip that tastes like haggis, Scotland's national delicacy. Real haggis is a rare treat—a blend of various sheep organs (like the heart, liver, and lungs) traditionally simmered in the animal's stomach or intestines for several hours. It's more delicious than it sounds, but for those who aren't into sheep innards, we can now sample the taste in potato chip form.

It's also amazing what the world wants to put into our minds. Just as our bodies need nourishment, our minds need to be well fed. We need the milk of the Word, the meat of sound doctrine, the Bread of Life, and the sustenance of Scripture. Instead, many people are addicted to video games, the Internet, movies, and television programs. According to the *New York Times*, people consume an average of twelve hours of media a day.

Stop filling your mind with junk food. Develop a personal plan to study your Bible every day. Eat His Book.

Reading is an immense gift, but only if the words
are assimilated, taken into the soul—eaten, chewed,
gnawed, received in unhurried delight.*

EUGENE PETERSON

---

*Eugene Peterson, *Eat This Book* (Grand Rapids: Eerdmans, 2006), 11.

CAREFUL OF COUNTERFEITS

*The coming of the lawless one will be in accordance
with the work of Satan displayed in all kinds of
counterfeit miracles, signs and wonders.*

2 THESSALONIANS 2:9, NIV

In Chicago, police raided a small store and found more than sixteen thousand counterfeit CDs and DVDs. Police near Atlanta arrested thirteen coconspirators on charges of making counterfeit copies. Police in North Wilkesboro, North Carolina, arrested two local men for possessing thousands of counterfeit CDs and DVDs. It is said that, in China, counterfeit CDs and DVDs are available before the originals are even released in the United States. And the counterfeit packaging is excellent quality! Many people can't tell the difference—until they play the movie or listen to the music. Even then, the counterfeits can be deceiving.

Satan is good at counterfeiting in the spiritual realm. He can produce signs and wonders and make his apostles look like Christ's apostles. Christians must be careful. Spiritual appearance is not a guarantee of spiritual integrity. We must "test the spirits to see whether they are from God," as John writes (1 John 4:1, NIV).

There are powers that can counterfeit
almost anything in the Christian life.

D. MARTYN LLOYD-JONES

CALLED TO LIVE

[The mob shouted,] "These who have turned the world upside down have come here too."

ACTS 17:6

Many of Jesus' disciples suffered horrific deaths. Peter was crucified upside down. James was beheaded. Andrew was crucified on an X-shaped cross. Philip, Jude, and Simon were also crucified. Bartholomew was skinned alive and beheaded. Matthew was stabbed to death. Thomas was speared to death. James was stoned, crucified, and beaten to death. Matthias (the replacement for Judas Iscariot) was stoned and beheaded.

Jesus warned His original disciples before He was killed, "If they persecuted Me, they will also persecute you" (John 15:20). And when their faith was finally tested when Jesus was arrested in the Garden of Gethsemane, "they all forsook Him and fled" (Mark 14:50). What happened to turn a group of cowards into a core of courageous couriers of the gospel who turned the world upside down and were willing to die for their beliefs? One thing: they witnessed the Resurrection. This event had a transforming effect on the disciples, transforming them into apostles—"sent ones." When they saw the risen Christ (1 Corinthians 15:3-8), they were no longer afraid.

You may not be called to die for Christ, but you are called to live for Him.

The Christian church has the resurrection written all over it.

E. G. ROBINSON

HAVE MERCY!

They lifted up their voices and said,
"Jesus, Master, have mercy on us!"

LUKE 17:13

If you grew up decades ago in the southern United States, you likely remember hearing the expression "Lord, have mercy!" whenever life took a turn for the worse. It was a familiar expression in the Deep South because the South is synonymous with the Bible Belt, and "Lord, have mercy!" is a biblical expression.

"Have mercy" occurs forty-six times in Scripture, twelve times in Psalms alone—the book in which authors were often found imploring God for relief or help. On several occasions, Jesus was called upon to "have mercy" by those in need. And He responded by granting healing or deliverance as required.

What is mercy? It is not getting what we deserve. Being sinners, we deserve all manner of judgment. So when we feel we're in the middle of a judgment of circumstances, we call out to God to "have mercy" and take the bad situation away. By grace, God often does—giving us something (in this case, relief) that we don't deserve. Grace and mercy are both sides of God's love.

Find someone this week to show mercy to. If someone does something wrong and thus deserves judgment, extend mercy instead.

The name Jehovah carries majesty in it,
the name Father carries mercy in it.

THOMAS WATSON

WINNING THE BATTLE

Put on the whole armor of God, that you may be able to stand against the wiles of the devil.

EPHESIANS 6:11

Many people misunderstand the purpose of the spiritual warfare Job experienced (Job 1–2). The point of Satan's attack was not to destroy Job or ruin his life by destroying his family and property. Satan's desire was that Job would curse God for letting such bad things happen to him. Job's wife became so exasperated that she fell right into Satan's hands and said to her husband, "Do you still hold fast to your integrity? Curse God and die!" (Job 2:9). But Job kept his spiritual integrity and would not blame God for his troubles.

The point is this: Satan's primary purpose is to make God, not us, look bad. But he attacks us in order to tempt us to attack God. And he will use any situation to test us—including our finances. If you become so anxious over money that you lose your faith in God, Satan has won the battle. We win by giving thanks in everything (1 Thessalonians 5:18).

Don't let anything—including finances—cause you to "curse God." Rather, say what Job said: "Shall we accept good from God, and not trouble?" (Job 2:10, NIV)

Scars are the price which every believer
pays for his loyalty to Christ.

WILLIAM HENDRIKSEN

SOWING SEEDS OF KINDNESS

*Let us not grow weary while doing good, for in
due season we shall reap if we do not lose heart.
Therefore, as we have opportunity, let us do good to all,
especially to those who are of the household of faith.*

GALATIANS 6:9-10

Good deeds have a way of coming back to bless us. John Wooden, the great basketball coach at UCLA, was admired for his inspirational influence on players and fans alike. His life was shaped by a seven-point creed his father had given him upon graduation from grammar school, and he often passed it along to others.

Be true to yourself. Make each day your masterpiece. Help others. Drink deeply from good books, especially the Bible. Make friendship a fine art. Build a shelter against a rainy day. Pray for guidance and give thanks for your blessings every day.

When we are kind to others and practice a merciful attitude, we become recipients of mercy ourselves. Just as the sower reaps the crop he has sown, so do merciful people reap what has been planted in the lives of others.

Don't get tired of doing good!

Talent is God-given; be humble. Fame is man-given;
be grateful. Conceit is self-given; be careful.

JOHN WOODEN

HERE I STAND

*Do not be ashamed of the testimony of our Lord, nor
of me His prisoner, but share with me in the sufferings
for the gospel according to the power of God.*

2 TIMOTHY 1:8

When Martin Luther was asked to recant his teachings against the church, he made this bold statement to the Diet of Worms in 1521: "Unless I am convinced by proofs from Scriptures or by plain and clear reasons and arguments, I can and will not retract, for it is neither safe nor wise to do anything against conscience. Here I stand. I can do no other. God help me. Amen."*

In his farewell address to the Israelites, Joshua urged them to take a stand and commit themselves to the Lord. He laid out their two options: choose to serve the God of Israel or choose idols. The choice would determine Israel's history and shape future generations. Leading by example, Joshua proclaimed his commitment to God: "As for me and my house, we will serve the LORD" (Joshua 24:15).

Perhaps today you need to renew your commitment to God. Take a stand. Declare, "Here I stand. I can do no other. God help me."

Our strength is seen in the things we stand for;
our weakness is seen in the things we fall for.

THEODORE EPP

---

*"English Bible History: Martin Luther," Greatsite, http://greatsite.com/timeline-english-bible-history/martin-luther.html.

MAY

ORGANIZED FOR BATTLE

[David] took his staff in his hand; and he chose for himself
five smooth stones from the brook, and put them in a
shepherd's bag, in a pouch which he had, and his sling
was in his hand. And he drew near to the Philistine.

1 SAMUEL 17:40

When we think of the story of David and Goliath, we empha-size the slingshot. But notice David's other equipment. He had a staff in his hand and a shepherd's bag tied around his body. Into the shepherd's bag he dropped the stones chosen from the nearby brook. David didn't want Saul's armor, but he couldn't do without his own simple equipment: a sling, a staff, some stones, and a shepherd's bag.

Without the stones, the slingshot would have been useless, and without the shepherd's bag, the stones would not have been accessible. David was organized for the battle.

In our battles in life, we need our ammunition near at hand. Do you carry a Bible on your phone or a small New Testament in your purse or pocket? Is there a Bible by your bed or on your desk? Have you memorized a verse recently? Do you have it tucked away safely in your heart?

God's Word is a potent weapon, but only if we keep it read-ily accessible.

The one who neglects his Bible is bound to
make a failure of the Christian life.*

R. A. TORREY

_____
*R. A. Torrey, *How to Succeed in the Christian Life* (Chicago: Moody Press, 1979), 48.

A WAY OF ESCAPE

*I also will keep you from the hour of trial
which shall come upon the whole world,
to test those who dwell on the earth.*

REVELATION 3:10

The fall of Saigon—April 30, 1975—marked the end of America's involvement in the Vietnam War and the final departure of Americans from the city. As US Army helicopters evacuated the last American employees from the embassy in Saigon, thousands of South Vietnamese begged to be included, fearful of life under the North Vietnamese Communist regime.

The inhabitants of planet Earth will one day beg for a way to escape the terror unleashed during the seven-year Tribulation. Those not taken in the Rapture of the church may come to faith in Christ during the Tribulation, but they will still endure the trials of that dark time. Through trusting our Savior now, we can avoid the trials that will visit the earth during the Tribulation. Rejoice in the knowledge that you are a child of God and that He has provided a way of escape for you.

Just as God provided Noah's family an ark of refuge, so Christ becomes an ark of deliverance for all who believe.

Oh, how I wished that I had a tongue like thunder, that
I might make all hear; or that I had a frame like iron,
that I might visit every one, and say, "Escape for thy life!"

ROBERT MURRAY MCCHEYNE

BE A PEACEMAKER

*The fruit of righteousness is sown in
peace by those who make peace.*

JAMES 3:18

Our planet is not a peaceful place. The University of Oslo and Norwegian Academy of Sciences have determined that there have been more than 14,000 wars in the world since 3600 BC. Surprisingly, the world has known relative peace only 5 percent of the time over the last 5,600 years.

It is painfully obvious to everyone on the planet that peace is rare these days—and not just between nations. There are innumerable wars going on between individuals, within families, in business, and in government. Interestingly, the Bible puts the responsibility for peace in the world on individuals: "If it is possible, as much as depends on you, live peaceably with all men" (Romans 12:18). Hebrews tells us to "pursue peace with all people" (12:14). Obviously, if every individual purposed to live in peace, then nations could live in peace as well.

Today, try to create peace wherever you go. Be a peacemaker, befitting a son or daughter of God.

The peacemakers are those who are at peace with God
and who show that they are truly children of God by
striving to use every opportunity open to them to effect
reconciliation between others who are at variance.

R. V. G. TASKER

PAIN TODAY, REWARDS FOREVER

*All who desire to live godly in Christ
Jesus will suffer persecution.*

2 TIMOTHY 3:12

For two thousand years, followers of Jesus Christ have been persecuted. For example, Martin Luther and his supporters were persecuted for protesting abuses in the established church in sixteenth-century Germany. We are reminded throughout God's Word that there is a cost to following our Savior, but the rewards are also great.

The probability of persecution is not the focal point of the gospel message, but followers of Christ should understand that "all who desire to live godly in Christ Jesus will suffer persecution." Jesus told His original disciples plainly, "If they persecuted Me, they will also persecute you" (John 15:20). Although persecution is unpleasant, Jesus called those who are persecuted for His sake "blessed." Why? Because their reward in heaven will be great (Matthew 5:12).

Persecution is painful, but the anticipation of eternal rewards for faithfulness is a balm for the wounded body and soul. Your Savior will be with you through it all.

Persecution is the legacy bequeathed by Christ to His people.

THOMAS WATSON

JOCHEBED: A COURAGEOUS MOTHER

By faith Moses, when he was born, was hidden three months by his parents, because they saw he was a beautiful child; and they were not afraid of the king's command.

HEBREWS 11:23

You may never have heard her name, but Moses' mother was one of the greatest mothers of all time. Jochebed was a woman of courage.

When Moses was born, Pharaoh had decreed that all Hebrew baby boys would be killed. Willing to risk the wrath of the king, Jochebed made a watertight basket and placed Moses in the river at a time when the Egyptian princess would be at the banks. With her daughter watching from a distance, Jochebed trusted that the baby's cries would warm the heart of the princess in time to save her son.

By placing her precious infant in the Nile River, Jochebed showed great courage and faith. She risked much to save her son so she could raise him to honor God. She became the palace nurse and reared her own son to fear God in spite of the Egyptian godlessness.

Christian parenting takes courage. Society will draw our children away from the godly values that we want to instill in them. Like Jochebed, we can set our fears aside and risk anything necessary to teach our children to follow Jesus Christ.

The mother's heart is the child's schoolroom.

HENRY WARD BEECHER

CHRIST'S RETURN

*This same Jesus, who was taken up from you into heaven,
will so come in like manner as you saw Him go into heaven.*

ACTS 1:11

Since we can't even see one minute into the future, human beings are poor fortune-tellers. Thomas Watson, chairman of IBM, said in 1943 that he foresaw no world market for computers. *Popular Mechanics* ran an article in 1949, predicting that one day computers would weigh no more than 1.5 tons. Ken Olsen, president of Digital Equipment Corporation, declared in 1977, "There is no reason anyone would want a computer in their home." And even Bill Gates is reported to have said in 1981, "640K memory ought to be enough for anybody."

Humans may not know about the future, but God, who is omniscient, eternal, and truthful, has given us an accurate set of predictions about days to come. Biblical prophecies contain no inaccuracies or errors in judgment.

The greatest prophecy of all has to do with the glorious return of Jesus Christ to the earth. Just after Jesus ascended to heaven, His followers were told that He would be coming back again (Acts 1:11). Because God's Word can be trusted, we can believe in this promise.

Live today with the assurance that His coming is sure, certain, and soon!

Some are looking merely for something to
happen, not for Someone to come.

VANCE HAVNER

CONDITIONS FOR HAPPINESS

Taste and see that the L ORD is good;
blessed is the man who trusts in Him!
PSALM 34:8

In the Old Testament, the word for *blessed* or *happy* comes from a verb that means "to go straight; to advance." It was originally used to refer to leading others straight ahead or in the right path, then to setting things right, and then to being right oneself—in other words, it referred to being happy, blessed, or in the best place.

There is lots of advice in the world about how to be happy or how to live a happy life. One popular lifestyle guru talks about "living your best life." But none of this advice squares with how the Bible describes true happiness or blessedness. Thirteen times in Scripture, the phrase "Blessed is the man who . . ." is used, and few of the conditions for happiness would be recommended by the world: meditating on God's Word, having a pure spirit, trusting in God, learning God's precepts, fearing God, listening to God, enduring temptation. Drawing on the Old Testament examples, Jesus created His own list of nine conditions for happiness—the Beatitudes, or "be-attitudes," as they have been called.

What are your conditions for happiness? If they line up with the Bible's, nothing else will make you happier.

To seek God is to desire happiness;
to find Him is that happiness.

AUGUSTINE

OPERATION DYNAMO

Occupy till I come.

LUKE 19:13, KJV

On May 23, 1940, Vice Admiral Bertram Ramsey rubbed his eyes in the caves beneath Dover Castle overlooking the English Channel and then jotted a quick note to his wife: "No beds for any of us last night," he wrote, "and probably not for many nights. I'm so sleepy I can hardly keep my eyes open." But he did keep his eyes open as he presided over Operation Dynamo, which rescued the British Expeditionary Force at Dunkirk. In what Winston Churchill later called "a miracle of deliverance," Operation Dynamo successfully evacuated a third of a million troops who were trapped in France by Hitler's forces.

Everyone needs time to rest and relax. But the devil has millions of people trapped. The church of Jesus Christ is mounting the greatest evacuation effort in history, seeking and saving those who are lost. We need to remain vigilant so that our focus isn't diverted by "breaking news" about the latest movie, electronic gadget, or political debate. Let's live with a sense of urgency regarding the Lord's work until He comes. Let's win souls, even if in the process we lose a little sleep.

Because He is coming, I want to be pleasing Him when
He comes. I want to go out and suffer, work, and win
souls, and if necessary, die to save some lost one.

R. A. TORREY

SEASIDE SHORES

*Do not be afraid. Stand still, and see the salvation
of the LORD, which He will accomplish for you
today. . . . The LORD will fight for you.*

EXODUS 14:13-14

Who can imagine the terror that gripped the families of Israel in Exodus 14? The joy of their emancipation was overwhelmed by sudden crisis. Before them was the Red Sea; behind them was the flash of Pharaoh's swords. With no way out, they seemed to be facing annihilation. Yet the Lord said, "Don't be afraid. See what I will do. Stand still and watch while I fight for you." As Moses raised his rod over the water, the winds of heaven blew, and the sea parted before them.

God can make a way where there seems to be no way. Isaiah 43:19 (KJV) says, "I will even make a way in the wilderness, and rivers in the desert." The apostle Paul promised that God will not allow us to be tempted beyond our ability but will make a way of escape (1 Corinthians 10:13).

If you're facing a challenging problem, don't be afraid. Stand still and see what God will do. He will make a way.

The Lord will make a way for you where no foot
has been before. That which, like a sea, threatens
to drown you, shall be a highway for your escape.

CHARLES H. SPURGEON

WHEELS OF JUSTICE

The devil, who deceived them,
was cast into the lake of fire and brimstone
where the beast and the false prophet are.

REVELATION 20:10

The Sixth Amendment of the US Constitution guarantees that "the accused shall enjoy the right to a speedy and public trial." But legal proceedings can take many months, if not years, to finally be resolved in court. When a trial is finally ended, those seeking justice rejoice with a sense of relief.

The Bible says rejoicing is heard in heaven when a sinner is saved (Luke 15:7), but there will no doubt be rejoicing for another reason: when justice is finally applied to Satan and he is confined to "the lake of fire and brimstone . . . forever and ever" (Revelation 20:10). Satan's crimes and character will be laid bare before the bar of God's justice at the end of the coming Millennium, and he will be consigned to an eternal prison from which there is no escape.

Be assured that though the wheels of God's justice do not turn at a human pace, they turn nonetheless. All injustice will be set to right in due time.

God is not always a God of immediate justice,
but he is a God of ultimate justice.

JOHN BLANCHARD

WHAT'S PRECIOUS TO YOU?

To you who believe, He is precious.

1 PETER 2:7

During the Great Recession, the *Wall Street Journal* reported that investors were turning out in droves to purchase precious metals or precious stones as a hedge against uncertainty in the global economy. The word *precious* conveys the idea of being valuable, highly esteemed, and dearly loved.

The Bible uses the word *precious* to describe the value of our lives (Psalm 22:20), God's lovingkindness (Psalm 36:7), His thoughts toward us (Psalm 139:17), His wisdom on our lips (Proverbs 3:15; 20:15), and a good reputation (Ecclesiastes 7:1).

In the New Testament, Peter uses this word more than anyone else. In his letters, he calls our faith precious. A gentle and quiet spirit is also precious. Our Lord Jesus is precious, as is His redeeming blood. And we've been blessed with His "great and precious promises" (2 Peter 1:4).

Precious metals will burn up one day; precious stones will be left behind. But our most precious possession, Jesus Christ, is ours eternally; for where He is, there we will be also.

No one ever lost out by excessive devotion to Christ.
Christ is a substitute for everything, but
nothing is a substitute for Christ.

H. A. IRONSIDE

THE BATTLEFIELD OF THE MIND

*Though we walk in the flesh, we do not
war according to the flesh.*

2 CORINTHIANS 10:3

*T*he *American Heritage Dictionary* defines *battleground* as "an area where a battle is fought; a sphere of contention." But the pictures in the daily news make us think otherwise—that battlegrounds are only places where guns are fired, bombs are dropped, people are physically killed and wounded, and landscapes are destroyed. The danger is that, if we look around us and don't see those things happening, we think we are not living in a battlefield.

But nothing could be further from the truth. Paul wrote to the Corinthians that our battle is not like the world's battles. Rather, it is a battle of ideas, fought on the battlefield of the mind. Our enemy's strategy is to tempt us to deny God's truth and to deceive and discourage God's people so they lose faith in the goodness and providence of God. Yes, Satan stirs up physical wars between nations and peoples, but even those wars begin with thoughts.

Follow Paul's admonition to take every thought captive, submissive to the will of God in Christ Jesus (2 Corinthians 10:5). Thoughts must be tested by the Word of God.

How sad our state by nature is! Our sin, how deep it stains!
And Satan binds our captive minds fast in his slavish chains.

ISAAC WATTS

DEFENSE AGAINST DECEIT

I fear, lest somehow, as the serpent deceived
Eve by his craftiness, so your minds may be
corrupted from the simplicity that is in Christ.

2 CORINTHIANS 11:3

When a Wall Street investment manager defrauded investors out of billions of dollars, the guilty financier himself described it as "one big lie." He caused his investors to believe something that was not true.

That's a good way to describe the devil's primary strategy against the children of God: tempting them, influencing them to believe something that is not true. While Satan will attack truth wherever it is found—anything to promote discord and confusion on earth—it is the truth of God's Word that Satan most wants to negate. In the biblical account, the first time we see him on earth, he is in the Garden of Eden convincing Eve that she will not die if she disobeys God's explicit instruction. Satan deceived Eve, causing her to believe what was not true. And Eve died spiritually on the spot.

The best way for a Christian to defend against Satan's deceit is with the sword of the Spirit, the Word of God (Ephesians 6:17). Confidently correcting Satan's lies with God's own words will cause the devil to flee (Matthew 4:11; James 4:7).

No wickedness on earth is more common
than the various forms of deceit.

WILLIAM S. PLUMER

JUSTICE IN TIME

*If then you count me as a partner,
receive him as you would me.*

PHILEMON 1:17

Forgiving someone who has wronged you is hard to do, even at the best of times. Sometimes, in our humanity, we'd rather seek our own justice.

Yet forgiveness is what Paul asked of Philemon. He wanted Philemon to forgive Onesimus, his slave who stole from him and ran away. According to the law of that day, Philemon could have enacted a heavy punishment due to Onesimus's theft and desertion. Paul, however, pleaded with Philemon to follow the higher law of forgiveness. Receive him as "a beloved brother," Paul wrote (verse 16).

When Onesimus returned to his master, Philemon heard his confession and plea. And heeding Paul's request, Philemon forgave him and freed him. As a result of this forgiveness, Onesimus became a prominent leader in the early church.

Philemon's story shows us that forgiveness is a way of life for the believer. As we forgive and are forgiven, we grow in God's grace.

Is there someone in your life whom you need to forgive? A family member, friend, or colleague? Remember that God will exercise His wise justice in His own time. Ask God to bring the person to mind, and take the bold step of forgiveness today.

The only thing harder than forgiveness is the alternative.

PHILIP YANCEY

FIT FOR VICTORY

Stand therefore, having girded your waist with truth.

EPHESIANS 6:14

The English word *gird* reminds us of a girdle, but that conjures up the wrong image. Though older translations used the word *girdle*, they were referring to the belt or sash worn in biblical times around the waist or chest. When running, people tucked their robes into their belts to race more freely (1 Peter 1:13). The girdle was the sash that held the rest of the clothing together. Sometimes weapons, like one's sword, were attached (Psalm 45:3).

Paul writes of girding our waist with another weapon—*truth*. In a day when many people believe truth is relative, the Bible teaches that God's truth—found in His Word—is absolute. It's the truth that holds the rest of our armor together and enables us to fight with mental freedom. When we're convinced that the Bible is altogether true, our minds are composed; our weapons are in place; we're outfitted for victory.

Wear the truth, say it, sing it, and you will be
amazed how the difficulty will be subdued;
for the mouth of the Lord hath spoken it.*

JOHN HENRY JOWETT

---

*John Henry Jowett, *The Whole Armour of God* (New York: Revell, 1916), 37.

DESERT SANDS

Jesus said to him, "Away with you, Satan!
*For it is written, 'You shall worship the L*ORD
your God, and Him only you shall serve.'"

MATTHEW 4:10

We're often told that Jesus quoted Scripture to the devil and thereby defeated him. But it wasn't quite that easy. There were other factors involved in gaining victory. Through reading the story of the Temptation in Matthew 4, we notice that Jesus also relied on the Holy Spirit, who was leading Him at every point (verse 1). Christ was maintaining the spiritual discipline of fasting, and we can assume He was in the middle of a season of prayer (verse 2). Our Lord was also determined to say, "No! No! No!" to Satan's three enticements. Verse 11 tells us that Jesus outlasted the temptation and Satan limped away in defeat after being worn out by our Lord's unflinching righteousness. Within that context, Jesus quoted Scripture three times to Satan and thereby won the victory.

To win against sin, we need the Holy Spirit's power, the practice of regular spiritual disciplines, a determination to live righteously, tenacity, and a handful of crucial Scriptures to quote in times of temptation.

With our spiritual tools ready, we, too, can resist the devil, and he will flee from us.

Fight manfully onward, dark passions subdue,
look ever to Jesus, He'll carry you through.

HORATIO R. PALMER

THE POWER OF ONE

He asked Philip to come up and sit with him.

ACTS 8:31

As Philip and the Ethiopian eunuch talked about a prophecy from Isaiah, God's Spirit moved. Philip shared the gospel, which resonated with his listener. The eunuch asked to be baptized, and he made his simple confession of faith. Changed forever, the Ethiopian rejoiced (Acts 8:39).

Two ordinary individuals—that's the simple relationship of the story. God used one of His followers to minister to one person. He took Philip from the crowds of Samaria to a lone traveler on a country road in order to help a man searching for meaning.

This beautifully illustrates the heart of God. He cares for the individual, and He searches out the one lost sheep, leaving the others in the wilderness (Luke 15:4-7). He deeply loves every one of His children and knows each of them intimately (Psalm 139:1).

When you know Christ, you can reflect this same love. Who do you know who needs to know Christ? Ask God to lead you to someone who needs Him, and open the Scriptures to him or her. You can rejoice when that individual responds to His call.

The essence of faith is "being satisfied with
all that God is for us in Jesus."

JOHN PIPER

PUTTING ON TRUTH

Jesus said to him, "I am the way, the truth, and the life.
No one comes to the Father except through Me."

JOHN 14:6

Think of all the ways we are told to relate to "truth" in our modern world: *study* the truth, *find* the truth, *explore* the truth, *know* the truth, *discover* the truth, *reveal* the truth—and the list goes on. But before we can put any of those verbs into action, we must answer the question raised by Pontius Pilate when he asked Jesus of Nazareth, "What is truth?" (John 18:38). We can only study and learn that which we can identify.

Had Pilate known Jesus better, he would have known that Jesus had already answered that question when He said, "I am . . . the truth." Marrying that statement with Paul's description of truth as one of the elements of the Christian's spiritual armor brings us to this conclusion: Jesus Christ is the believer's spiritual armor. Paul says in Romans 13:14 that we are to "put on the Lord Jesus Christ." When we put on (believe in, submit to) Christ, who is truth, we clothe ourselves with truth; we protect ourselves from Satan's lies and deceit.

If you are clothed with Christ and His Word today, you are clothed in truth, defended against the subterfuge of Satan.

The truth of Scripture demolishes speculation.

R. C. SPROUL

FREE FROM ACCUSATIONS

*If anyone sins, we have an Advocate with the
Father, Jesus Christ the righteous.*

1 JOHN 2:1

At this very minute, accusations are flying around all over the world: in a court of law, in a political body, perhaps in a living room. Accusations can carry tremendous weight depending on the stature of the person making them.

There is another place where accusations never stop flowing—in the throne room of heaven. Revelation 12:10 calls Satan the "accuser of [the] brethren." He accuses Christians "before our God day and night." Given the power of the Accuser, the accusations against us as sinners, unworthy of forgiveness and grace, must be taken seriously. And the allegations are true: we are sinners. But because we have put on "Jesus Christ the righteous" (1 John 2:1), our Advocate enters these facts as evidence: He paid for our sins, and we have been credited with His righteousness.

When Satan tries to convince you of your unworthiness before God, agree that you are a sinner—then show him the breastplate of Christ's righteousness you are wearing.

When God declares a man righteous he instantly
sets about to make him righteous.

A. W. TOZER

HUMILITY RULES

*I wrote to the church, but Diotrephes, who loves to have
the preeminence among them, does not receive us.*

3 JOHN 1:9

Humility is an elusive quality. The moment you believe you've mastered it, it vanishes! Control is the opposite. When someone seeks to control a situation, a group, or a meeting, everyone knows immediately who is in charge.

In John's third letter, he writes stinging words about a forceful man named Diotrephes. It seems that Diotrephes sought the limelight and ordered everyone else around. When it came to the exercise of hospitality, he directly countered John's instructions. Worse yet, Diotrephes spoke ill of others and tried to manipulate them to do exactly what served his purpose, not what their church leaders had instructed them to do.

Does this situation sound familiar to you—even just a little bit?

We can sometimes be tempted to think that controlling a situation or group is satisfying. The truth is that whether it is the first century or the twenty-first century, God is always in control of His church. He wants to use humble and willing people who can set aside their personal agenda and follow as He leads. Does that describe you?

*Give me humility, in which alone is rest, and deliver
me from pride, which is the heaviest of burdens.*

THOMAS MERTON

DON'T BE OUTFOXED

Put on the breastplate of righteousness.

EPHESIANS 6:14

There once was a hunter in Belarus who shot a fox from a distance, but when the man approached the wounded animal, it sprang on him. As the two scuffled, the fox got its paw on the trigger of the rifle and shot the man in the leg. The hunter was transported to the hospital, and the fox escaped.

In our struggle with sin, we've got to make sure Satan doesn't turn the tables on us. The Bible warns us to beware of the little foxes that can spoil the vines (Song of Solomon 2:15).

We're safe if we're always clad in the breastplate of righteousness. The word *breastplate* is misleading, since this piece of armor also protected the back, neck, and hips. It was like a wraparound shield that encased the body's vital organs. The breastplate of righteousness is the Bible's symbol for a holy life. Living righteously requires us to be in constant submission to the will of God with hearts open to His righteousness, lest we be outfoxed.

Lay hold on the Bible until the Bible lays hold on you.

WILL H. HOUGHTON

FOR ALL WALKS OF LIFE

He will not allow your foot to be moved;
He who keeps you will not slumber.

PSALM 121:3

A tire shop in Milwaukee advertised, "Invite us to your next blowout." An optometrist said, "If you don't see what you're looking for, you've come to the right place." And a California landscaper boasted, "We're easy to get a lawn with." But when it comes to clever slogans, maybe the podiatrist had the best one when he said, "Put your feet in our hands!"

Most of us have learned that if our feet hurt, we hurt all over—and our feet hurt when we're wearing the wrong shoes. (Another podiatrist said, "Time wounds all heels," but that's enough slogans for now!) The point is that when we slip our feet into gospel shoes, we feel good all over. When we are shod with the gospel of peace, we needn't be anxious as we walk through life. We can cast all our cares on the One who said, "Do not worry about your life" (Matthew 6:25).

God's shoes are easy on our souls!

If you are at peace with God through Jesus,
then you are shod with peace. . . . His Presence
is an abiding reality in your experience.

C. A. FOX

GOOD, GOOD, NOT GOOD

The LORD God said, "It is not good that man should be alone; I will make him a helper comparable to him."

GENESIS 2:18

When we read the wonderful story of God's creation of the heavens and the earth, we are struck by the satisfaction He expressed after each movement in His creative symphony. Day one: the light was good. Day two: the earth and the seas were good. Day three: the plants were good. God's smiling contentment is woven through each moment of creation.

Did you know there was a point at which God said, "Not good"? Yes, when He looked on the loneliness of Adam, without a companion, He declared that it was not good! And He did something about it, creating a wonderful counterpart, Eve, to join with Adam.

God's plan for His creation is that we be in relationships with each other. Relationships are important to Him, and people take priority! Families may struggle with wanting more possessions, believing they will enhance the quality of their lives, but God makes it clear: people are more important than things.

The people God has placed in your life are your first priority. Put them first by giving them your time, attention, and energy today.

The Most High rules in the children of men.

GEORGE FOX

COUNCIL CHAMBERS

All who sat in the council, looking steadfastly
at him, saw his face as the face of an angel.

ACTS 6:15

When Stephen was dragged before the Jewish ruling council for his faith in Christ, the charges flew like daggers. But he never lost his poise, simplicity of faith, or glowing countenance. His words that day were memorable, but his love for Jesus was his greatest testimony.

In his book *The Changed Life*, Henry Drummond shares the story about a woman of sterling character and radiant attitude who wore a locket around her neck. The woman's friends were curious about whose picture it contained, but the woman never opened it or revealed its contents. Only later did a friend, with permission, look inside the locket and learn the secret of the woman's moral radiance. Written within were the words "Whom having not seen, I love." That was the secret of her beautiful life.*

Amid all life's conflicts, our greatest secret is our devotion to the One we have not seen but love. The world has no answer to Christ in us. It's one of our most valuable weapons.

O how I love Jesus, O how I love Jesus,
O how I love Jesus, because He first loved me!

FREDERICK WHITFIELD

---

*Henry Drummond, *The Changed Life* (NY: James Pott and Company, 1891), 20.

FOUNDATIONS OF FAITH

All the families of the nations shall worship before You.
PSALM 22:27

Every home builder understands the importance of a solid foundation when it comes to constructing a quality building. For a building to stand firm through time and all kinds of weather, it must be built on strong footings.

Families are the same. Without the foundation of faith, it's easy to fall apart when times get tough. Building a family without faith in God is often an exercise in futility!

It is during times of crisis that the true values of a family come into focus. Whether Grandma becomes ill, Dad works long hours, or someone loses a job, the families that remain strong in a crisis do so because of a firm foundation of faith. They honor God and look to Him for strength in difficult circumstances.

The same was true in Moses' day—families were instructed to love the Lord with everything in them and to teach this principle to their children daily so their footing would be strong. Make sure that your family is also built on the foundation that will pass the test of time—the foundation of faith.

The customs of society will lead us away unless the
grace of God rules in us with divine power.
CHARLES H. SPURGEON

THE SHIELD OF FAITH

*Take up the shield of faith, with which you can
extinguish all the flaming arrows of the evil one.*
EPHESIANS 6:16, NIV

Ancient and medieval soldiers went into battle with shields the size and shape of small doors, large enough to hide behind. A phalanx of soldiers could interlock their shields in front of them or over their heads to form a wall of protection against incoming missiles.

The "shield of faith" is a Christian's most important defensive weapon for this reason: if faith is defined as confidence in God and His Word, then it is faith that will deflect Satan's twisting, counterfeiting, and denying who God is and what God has said. If a lie of Satan is like a fiery arrow coming directly at the Christian, then faith is like the shield that keeps the arrow from finding its mark. Faith is how we walk daily (2 Corinthians 5:7). Faith is how we please God (Hebrews 11:6). And faith in Jesus Christ is the basis for "the life [we] now live in the flesh" (Galatians 2:20). But faith is more than belief—it is belief put into practice.

When thoughts of doubt or despair come, raise your shield of faith—faith in God and the promises of His Word.

I do not seek to understand in order that I may
believe, but I believe in order to understand.

ANSELM

HELMETS AND CAULIFLOWERS

Take the helmet of salvation.
EPHESIANS 6:17

Each of us owns a jewel more valuable than any displayed at Cartier or Tiffany's. It's a three-pound blob of gray pulp resembling a rotting cauliflower. This jewel is the most incredible creation in God's universe, a fabulous, living supercomputer with unfathomable circuitry and unimaginable complexity. It's the human brain—a collection of billions of neurons, each as complex as a small computer. Yet the brain is only as useful as the material it feeds on. Our thoughts should be fixed on Christ and filled with His Word.

The Bible tells us to set our minds on things above, not on the things of earth (Colossians 3:2). Wearing the helmet of salvation means our minds are protected by the saving truth of Christ. We're transformed by the renewing of our minds (Romans 12:1-2), for those who live according to the Spirit set their minds on what the Spirit desires (Romans 8:5).

Psalm 37:3 tells us, "Feed on His faithfulness." Be careful what goes into your mind today. Remember that it's the battleground of the soul—and by focusing on Christ, we can win the victory.

Our defeat or victory begins with what we think,
and if we guard our thoughts we shall not have
much trouble anywhere else along the line.*

VANCE HAVNER

---

*Vance Havner, *Pleasant Paths* (New Tappan, NJ: Revell, 1945), 72.

SALTY LANGUAGE

Let your speech always be with grace, seasoned with salt,
that you may know how you ought to answer each one.

COLOSSIANS 4:6

There's an old saying: "What's down in the well comes up in the bucket." That's another way of making our Lord's point in Matthew 12:34: "For out of the abundance of the heart the mouth speaks."

When we have the Scriptures wrapped around our brains like a helmet—especially through Scripture memorization and meditation—our minds become filled with God's Word. It saturates our thoughts. As we fall asleep thinking on His promises and wake up with Him on our minds, it changes the patterns of our brains. We discover that we often have a word of encouragement for someone else. If we continually fill our minds with the knowledge of Christ, He will bring the needed words to mind in every situation.

Every good cook knows that salt enhances the flavor of food. It's not just a matter of giving your meals a salty taste. There's something about salt, used in proper amounts, that brings out the taste of other ingredients and makes them more flavorful.

May God help us salt our conversations today with the flavor of His Word.

Broadly speaking short words are best and
the old words when short, best of all.

WINSTON CHURCHILL

WELL ARMED

Take . . . the sword of the Spirit, which is the word of God.
EPHESIANS 6:17

When the apostle Paul describes the Word of God as the sword of the Spirit, he uses an interesting Greek term for "word." He doesn't employ the common word *logos*, but the word *rhema*. The meaning of *rhema* tends to emphasize the many sayings of God rather than the unified, whole book. All of the Bible is God's inspired and infallible Word, but often in our hand-to-hand combat in daily life, the specific verses and sayings of Scripture are what we need.

Think of the Bible itself as the armory where the individual swords and daggers are stored. Paul's point isn't that we should always carry around a large black Bible for thumping and beating the devil, but that we should have individual verses and statements from Scripture unsheathed in our minds and ready to use at a moment's notice.

When we memorize the many truths of the Bible and are prepared to use them, we've got a set of weapons to plunge into Satan as he tries to fill us with doubt, pride, and selfishness.

Are you working on a memory verse today?

Bible verses, well memorized, are stabilizers for our nerves, strengthening our attitudes and improving our emotions.

ROBERT J. MORGAN

POWER OF THE SWORD

For the word of God is living and powerful, . . . piercing
even to the division of soul and spirit, . . . and is a
discerner of the thoughts and intents of the heart.

HEBREWS 4:12

In his book *The Lost Art of Disciple Making,* LeRoy Eims describes his personal battle with anger. It was not until he made a covenant with God, which included memorizing and meditating on Colossians 3:8 ("You yourselves are to put off all these: anger, wrath . . ."), that anger loosened its grip on his emotions. He reviewed the verse daily and asked the Lord to bring it to mind whenever he was tempted to lose his temper. The Word of God became a sword with which he was able to win his spiritual battle.

Jesus used Scripture in a similar way. When He was tempted for forty days and nights in the wilderness by Satan, Jesus rebuffed every temptation by quoting an appropriate verse from Deuteronomy (Matthew 4:1-11). If you are in a spiritual battle, your sword is to be the Word of God—the sword of the Spirit (Ephesians 6:17). If there is a persistent spiritual battle you fight, memorize a portion of God's living and active Word to gain the victory.

The Bible is alive, it speaks to me; it has feet,
it runs after me; it has hands, it lays hold on me.

MARTIN LUTHER

BATTLEFIELD COMMUNICATION

*Praying always with all prayer and supplication in the
Spirit, being watchful to this end with all perseverance and
supplication for all the saints—and for me, that utterance
may be given to me, that I may open my mouth boldly.*

EPHESIANS 6:18-19

In Ephesians 6:18-19, we have one of history's first missionary prayer requests. The apostle Paul, having written about the armor of the believer and the urgency of prayer, asks the Ephesians to pray that God will give him the ability to share the gospel boldly at every opportunity.

Notice the *all*s in this passage. We're to pray always—at *all* times. We're to offer *all* prayer and supplication in the Spirit. We're to pray with *all* perseverance. And we're to remember *all* the saints.

In his book on prayer, Samuel D. Gordon wrote that this world is God's prodigal son and that God has devised a plan for winning His prodigal back. He wants to use us in the process, and our greatest agency is prayer, which, Gordon says, is communication between God and His allies in the enemy's country. We're behind enemy lines, but prayer is our connection with the Commander.

Let's take prayer seriously and always offer all prayer in the Spirit with all perseverance for all the saints.

Communion is the basis of all prayer. It is the
essential breath of the true Christian life.

S. D. GORDON

JUNE

LOVE IS A VERB

Husbands, love your wives.
EPHESIANS 5:25

Every married woman longs to be cherished by her husband. Knowing that she is loved unconditionally gives the wife the greatest sense of security she can know. A husband who runs off to meetings every night, no matter how worthwhile his activities may seem, or a husband who spends his weekends with people other than his wife is robbing his spouse of an important source of security.

Security in a marriage relationship brings about companionship in a kind of closeness known as intimacy. Intimacy comes through two partners sharing their thoughts and feelings—being vulnerable in a relationship of complete trust. Intimacy is more than sexual closeness. It is the acting out of genuine love.

While we think of love as a noun, we need to remember that love is also a verb—an action word. That means love is based not on feeling but on doing. By a husband's actions, he can bring about the closeness his wife longs for. The biblical imperative "Husbands, love your wives" is not a suggestion; it is a command. When a wife knows her husband is committed to her, their home becomes a place where they'll both enjoy intimacy based on security and love.

In Marriage do thou be wise; prefer the Person before Money; Virtue before Beauty; the Mind before the Body.

WILLIAM PENN

SAVE THIS DATE!

*Watch therefore, for you do not know
what hour your Lord is coming.*
MATTHEW 24:42

"Save this date!" That could be the slogan of those who have proffered specific dates for the return of Jesus Christ to earth.

The fourth-century Christian writer Lactantius determined Jesus would return in AD 520. Many believed Jesus would come in the year 1000, causing adherents to stay up all night on New Year's Eve of 999, awaiting the great event. Some among the Anabaptists believed Christ would come in 1533—exactly 1500 years after His death, according to their calculations. Archbishop Ussher believed our Lord would come on a particular day in 1644. George Rapp, a religious teacher in Pennsylvania, predicted Christ's return on September 15, 1829. William Miller caused widespread panic throughout America by announcing October 22, 1844, as the date of Christ's return. In the 1980s, a popular booklet gave eighty-eight reasons why the Rapture would occur in 1988.

No one knows when Jesus will return, not even the angels. But Jesus told us to be ready at any time: "Take heed, watch and pray; for you do not know when the time is" (Mark 13:33).

It might be today! Are you ready?

To be ever looking for the Lord's appearing is one
of the best helps to a close walk with God.

J. C. RYLE

GOD'S GRANDCHILDREN?

His delight is in the law of the LORD,
and in His law he meditates day and night.

PSALM 1:2

The great preacher Charles Spurgeon is reported to have said, "A child who knowingly sins can savingly repent." Since our salvation is an individual responsibility, it is important that every person comes to the Lord on his or her own. Another has said, "God doesn't have grandchildren." In other words, no one can depend on the faith of his or her parents or grandparents for salvation.

Take heart if your children are slow to come to faith. Remember the final chapter is not yet written, and God has time to bring our loved ones to Himself. Be like the woman who never gave up on her wayward son, but continued to pray. Years after she died, the aging son committed his life to God.

Do everything in your power to share your personal faith story with your children and grandchildren. Model your faith through your lifestyle, your literature, your music, and your activities.

Exodus 20:5 says certain sins can go on to the third and fourth generation. But Deuteronomy 7:9 tells us that God keeps His covenant for "a thousand generations with those who love Him and keep His commandments." By sharing our faith with our children and their children, we can impact the world beyond our years.

Never mind the scribes; what saith the Scripture?

MARTIN LUTHER

LOOKING FORWARD

Looking forward to these things,
be diligent to be found by Him in peace.

2 PETER 3:14

Whatever problems you're facing, news you're dreading, or burdens you're bearing—all will be resolved within two seconds of Christ's return. This world brings tribulations, but we can be of good cheer because Christ has overcome the world (John 16:33). When He comes, He will give rest to the troubled, and an eternal weight of glory for those facing "light momentary affliction" (2 Corinthians 4:17, ESV). Then we will see that "the sufferings of this present time are not worthy to be compared with the glory which shall be revealed in us" (Romans 8:18).

One day soon, our sighs will become songs, our heartaches will become hallelujahs, and our worldly woes will be swallowed up in everlasting joy. There will be no heavy hearts in our heavenly homes. That's why the Bible tells us to "seek those things which are above, where Christ is, sitting at the right hand of God" (Colossians 3:1).

Let's set our minds on things above (Colossians 3:2). Great joy comes to those who look forward to the Lord's return. Learn to visualize it, meditate on it, speak of it, study it, and pray, "Even so, come, Lord Jesus!" (Revelation 22:20).

Beyond the bounds of time and space,
look forward to that happy place.

CHARLES WESLEY

HUDSON TAYLOR

*Abide in Me, and I in you. As the branch cannot bear fruit
of itself . . . neither can you, unless you abide in Me.*

JOHN 15:4

Missionary pioneer Hudson Taylor worked so hard in China that his health was impaired. One day a letter came from a friend who wrote about the joy of abiding in Christ. The letter said, "Abiding, not striving nor struggling; looking off unto Him; trusting Him for present power . . . this is not new, and yet 'tis new to me."

When he read this at his mission station at Chinkiang on September 4, 1869, Taylor's eyes were opened. "As I read," he recalled, "I saw it all! 'If we believe not, He abideth faithful.' I looked to Jesus and saw (and when I saw, oh, how joy flowed!) that He had said, 'I will never leave thee.' . . . Jesus is . . . ten thousand times more than we have ever dreamed, wished for or needed." Writing to his sister, he said, "As to work, mine was never so plentiful, so responsible, or so difficult; but the weight and strain are all *gone*. The last month or more has been, perhaps, the happiest of my life; and I long to tell you a little of what the Lord has done for my soul."

This became known as "Hudson Taylor's Spiritual Secret." Proclaiming the Word is not something we do for Christ but something He does through us as we abide in Him.

The branch . . . rests in union and communion
with the vine; and at the right time, and in the
right way, is the right fruit found on it.

HUDSON TAYLOR

WHEN THINGS LOOK DARKEST

False christs and false prophets will rise and show signs
and wonders to deceive, if possible, even the elect.
But take heed; see, I have told you all things beforehand.

MARK 13:22-23

The ever-present turmoil among the Arab states in the Middle East is a reminder that the nation of Israel and its neighbors dominate the agenda of history. We cannot predict the reverberations of every conflict or the aftereffects stemming from every shift of power. It may be that the youth movements among Arab states will provide new openness for the gospel. On the other hand, the shifting political structures may lead to increased radicalism, setting the stage for the Antichrist.

It's not wise to be dogmatic as we try to interpret current events. The twists and turns of history are under God's providential control, and it's best to watch prayerfully so we can take advantage of open doors for evangelism while awaiting our Lord's return.

Although we can't be dogmatic about specific events in the headlines, we can be fully assured that history is His-story, and that the stage is being set for His soon return. We can live every day with confidence and excitement because no matter how disturbing the news reports, our sovereign Lord is in control.

When things look darkest to the world, they look
brightest to the Christian. Our King is coming back!*

VANCE HAVNER

---

*Vance Havner, *Day by Day* (New Tappan, NJ: Revell, 1953), 219.

READY FOR ANYTHING

Be ready, for the Son of Man is coming.
LUKE 12:40

Mike Yardley had just left his network's studios when his city began to shake. As the ground convulsed, a cloud of dust rose all around. Pieces of the city center of Christchurch, New Zealand, were raining down on the sidewalks. Looking back at his news building, Yardley saw nothing but dust. The building had collapsed in the February 2011 earthquake, killing seventeen of his colleagues. "My heart has been torn by the unwieldy weight of grief," he said, "as I reflect on 17 much-loved workmates who I will never share a TV studio with again."*

Jesus warned of an increasing number of earthquakes, along with famines and pestilences, as we grow closer to His return. We may see all these disasters today and marvel at the state of the world. But we shouldn't fear. We should take these things as reminders to be watching, waiting, and praying. We should be ready!

The world is in trouble, but Jesus came
to rescue us from its final consequences.**

ERWIN LUTZER

---

*Mike Yardley, "CTV Reporter Torn with Grief," CNN, February 24, 2011,
http://www.cnn.com/2011/WORLD/asiapcf/02/24/nz.yardley.ctv.
**Erwin W. Lutzer, *Where Was God?* (Carol Stream, IL: Tyndale, 2006), 111.

ABRAHAM: THE OBEDIENT FATHER

*Because you have . . . not withheld . . . your only son, I will
surely bless you and make your descendants as numerous as
the stars in the sky . . . and through your offspring, all nations
on earth will be blessed, because you have obeyed me.*

GENESIS 22:16-18, NIV

It fills a father's heart with joy to see his children obey. The younger our children are, the more remarkable their obedience is! In our desire to build godliness into our children's lives, we want to be sure obedience is on their list of character qualities.

If the obedience of our children is meaningful to us humans, how much more it must please God when we obey Him, whether we know the outcome or not. Abraham obeyed without questioning. When God asked him to take Isaac to Mount Moriah and sacrifice him, Abraham followed His request. We aren't told of the emotions he felt or the sleeplessness he may have endured through the long night before. We just know that he obeyed and trusted in God.

When a godly father has a heart that is obedient to the Lord, it is a gift to his children. Are you ready to do whatever God asks, immediately and without hesitation? It may be very difficult, and we may not understand why God is asking us to do something, but God blesses His children when they obey.

One act of obedience is better than one hundred sermons.

DIETRICH BONHOEFFER

ZEALOUS FOR SOULS

*This gospel of the kingdom will be preached in all the world
as a witness to all the nations, and then the end will come.*

MATTHEW 24:14

The great commission tells us to go and preach the gospel to every creature. But the fulfilling of the great commission is not necessarily a sign of Christ's imminent return. When we compare the prophetic events of Matthew 24 with the book of Revelation, we learn that after the Rapture of the church, the task of world evangelism will continue under the ministry of the 144,000 Messianic Jewish preachers, leading to the salvation of people during the Great Tribulation.

Just imagine! Only twelve Jews (the disciples) turned the world upside down after the resurrection and ascension of Christ in the first century. Think of what 144,000 Jewish evangelists can do after the return of Christ to rapture the church!

But until then, we can do our part. We're to preach and proclaim the Word to the world. As followers of Christ, we're to be fishers of men. Think of the value of one soul into whose heart you were able to drop the seed of the gospel. Be zealous for souls!

While we are creating sophisticated organizations
and employing the latest technology to win the
world to Christ, let us not forget that our neighbor
judges Jesus Christ by what he sees in us.

CHUCK COLSON

NOW!

*"Come now, and let us reason together," says the L*ORD.
ISAIAH 1:18

There was a pastor who took a visiting evangelist with him to meet with a farmer and his family. Everyone but the farmer had been converted during revival meetings, and the pastor and evangelist hoped to witness to the man. But when they arrived, the farmer was offended. "I didn't ask you to bring anyone out here to preach to me," he said. "I know where the church is. Anytime I want to hear anybody preach, I'll go to church. I'm going to be saved sometime, but not till I'm good and ready."

The next Monday the pastor's phone rang with an urgent message to come to the farmer's house. In a freak accident, he had fallen from the hayloft and died instantly. He fell at the very spot where two days before, he'd declared, "I'll get saved when I'm good and ready."*

We have no promise of tomorrow. Today is the day of salvation, and we must call upon the Lord while He is near. If you need Christ, don't wait another moment. Come to Him today, while there's still time. And don't delay in sharing God's grace with others who need to hear His plan of redemption.

The little word "now" is a very important word
in God's vocabulary of salvation.**

J. C. MACAULAY

---

*Leslie B. Flynn, *Come Alive with Illustrations* (Ada, MI: Baker Publishing Group, 1988), 143.
**J. C. Macaulay and Robert H. Belton, *Personal Evangelism* (Chicago: Moody, 1956), 168.

LET THE READER UNDERSTAND

"Therefore when you see the 'abomination of desolation,'
spoken of by Daniel the prophet, standing in the holy place
. . . then let those who are in Judea flee to the mountains."

MATTHEW 24:15-16

Many Bible readers are troubled by this passage because we are warned to understand Jesus' words, yet they are mysterious and difficult to understand. The "abomination of desolation" Jesus is referring to is an event that will take place in the future, when an abominable image will be erected in the rebuilt Temple in Jerusalem. The abomination of desolation will trigger the horrific three and a half years of Great Tribulation.

This disgusting image is mentioned elsewhere in the Bible. The Daniel mentions it in chapters 9, 11, and 12 of his book. Paul makes reference to it in 2 Thessalonians, as does John in Revelation 13. We have been warned of Satan's plans for the end times.

Satan isn't waiting until then, however, to lead multitudes of people into idolatry. An idol isn't necessarily a statue or image; it's anything that we love more than we love Jesus Christ. Both now and then, Jesus Christ must be the unrivaled Lord of our hearts.

Let Him reign without equal in the temple of your life today.

Let Jesus be first and uppermost in thought and
life and let all other things trail on after.*

S. H. HADLEY

---

*J. Wilbur Chapman, *S. H. Hadley of Water Street* (New York: F. H. Revell, 1906), 97.

GEOFFREY BULL

Feed on His faithfulness.

PSALM 37:3

The Book that missionaries proclaim throughout the earth is also the Book that sustains them in their work of proclamation. Geoffrey Bull, a British missionary to Tibet, was imprisoned by Chinese Communists, who seized his Bible and made him suffer terribly for three years. Bull was subjected to so much psychological torture that he feared he would go insane.

But the missionary devised a plan to help him cope: he systematically went through the entire Bible in his mind. He began with Genesis and made his way to Revelation—a process that took him approximately six months. He brought to mind each story he could recall from Scripture, starting with the Creation account. First he focused on the content of each story; then he reflected more deeply on certain points. Once he pieced together each book and chapter as closely as he could, he started over again. Later, after he was released, he wrote, "The strength received through this meditation was, I believe, a vital factor in bringing me through, kept by the faith to the very end."*

In all our labors and trials, the Book we proclaim is also the Book that restores our souls. It should be both our decree and our diet.

> In the Bible God has given us thoughts of His power and His love, and He has given them to us that we may think about them and have food for our souls.
>
> **WILLIAM WILBERFORCE NEWTON**

---

*Clarence E. Warner, *The Promises of God* (Maitland, FL: Xulon Press, 2005), 267.

HISTORY'S MONSTER

*The people who know their God shall
be strong, and carry out great exploits.*

DANIEL 11:32

In Daniel 11, we're given a prophecy about a man known to history as Antiochus IV, a Syrian general who is the biblical prototype of the coming Antichrist. Antiochus is among history's most despicable characters. He tried to force the people of Israel to forsake their religion, burn their Scriptures, paganize their children, and disavow their God. He desecrated the Temple by stopping the daily sacrifices and setting up an altar or idol devoted to Zeus (the "abomination of desolation" that previewed the future actions of the Antichrist). In his fury at Jewish resistance, Antiochus massacred eighty thousand men, women, and children. It was an indescribable reign of terror. But even then, there were faithful Jews (those who knew their God) who amid the carnage were strong and did great exploits. As a result, Israel regained its freedom until the days of the Roman Empire.

Every generation of believers faces opposition and persecution. But those people who know their God will be strong and do great exploits. With Christ beside us, we cannot be conquered or cowed—never forget that the power of God working through a faithful servant is a mighty thing.

The right knowledge of God is the strength of the soul,
and, in the strength of that, gracious souls do exploits.

MATTHEW HENRY

GOD-PLEASING FAITH

*Without faith it is impossible to please Him, for he
who comes to God must believe that He is, and that
He is a rewarder of those who diligently seek Him.*

HEBREWS 11:6

Almost everything we as believers hold dear has to do with the invisible. In fact, the great truths of our faith involve things we can't see—God, Jesus, eternity. Yet, by faith, we know that God exists, Jesus was raised from the dead, and heaven is real.

Believing God exists is not enough. Faith is also seeking God. In fact, throughout Scripture, having faith and seeking God are synonymous. True faith means we don't stop believing after our salvation. Instead, we entrust our whole selves to God, seeking Him daily to fulfill His promises in and through our lives and circumstances.

Faith that actively believes and diligently seeks is the kind of faith that pleases God. That's why the heroes of Hebrews 11 are commended for their faith. They believed God wholeheartedly. They trusted His promises unconditionally. And they sought His purposes solely. Are you active in your belief? Diligent in your seeking? This pleases God.

Faith enables the believing soul to treat the
future as present and the invisible as seen.

J. OSWALD SANDERS

THE RIVAL BROTHERS

By faith Abel offered to God a more excellent sacrifice.

HEBREWS 11:4

Abel, a shepherd, is the first person in Hebrews 11 commended for his faith. Cain, his elder brother, receives no such praise.

Genesis 4 relates how each of the brothers offered a sacrifice to God. Cain, a farmer, presented a portion of his harvested field, and Abel brought a firstborn of his flock. God, however, accepted Abel's sacrifice but rejected Cain's.

What was the difference? God saw that Abel was willing and obedient. He did everything in his power to please God with his sacrifice, and he brought to the altar exactly what had been asked, without argument or question. As a result, God was pleased and declared him righteous.

Although Cain presented a sacrifice to God, he became angry and jealous of Abel when God showed His disfavor. Refusing an opportunity to get right with God, Cain chose his own stubborn ways. The result? He killed his brother, refused to repent, and was banished from God's presence.

The message is simple. Faith pleases; sin separates. By faith, Abel became a hero. Through sin, Cain became an outcast. Choose the way of Abel. Act in faith today.

Our prayers may be awkward. Our attempts may be feeble. But since the power of prayer is in the One who hears it and not in the one who says it, our prayers do make a difference.

MAX LUCADO

JOY IN THE MORNING

Unless those days were shortened, no flesh would be saved;
but for the elect's sake those days will be shortened.

MATTHEW 24:22

The Great Tribulation will last three and a half years, and not a moment longer. If this period of calamity were to last longer, no one would survive. For the elect's sake, there's a termination point; it will not go on forever.

That's true of our current troubles, too. Sometimes we feel our problems have no end. There's no light at the end of the tunnel, no dawn at the end of the night, and no joy at the end of our sadness. The psalmist expresses this when he cries, "How long, O LORD? Will You forget me forever? How long will You hide Your face from me? How long shall I take counsel in my soul, having sorrow in my heart daily?" (Psalm 13:1-2). But keep reading. By verse 5, the psalmist writes, "I have trusted in Your mercy," and in the final verse he exclaims, "I will sing to the LORD, because He has dealt bountifully with me."

In Christ, all our problems are temporary; all our blessings are eternal. Don't give up. There will be joy in the morning.

O my soul, what need it trouble thee to have heaviness in the evening, so long as thou art sure to have joy in the morning?

SIR RICHARD BAKER

THE POSSIBILITIES OF FAITH

By faith Enoch was taken away so that he did not see death,
"and was not found, because God had taken him."

HEBREWS 11:5

While it may seem like a bit of a dark thought, have you ever wondered what people might say about you at your funeral or memorial service? What do you want them to say?

In Hebrews 11:5, we read that Enoch "pleased God." Most Christians would be elated to have those words spoken about them. Enoch had this testimony because he was a man of faith who walked in obedience to God and compliance with His laws for more than three hundred years.

Enoch didn't die. One moment he was here on earth living life. The next moment, poof! He was gone. To his family and friends who searched high and low, Enoch had literally disappeared off the face of the earth. So closely was he linked to the heavenly Father that he simply transferred his presence from this life to God's presence in a heartbeat. No wonder the Scriptures say, "He pleased God"!

What will people say about you after you are gone? Walk with God today.

I fear no foe, with Thee at hand to bless; ills have no
weight, and tears no bitterness. Where is death's sting?
Where, grave, thy victory? I triumph still, if Thou abide with me.

HENRY FRANCIS LYTE

THERE'S LIGHT FOR A LOOK AT THE SAVIOR

They came to Philip, who was from Bethsaida of Galilee, and asked him, saying, "Sir, we wish to see Jesus."

JOHN 12:21

After years of research, scientists at the University of Michigan have developed the world's smallest computer system to help treat glaucoma patients. This tiny unit, about the size of a single letter on a penny, contains a microprocessor, sensor, memory, battery, solar cell, and wireless radio with an infinitesimal antenna. Though it won't be available for actual use for years, it is designed to be implanted in a person's eye to track the progress of glaucoma and preserve vision.

According to the Bible, the god of this age has blinded the minds of the perishing, lest the light of Christ's glory shine on them (2 Corinthians 4:4). But as Christians, we have the Scriptures implanted in our vision. We look at the headlines through the computer of God's Word. We understand that Christ is coming again according to Scripture. Though the times are perilous, we have the peace of saying, "We see Jesus, who was made a little lower than the angels, for the suffering of death crowned with glory and honor" (Hebrews 2:9).

Look to Jesus for healthy vision.

Turn your eyes upon Jesus; look full in His wonderful face.

HELEN H. LEMMEL

THE DAYS OF NOAH

*As the days of Noah were, so also will the
coming of the Son of Man be.*

MATTHEW 24:37

Noah's arks are popping up all over the place. A Dutch builder
has a full-size replica on the Maas River in the Netherlands.
Another full-size replica is in Kentucky. There's a life-size fiber-
glass copy in Hong Kong. And smaller-scale versions sit here and
there on sites around the world.

Perhaps in the providence of God, we need to be reminded
that we're living in the days of Noah. Both Jesus and Peter compare the days before the Flood to those preceding the return of
Christ. Jesus says, "They ate, they drank, they married wives,
they were given in marriage, until the day that Noah entered the
ark, and the flood came and destroyed them all" (Luke 17:27).
Peter says, "The world that then existed perished, being flooded
with water." In the same way, he said, the current earth is facing
imminent judgment by fire (2 Peter 3:6).

We are Noahs—preachers of righteousness in an evil age,
warning others of the judgment to come. Noah persevered in his
day, and we must do the same. Let's flood the world with gospel
truth! Today is a good day to share the Good News.

The judgment of God shall come. . . . And that judgment is
swift and sure and certain, as it was in the days of Noah.

W. A. CRISWELL

THE MIDNIGHT CRY

At midnight a cry was heard: "Behold, the
bridegroom is coming; go out to meet him!"

MATTHEW 25:6

An old campfire song says, "Give me oil in my lamp; keep me burning." That's a good prayer to offer. It's from Jesus' story in Matthew 25 about the ten virgins assigned to accompany the bridegroom to the wedding. They were to illumine the way. They didn't know the hour of his arrival, so they were to remain ready. Half the virgins did so, with their lamps filled with oil and their wicks trimmed for the procession. The other five were unprepared for his coming.

All ten women looked the same, but when the hour came, only half were ready. The other half were excluded from the wedding supper and locked outside the house. The door was closed. "Watch therefore," says Jesus, "for you know neither the day nor the hour in which the Son of Man is coming" (verse 13).

Paul told the church members in Corinth, "Examine yourselves as to whether you are in the faith" (2 Corinthians 13:5). Make sure the oil of the Holy Spirit is in your heart and that you are prepared for the arrival of our Savior and Lord.

O Christian . . . wait for the coming of your Lord, but let it
be with your lamps trimmed and your lights burning.

CHARLES H. SPURGEON

TWO EARS, ONE MOUTH

My dear brothers and sisters, take note of this: Everyone should be quick to listen, slow to speak and slow to become angry, because human anger does not produce the righteousness that God desires. Therefore, get rid of all moral filth and the evil that is so prevalent and humbly accept the word planted in you, which can save you.

JAMES 1:19-21, NIV

It is better to keep silent and appear foolish than to open your mouth and remove all doubt." This humorous phrase has an element of truth to it. To be human is to want to be heard. It is said that on one occasion, a young man came to the great philosopher Socrates to be trained as an orator. In his first meeting with his teacher, he talked without stopping. When Socrates could get a word in, he said, "Young man, I will have to charge you a double fee."

"A double fee? Why is that?"

"I will have to teach you two sciences. First how to hold your tongue, and then how to use it."

The book of Proverbs contains many references to the silence of the wise and the noisiness of the foolish. James reminds us that our readiness to understand is directly related to our deliberate reflections—not our immediate reactions.

The tongue is the only tool that gets sharper with use.

WASHINGTON IRVING

GOD'S OPEN-DOOR POLICY

By faith Noah . . . condemned the world and became heir to the righteousness which is according to faith.

HEBREWS 11:7

One of the most welcoming signs is an open door. At home, an open door says, "You're welcome inside." At work, it means, "I have time for you." We also see an open door in Genesis 7:1 when God extends an invitation to Noah and his family: "Come into the ark, you and all your household." It's God's open-door policy.

Throughout Scripture and down through history, God never sends judgment without providing a way of salvation. Yes, God flooded the earth to rid the world of a sinful generation, but He also provided a lifesaving ark to all who would enter the open door.

Everyone in Noah's time heard the message of judgment and was given the opportunity to be saved. Yet only eight people accepted God's provision of safety from the rising waters—Noah, his wife, his three sons, and their wives.

We have the same mission as Noah. Saved by faith in Christ, we are to relay God's open-door invitation to the world: "Come to Jesus, for He is the way, the truth, and the life. He is the door."

Man is capable of nothing, it is God who gives everything, who gives man faith.

SØREN KIERKEGAARD

FAITHFUL IN LITTLE THINGS

Well done, good and faithful servant;
you have been faithful over a few things.

MATTHEW 25:23

Puritan Richard Baxter said, "It will be an unspeakable comfort to look back on a life well spent. And to be able to say in humble sincerity, 'My time was not cast away. . . . It was spent in sincere labors for my God—in making my calling and election sure, in doing good to men's souls and bodies, it was entirely devoted to God.'"

In His parable of the talents in Matthew 25, Jesus stresses the importance of being faithful to the work assigned us. We want to hear Him say, "Well done, good and faithful servant."

It's not the amount of our work that's important, or its status or notoriety. It's the faithfulness with which we do exactly what He has assigned us. Our lives and labors call for perseverance, persistence, patience, and prayer.

If God has assigned our daily tasks, He'll produce an eternal harvest. Don't give up, and don't worry if the work seems small, the costs large, or the results meager. Just be faithful to the will of God—nothing more, nothing less.

Seeking to please God in little matters, is a test of real devotion and love. . . . Let your aim be to please our Dear Lord perfectly in little things.

JEAN NICOLAS GROU

GOD'S MAP OF OBEDIENCE

By faith Abraham obeyed when he was called. . . .
And he went out, not knowing where he was going.

HEBREWS 11:8

How often do you leave home not knowing where you're headed? When Abraham received God's call to leave Haran in Genesis 12, he responded to God's directive with obedience.

Abraham promptly packed up his family and left Haran without knowing where they were headed. The only thing Abraham knew was that God had asked him to go.

From then on, two things characterized Abraham's journey of faith. The first was his tent—evidence of his earthly pilgrimage and a symbol of his heavenly citizenship. He knew that the promises of God were far greater than building a permanent home in a new homeland.

The second symbol was the altars Abraham built—physical structures showing his spiritual dependency upon God. Day after day, as Abraham walked with God, His purposes were revealed.

Wherever God leads you in life, remember that you are always "at home" with Him.

Guide me, O Thou great Jehovah, pilgrim through
this barren land. I am weak, but Thou art
mighty; hold me with Thy powerful hand.

WILLIAM WILLIAMS

ACCOUNTABLE

It is required in stewards that one be found faithful.

1 CORINTHIANS 4:2

Taxpayers around the world are in a feisty mood. They're demanding that civic leaders and public employees be accountable for managing the common good. They expect politicians and governments to be accountable to the voters. And they want teachers to be accountable for the success of students. Suddenly taxpayers are coming to the realization that without accountability, there's little restraint in our world.

Christ requires that His people be responsible also. Like the owner of an estate who expects his employees to be good stewards of the things entrusted to them, God has given us time, talents, and treasures. Because we belong to Him, we're stewards on His behalf. One day we'll be judged on the basis of our faithfulness with what has been entrusted to us.

When we see Christ, we will show Him what we have done with what He has given us. All that we have will be a meager offering to the King of kings and Lord of lords, but it will be accepted and blessed because we have been faithful with whatever talent or treasure He has entrusted to us. What a day that will be when we hear Him say, "Well done, thou good and faithful servant."

Truehearted, wholehearted, faithful and loyal,
King of our lives, by Thy grace we will be.

FRANCES HAVERGAL

YOU ARE BEING WATCHED

He is the One who goes before you.
He will be with you, He will not leave you nor
forsake you; do not fear nor be dismayed.

DEUTERONOMY 31:8

A little guy was nervous about riding the bus to school for the first time. For reassurance, his dad waited with him at the bus stop. After his son was safely on the bus, the father quickly got in his car, followed the bus to the school, and parked close to where the bus would unload. When his son got off, he saw his father giving him a thumbs-up. His father was the last person he saw before boarding the bus and the first person he saw getting off. It was as if the father had been there the whole time.

And in a sense, he had been. Even though the child couldn't see his father during the trip, he knew his father had made sure he was safe. And it's the same way with God. We don't see Him with us physically, but the witness of the Spirit lets us know that we are children of a Father whose care never ceases (Romans 8:14-17).

You are never alone. The Father is watching over you—at this very moment and wherever you go today.

The presence of God in the flood is better than a ferryboat.

CHARLES H. SPURGEON

COME, YOU BLESSED!

*Come, you blessed of My Father, inherit the kingdom
prepared for you from the foundation of the world.*

MATTHEW 25:34

In Matthew 25, Jesus warns of a day when He will return to judge the nations. He will separate people as a shepherd divides his sheep from the goats. He will say to the "sheep," "Come, you blessed of My Father, inherit the kingdom prepared for you" (verse 34). To the others He will say, "Depart from Me, you cursed, into the everlasting fire prepared for the devil and his angels" (verse 41).

The former group is saved by grace through faith. Out of their salvation flow their good works—they feed the hungry, clothe the naked, visit the sick, care for the imprisoned, and minister to "the least of these." We aren't saved on the basis of those deeds, for no amount of good works can save us. We engage in them because we have *been* saved, and our kindness is evidence of the grace of Christ in our hearts.

Our days should be filled with blessing those around us, living in expectation of the day when we hear the words of Christ calling us to come and inherit the Kingdom that has been prepared for us.

The seeming peace a sinner has, is not from the knowledge
of his happiness, but from the ignorance of his danger.

THOMAS WATSON

FRIENDS AND OTHERS

Faithful are the wounds of a friend.

PROVERBS 27:6

One of two things is true about the person who has never received guidance from another person: either that person is perfect and has never needed guiding or correcting, or that person doesn't have anyone in his or her life willing to risk the possibility of a negative response from the "correctee." Since we know there are no perfect people, guess which one is true?

The book of Proverbs says, in more than one way, that we are fortunate if we have a friend who loves us enough to guide and correct us. No one would allow another person to unknowingly make a serious mistake, like taking the wrong turn on a long car trip. Yet how often do we fail to give guidance to others when they are threatening to derail their own spiritual journeys? When we need guidance, we should ask someone who has been where we are or has a deeper knowledge of God and His Word. We should receive it gently, humbly, and with love. Guidance—especially unsolicited guidance—should be given with the same characteristics.

Do you need guidance or know someone who does? God gives "parts" to the body of Christ so the whole may be healthy. Don't fail to do your part when it comes to guidance—whether giving or receiving.

Men give advice; God gives guidance.

LEONARD RAVENHILL

THE REAL UTOPIA

*God will wipe away every tear from their eyes; there shall
be no more death, nor sorrow, nor crying. There shall be
no more pain, for the former things have passed away.*

REVELATION 21:4

In 1516, the English statesman Sir Thomas More wrote a book called *Utopia*. It described a fictional island in the Atlantic Ocean where there existed a perfect world—socially, politically, and economically. Since then, the idea of "utopia" has become entrenched in Western thought.

Unfortunately, many people equate utopia—a fictional place—with the biblical heaven. But nothing could be further from the truth. The Bible definitely describes a perfect place—no tears, no death, no sorrow, no crying, no pain—but it is not fictional! It is as real, from the perspective of our five senses, as the life we are now living but without the effects of sin. When we think of it that way—a place we can touch and feel—it changes our perspective on the world we now live in, a world where pain is all too real. The world we experience today is nothing like the new heavens and new earth God has planned (2 Peter 3:13).

Live your life today in light of the life that is to come.

I doubt not but every gracious person finds
the nearer to heaven he gets *in his hopes*, the
farther he goes from earth *in his desires*.

WILLIAM GURNALL

GENERIC FAITH

If anyone among you thinks he is religious, and does not bridle his tongue but deceives his own heart, this one's religion is useless. Pure and undefiled religion before God and the Father is this: to visit orphans and widows in their trouble, and to keep oneself unspotted from the world.

JAMES 1:26-27

What is generic faith? Sometimes the generic brand seems just like the real thing. But what is a generic? It is an imitation of the original. When it comes to our Christian life, there is no substitute for authenticity.

James reminds us that many Christians think they engage in real religion, but they are actually fooling themselves. True faith—the real thing—requires the self-control, compassion, and clean heart that James talks about.

When we approach His Word with the right focus, God promises that it will change us. We must be willing to prepare ourselves completely, to examine His truths thoughtfully, and to apply His commands daily. Our faith must be authentic. God is challenging us to live a life of real faith—pure and undefiled.

God doesn't take us out of the world; He wants us to live in it, but to change our thinking.

RAY STEDMAN

JULY

FAITHFUL FRIEND OF GOD

You, Israel, are My servant,
. . . the descendants of Abraham My friend.

ISAIAH 41:8

When a president leaves office, work begins on his presidential library. It is where the legacy of his life is exhibited. His accomplishments, great and small, are on display so that scholars and schoolchildren alike can research his life.

As the founder of a great nation, Abraham would be worthy of a museum and archive, if he lived today. Instead, we have the words of Scripture that describe his greatness. We read that he was hospitable to strangers (Genesis 18:1-8), that he was obedient to God's laws (Genesis 26:5), and that the Lord blessed him in every way (Genesis 24:1). When the Scriptures refer to the Lord as "the God of Abraham" (Genesis 28:13), they esteem him. Can you imagine *your* name being used to describe God the Father?

Perhaps the greatest honor the Scriptures ascribe to Abraham is that he was a friend of God. Are you a friend of God? Do you respect Him, honor Him, love Him, and confide in Him? Abraham's example is for each of us today.

If God had a refrigerator, your picture would be
on it. If He had a wallet, your photo would be in it. . . .
Face it, friend. He's crazy about you.

MAX LUCADO

THE GLITTERING LURE

*Let no one say when he is tempted, "I am tempted by God";
for God cannot be tempted by evil, nor does He
Himself tempt anyone. But each one is tempted when
he is drawn away by his own desires and enticed.
Then, when desire has conceived, it gives birth to sin;
and sin, when it is full-grown, brings forth death.*

JAMES 1:13-15

Glassy waters, warm sun, the serenity of nature . . . The fisherman casts his line out across the water, and the little lure entices a brave passerby lurking under the surface. Within moments there will be a nibble of curiosity, then a violent struggle, and ultimately, dinner for the fisherman.

Just as a glittering lure attracts fish, so our lustful hearts are attracted to tempting things. Even while we are standing next to God, we can be tempted to sin. Who throws us the line with the deadly hook? Who maneuvers that enticing bait?

We should remember that all sin comes from Satan. God permits trials in order to strengthen us, but Satan tests us to expose our weaknesses. Let us strive to become careful and well prepared to identify and escape Satan's lure.

There are some who say that there is no Devil,
but if they would try to live just one day for God,
they would know that the Devil does exist.

HERSCHEL FORD

WATCHING AND WAITING

Take heed, watch and pray; for you do
not know when the time is.

MARK 13:33

Children wait for Christmas morning. Cooks wait for water to boil. Job seekers wait for the phone to ring. Young men on bended knee wait to hear their beloved say yes. Revelers wait for midnight on New Year's Eve. Everybody, every day, everywhere, waits for something. But how many people are waiting for the return of Jesus with the same enthusiasm?

Jesus made it clear that the moment He returns for His church will be a surprise. The surprise won't be *that* it happens but *when* it happens. We can imagine more than one reason why God didn't reveal the date or time of Christ's return. One good reason is that it is based on finishing a task, not an arbitrary time standard. Jesus did provide this insight: "And this gospel of the kingdom will be preached in all the world as a witness to all the nations, and then the end will come" (Matthew 24:14). So fulfillment of the great commission is a key marker relating to Christ's return. But not specific enough to mark on a calendar, which is why Jesus said, "Take heed, watch and pray."

Would you be ready to meet Jesus if He returned today?

It is later than it has ever been before, and the smartest thing any man can do is to set his watch by God's clock.

VANCE HAVNER

DIVINE IMPOSSIBILITY

By faith Sarah . . . bore a child when she was past the age,
because she judged Him faithful who had promised.

HEBREWS 11:11

What would you do if a couple in their nineties told you they were expecting their first child? Maybe you'd stifle a laugh or launch into all the reasons why that would be humanly impossible.

Years ago, Sarah and Abraham faced similar arguments. God had promised them a son, Isaac, in their old age. Although Sarah went through moments of disbelief, she ultimately believed God. She had hope when there was no logical reason to have hope.

Sarah weighed the human impossibility of becoming a mother in her old age against the divine impossibility of God breaking His promise. Like Sarah, you can say that it would be a divine impossibility for God to break any of His promises to you.

When the angel asserted that "with God nothing shall be impossible," the two negatives add up to a ringing positive.

A. W. TOZER

BLAMELESS, NOT PERFECT

*There was a man in the land of Uz, whose name
was Job; and that man was blameless and upright,
and one who feared God and shunned evil.*

JOB 1:1

It is often said that we live in an age without heroes. Too often, those in places of leadership—from government to business to religion to culture—are found to be less worthy of emulation than we once thought. We rarely hear the word *blameless* used to describe anyone anymore—and we are the poorer for it.

What does *blameless* mean? It certainly doesn't mean "sinless," since the Bible says all have sinned (Romans 3:23). Job was described as blameless, upright, fearing God, and shunning evil. He turned away from sin and turned toward God with fear and reverence. He cared about his own uprightness as well as that of his family, even offering sacrifices for his children (Job 1:4-5). Throughout Scripture we are expected to have the same high standards. In fact, it was Jesus Himself who said, "Be perfect, therefore, as your heavenly Father is perfect" (Matthew 5:48, NIV). Even if perfection is unreachable, being blameless is still the goal.

Is there any aspect of your life today that is not "perfect"? Ask God for the grace to turn away from sin and toward Him so you can be considered blameless.

Saints on earth are not perfect angels,
but only converted sinners.

J. C. RYLE

THE COMING SURPRISE

*Watch therefore, for you do not know when the master
of the house is coming—in the evening, at midnight,
at the crowing of the rooster, or in the morning.*

MARK 13:35

Every day was hard for the Padgett children while their dad was deployed to Afghanistan. They missed him terribly and sometimes tearfully. Then one day at school, Joseph and Cortney joined their classmates for a program in the cafeteria. The band struck up "America the Beautiful," and a soldier in combat fatigues stepped through the door. Instantly the two youngsters leaped up and ran through the crowd with tears in their eyes. Their dad, Spc. Buddy Padgett, had surprised his children with an early return home.*

We don't know the day or hour of our Lord's return, but what a glorious surprise awaits us! Jesus told us to watch, for we don't know if He'll come when the alarm clock rings, the dinner bell chimes, or the clock strikes midnight. We must be ready to leap to our feet with joyful shouts of "He's back! He's come to take us home!"

For nearly twenty years a spiritual enrichment has come
into my ministry because I have realized the great New
Testament revelation of the personal return of our Lord.**

DINSDALE YOUNG, ENGLISH METHODIST PREACHER

---

*Derrick Ek, "Soldier Surprises Children at School with Early Return," *The Leader*, February 17, 2011, http://the-leader.com/article/20110217/News/302179900.
**Denis Lyle, *Countdown to Apocalypse* (Belfast: Ambassador Publications, 1999), 24.

AN UNUSUAL LAST REQUEST

*By faith Joseph, when he was dying, made
mention of the departure of the children of Israel,
and gave instructions concerning his bones.*

HEBREWS 11:22

Have you ever wondered why Joseph took the time on his deathbed to talk about his bones?

To understand Joseph's unusual last request, we must go back to his circumstance. Although he had spent many years under the influence of Egyptian culture, he knew that Egypt was not his home. He didn't want to be buried there. By faith, he dreamed of going with the children of Israel when they entered the Promised Land.

Do you have the same awareness that Joseph had about his true home? It can be easy to grow comfortable with the way life works here on earth. Day-to-day activities can fill your calendar to the point that you forget to look at life with an eternal perspective. Like Joseph, do you have an eye on your heavenly home?

Joseph's bones were carried out of Egypt and buried in the plot of land that belonged to his inheritance. We, too, are strangers and pilgrims on the earth. The Promised Land for us is yet to come.

Let your heart not forget / We are not home yet.

STEVEN CURTIS CHAPMAN

CELEBRATE THE CHILD

*By faith Moses, when he was born, was hidden three
months by his parents, because they saw he was a beautiful
child; and they were not afraid of the king's command.*

HEBREWS 11:23

Normally the birth of a child is heralded with much joy and fanfare. Baby "necessities" are purchased while the baby's room is decorated. But for the parents of Moses, nothing could have been further from the truth. Male children lived under a death sentence from Pharaoh.

Yet during this difficult time in history, Moses' parents saw the potential in their son. Through the eyes of faith, they knew he was somebody important to God's plan.

Too often it takes a traumatic experience to show us the priceless treasures we have in our children. If you have children, do you look at them, whether small or grown, and see God's beauty? Do you celebrate the potential that they possess?

Even if you are not a parent, there are probably children that God has placed in your life. Seek out a child in your life who needs to hear how very special he or she is to you and to God.

The Psalms call children a "reward." Not a curse, not a tragedy, not an accident—they are the expression of God's favor.

HOWARD HENDRICKS

"WHEN YOU ARE DISCOURAGED . . ."

Do not fear or be discouraged.

DEUTERONOMY 1:21

Many of our favorite hymns tell us what to do when we are discouraged. One old standby by Johnson Oatman, Jr. advises, "When you are discouraged, thinking all is lost, count your many blessings, name them one by one."

Another asks, "Why should I feel discouraged, why should the shadows come?" Instead, we should remind ourselves, "His eye is on the sparrow, and I know He watches me."

The beloved hymn "What a Friend We Have in Jesus" gives us sound advice in saying we should "never be discouraged" over a burden, for we can "take it to the Lord in prayer."

The spiritual "There Is a Balm in Gilead" says, "Sometimes I feel discouraged and think my work's in vain, but then the Holy Spirit revives my soul again."

So if you're discouraged today, remember that a moment in the presence of our Lord can change your attitude. Count your blessings. Realize you're more valuable than the sparrows. Take it to the Lord in prayer, and let the Holy Spirit revive your soul again.

Do not fear or be discouraged.

I sing because I'm happy, I sing because I'm free.
For His eye is on the sparrow, and I know He watches me.

CIVILLA D. MARTIN

OUR PART, HIS PLAN

You shall march around the city, all you men of war;
you shall go all around the city once. This you shall do six days.

JOSHUA 6:3

It was a very unorthodox plan. Who had ever heard of conquering a city by walking around it? Picture the amazement on people's faces as they asked, "Let us get this straight. We're going to walk around Jericho, and the walls are going to fall down?"

Sometimes, we don't understand God's plan. One of the hardest things in the Christian life is when God directs you to do something, but you can't figure out why. Our part is to obey God's directions by faith, even if they don't make sense.

Perhaps God involves us in far-fetched plans so that when they succeed, no one but God can possibly claim the credit. After all, Joshua couldn't take credit for the fall of Jericho. That was a plan only God could have come up with. Remember that God has some amazing plans for your life. Walk in obedience to His direction. Believe that God has a wonderful purpose and a plan for you.

God moves in a mysterious way, His wonders to perform.
He plants His footsteps in the sea and rides upon the storm.

WILLIAM COWPER

PROVING YOUR PATIENCE

The testing of your faith produces patience.

JAMES 1:3

In our culture, the concept of testing immediately brings school days to mind. From the first grade on, we got used to the sweaty palms that accompanied the words "Clear your desk and take out a pencil." If we were well prepared, the test was an affirmation. If we were poorly prepared, the test was a rebuke—gentle or severe, depending on the grade.

Tests didn't end on graduation day, however. God has tests for us as well, like this one: "Describe nine ways to know if you are filled with the Holy Spirit." The answer is whether we manifest the nine dimensions of the fruit of the Spirit (Galatians 5:22-23). Consider patience, for instance. God allows us to experience times that test our patience in order to show us whether we are relying on ourselves or on the Holy Spirit. The more we are tested, the more evidence we have of the kind of power we are relying on—our own or the Spirit's. And the more opportunities we have to say, "Fill me with Your presence, Holy Spirit, that I may manifest patience in this situation."

If you are tested today, don't fail by relying on yourself. Let tests become affirmations of your reliance on the Holy Spirit in you.

Hope is the foundation of patience.

JOHN CALVIN

A FRIEND INDEED

A man who has friends must himself be friendly,
but there is a friend who sticks closer than a brother.

PROVERBS 18:24

There is no consensus as to the origin of the question "With friends like these, who needs enemies?"—but we all know what it means: sometimes those we thought were our friends act more like enemies. Anyone who has experienced such a reversal of "friendship" knows the pain and perplexity it can cause.

Job experienced such pain. When he was at the worst point of his life, his friends came to accuse and lecture him about his dishonesty before God and his failure to repent of whatever sins caused God to heap suffering upon him. They were not the kind of friends described in Proverbs 18:24—friends who stick closer than a brother. Anyone who has a brother or sister knows that siblings can act like enemies at times. But there is a friend who does what even a sibling cannot do, a friend who loves at all times. That's the kind of friend Job needed.

Jesus declared Himself to be the friend of those who follow Him (John 15:14). If you need a friend today, He is there for you. If you know others who need a friend, be one who sticks closer than a brother.

A rule I have had for years is, to treat the Lord Jesus
Christ as a personal friend. His is not a creed, a mere
empty doctrine; but it is He Himself we have.

D. L. MOODY

RISKS AND REWARDS

*By faith the harlot Rahab did not perish
with those who did not believe, when she
had received the spies with peace.*

HEBREWS 11:31

Rahab took a great risk when she hid two Hebrew spies from the king of Jericho and his army. Yet her risk was not impulsive or foolish. She had heard the stories of Israel's victories and the works of their God. She believed—by faith—that God would indeed destroy the city of Jericho. She knew in her heart that her risk would result in a great reward.

We know from Scripture that God honored Rahab's risk. She and her household were the only ones spared from destruction in Jericho. She began a new life, marrying a Jewish man, and eventually became a part of the genealogy of Christ.

At one time in your life, you took a risk like Rahab. You made a covenant based on faith to save you from the destruction of sin. Your decision to follow Christ might have been considered risky by some. But was the risk worth it? Yes! Unlike other risks in life, God always delivers on His promises. Thank God for the gift of your salvation!

For without risk there is no faith, and the
greater the risk the greater the faith.

SØREN KIERKEGAARD

JUDGE NOT

*Let us not judge one another anymore,
but rather resolve this, not to put a stumbling
block or a cause to fall in our brother's way.*

ROMANS 14:13

There is a fine line that separates an opinion from a judgment, and it's a line we must not cross. We can have opinions about the styles of music we listen to or our favorite foods to eat, but when we begin to judge others about their tastes, we can wound another brother or sister in Christ.

The early church in Rome had fallen prey to passing judgment on members with regard to food—a nonessential matter in the Christian faith. And Paul told them to stop. As Paul writes, "For the kingdom of God is not eating and drinking, but righteousness and peace and joy in the Holy Spirit" (Romans 14:17). Christians are free to form different views about matters of faith and practice that are not fundamental to Christian orthodoxy—such as diet, as in the case of the church in Rome. When we judge one another, our unity in Christ is disrupted. Yes, there will be judgment—but it will be by the Word of Christ, not the word of man (Romans 14:10).

If you have been judged by others, wait patiently for Christ to put things right. If you have judged others, seek to be forgiven.

In essentials, unity; in non-essentials,
liberty; in all things, charity.

AUGUSTINE

WHY?

*We know that all things work together for good
to those who love God, to those who are
the called according to His purpose.*

ROMANS 8:28

Every Christian eventually has an experience that seems totally inconsistent in the life of a child of a loving God. It may involve health, finances, relationships, career, property, or family. Whatever the experience, you will come through it with one nagging question: "Why, Lord?"

That question is acceptable to God; He is not angered by our desire for answers. As an example, Job was never rebuked by God for wanting to understand his own experience. But God did challenge Job's assumptions. Job thought he knew everything there was to know about God and His ways. Only after an extended period of questioning by God did Job realize he really didn't know God at all (Job 38–41). Job never received a good answer to his "Why?" question, but he received something better: the realization that God is so big and so wise that whatever He chooses to do will work out best in the end. Job learned what Paul eventually summarized in Romans 8:28: all things work together for good to those who love God.

If you have a "Why?" question of your own today, instead of seeking an immediate answer, seek the Answerer Himself.

I may not have the answers, but I do have Him.

DAVE DRAVECKY

LET IT SHINE

*All Scripture is given by inspiration of God, and is
profitable for doctrine, for reproof, for correction,
for instruction in righteousness.*

2 TIMOTHY 3:16

Is the Bible a road map you refer to when you need direction? Is it a spotlight that shines into the deepest corners of your heart and soul? Is it a coach that motivates you to persevere?

The Word of God is, in fact, all three. For it is through His Word that God directs you, convicts you, and encourages you.

The Bible is God's timeless love letter to you. Because Scripture is inspired and comes from the eternal heart of God, it is both universal (all its truth applies to all people and situations) and personal (all its truth applies directly to your life). Christians are uniquely blessed to have God's Word readily accessible so we can know truth (right doctrine), so we can stay on the right track (reproof and correction), and so we can live to please God in everything we do (training in righteousness).

Are you spending time in God's Word, allowing God to give you the direction, light, and motivation you need? Be sure you set aside time to let God speak to you personally through the wonderful light of His Word.

[God] has sent us sixty-six love letters etched in
heavenly handwriting. And the more we meditate upon
those words, the clearer his voice will resonate.

HANK HANEGRAAFF

KNOW THYSELF?

O Lord, You have searched me and known me.

PSALM 139:1

The ancient philosopher said, "Know thyself," but that's hard to do. Jeremiah 17:9 says, "The heart is deceitful above all things, and desperately wicked; who can know it?" The apostle Paul cautions us against being too quick to approve ourselves or condemn others, saying, "I care very little if I am judged by you . . . indeed, I do not even judge myself. My conscience is clear, but that does not make me innocent. It is the Lord who judges me" (1 Corinthians 4:3-4, NIV).

We must be careful about being overly introspective and too quick to criticize others. As fallen creatures, we're capable of wounding ourselves and others with misguided judgments.

Yes, be discerning about right and wrong and be willing to properly admonish someone when the Spirit leads, but remember there's only One who can actually read the heart. How much better to say with the psalmist, "Search me, O God, and know my heart; try me, and know my anxieties; and see if there is any wicked way in me, and lead me in the way everlasting" (Psalm 139:23-24).

The best of [us] are too apt to judge rashly,
and harshly, and unjustly; but [God's]
judgment is always according to truth.

MATTHEW HENRY

ALACK AND ALAS!

Is not your reverence your confidence?

JOB 4:6

Funny how some words go out of style. If you could go back in time and eavesdrop on your grandparents, you might hear them say words like *hark, hither, alack, fain, twain, betwixt, mayhap, nigh*, and *yon*. Few people miss those words now; they've been replaced by others. But another set of nearly forgotten terms isn't so expendable: *holy, reverence, God-fearing, devout*, and *piety*. How did we manage to lose *those* words?

The loss of *reverence* is particularly disturbing. We're to serve God with reverence and godly fear (Hebrews 12:28). The Lord told the Israelites, "You shall keep My Sabbaths and reverence My sanctuary" (Leviticus 19:30). The psalmist says, "God is . . . to be held in reverence by all those around Him" (Psalm 89:7). Proverbs 28:14 says, "Happy is the man who is always reverent." In Malachi's day, the Lord demanded, "If I am a Master, where is My reverence?" (Malachi 1:6).

In a world that has forgotten the meaning of the term, let's "lead a quiet and peaceable life in all godliness and reverence" (1 Timothy 2:2).

There is a communion with God, in which the soul
feels the presence of the unseen One, in the profound
depths of its being, with a vivid distinctness and a
holy reverence, such as no words can describe.

SAMUEL D. ROBBINS

FRIENDS FOR THE JOURNEY

Two are better than one. . . . For if they fall,
one will lift up his companion.

ECCLESIASTES 4:9-10

In John Bunyan's *The Pilgrim's Progress,* the main character, Christian, is blessed with two friends on his journey to the Celestial City: Faithful and Hopeful. At one point in the story, Christian and Hopeful are captured by Giant Despair and locked away in Doubting Castle. The symbolic names give wise counsel. Faith and hope are key companions when we encounter the twin destroyers of doubt and despair—especially in these desperate days of economic uncertainty, natural disasters, and international conflict.

Bunyan's allegory of the believer's struggle through life on the way toward heaven poignantly illustrates the difficult journey we face. But the indispensable lesson of faith and hope through Christian's traveling companions reminds believers of another important truth: we need friends along life's path to pick us up when we fall, encouraging us to keep on keeping on.

No burden is too great to carry with the heavenly promise of our Lord (John 14:1-2) and encouraging friends who help turn our despair into joy and our doubt into a stronger faith and hope. Look around your path today. There is probably someone not too far from you who needs your encouragement.

A true friend never gets in your way unless
you happen to be going down.

ARNOLD H. GLASGOW

LITTERED WITH BLESSINGS

*It is good to give thanks to the LORD, and to
sing praises to Your name, O Most High.*

PSALM 92:1

One March day, a motorist driving along Route 23 near Columbus, Ohio, called the police with an unusual sighting: a large amount of money was scattered alongside the highway. Although the exact amount wasn't announced, sources close to the case said it added up to tens of thousands of dollars. Officials had no idea where the money came from.

That story is reminiscent of the blessings in our lives. Just like the cash littering the highway, blessings are often unexpected and many times overlooked. The highway of life isn't free of obstacles or traffic jams. Sometimes there are exhausting grades and precipitous curves. But God litters our way with blessings. The psalmist proclaims, "Blessed be the Lord, who daily loads us with benefits" (Psalm 68:19).

Perhaps today we need to slow down and ponder how blessed we are. Tens of thousands of blessings attend our way. Goodness and mercy follow us all our days.

When God draws the curtain . . . mercy streams in
on the sunbeam! And when He shuts the eyelids
of the day . . . it is mercy that . . . bids us rest.
He "daily loadeth us with benefits."*

CHARLES H. SPURGEON

---

*Charles H. Spurgeon, "Daily Blessings for God's People" (sermon, Metropolitan Tabernacle, London, September 21, 1871), http://www.spurgeongems.org/vols61-63/chs3493.pdf.

MAKE FRIENDS AND LIVE LONGER

*Ointment and perfume delight the heart, and the sweetness
of a man's friend gives delight by hearty counsel.*
PROVERBS 27:9

According to the *New York Times*, researchers are paying attention to the role of friendship in our overall health. It reports, "A 10-year Australian study found that older people with a large circle of friends were 22 percent less likely to die during the study period than those with fewer friends." A study of middle-aged Swedish men found that those with quality friendships were much more likely to survive coronary heart disease. Another study of women battling breast cancer found that friendship circles had a dramatic influence on survival rates.

"Friendship has a bigger impact on our psychological well-being than family relationships," said one sociologist.*

Long ago, the writer of Proverbs said that a good friendship is to the heart what oils and medicines are to the body. Encouraging our friends—and being encouraged by them—is a conduit of blessing to our lives. We should cherish our relationships, pray for our friends, and fellowship warmly with those whom God brings across our paths. It's good for what ails us!

A real friend is one who walks in when
the rest of the world walks out.

WALTER WINCHELL

---

*Tara Parker-Pope, "What Are Friends For? A Longer Life," *New York Times*, April 21, 2009, http://www.nytimes.com/2009/04/21/health/21well.html.

THREE YET ONE

May the grace of the Lord Jesus Christ, and the love of
God, and the fellowship of the Holy Spirit be with you all.

2 CORINTHIANS 13:14, NIV

Have you ever considered the resemblance between an earthly family and the heavenly family—the Trinity? For some, the idea of the Trinity is difficult to grasp. There is one God, but He is revealed in three persons—the Father, Son, and Holy Spirit. They interact as one.

When you meet a family, you get to know each member individually, but you also see them work as one—in a shared meal or activity. Just as a human family works together in love to accomplish their goals, so God, three in one, acts to bring us to Him, inspire our growth, and help us walk in righteousness.

To know God, you must know the Father—God of the past, present, and future. You also need to know the Son—Jesus Christ, the Lamb of God. The third member is the Holy Spirit—the Comforter, the Guide, and the One who convicts us of sin. Do you know each member of the Trinity? Discover the loving presence of the Father, the Son, and the Holy Spirit in your life today!

The three Persons in the Godhead are Three in one sense,
and One in another. We cannot tell how—
and that is the mystery!

SAMUEL JOHNSON

GOD IN EXILE

I am with you always, even to the end of the age.

MATTHEW 28:20

Do you ever feel like you are far away from God?

John, the beloved apostle of Jesus Christ, though exiled to a barren island in the Aegean Sea, was not exiled from God. God, the Living One, went with him. Being shut away from the world on a prison island meant John could focus on God. While on Patmos, John received a magnificent revelation of heaven and humanity's future—the book of Revelation.

Across the centuries, God has walked with people of faith in dark circumstances. An innocent Joseph sat in a prison. Rizpah spent months guarding the dead bodies of her sons. Martin Luther walked through deep depression. In each case, the living God walked with them through these dark circumstances. These people came through their bend in the road because God was with them every step of the way.

God uses the difficult times in our lives to show us amazing things. You may feel exiled from everyone on earth, but you can walk in confidence. As God was with John on Patmos, He is with you. God won't desert you. You can trust Him fully through every difficult experience. You will never be exiled from God.

If we are shut in by life's troubles,
we can look to the open heaven above us.

JAMES M. CAMPBELL

IN HIS GRIP

Your hand shall lead me, and Your right hand shall hold me.
PSALM 139:10

We teach our children to grip our hand before crossing a busy street. Toddlers walk confidently as long as they remain hand in hand with Mom or Dad.

Joni Eareckson Tada understands the value of holding the hand of God. In fact, she signs all her correspondence, "In His Grip." It's where this writer claims she needs to be at every moment of her life. A diving accident at age seventeen left her a quadriplegic, and though her hands are immobile, she feels safest and most productive when she is hand in hand with God.

For Christians, there is no safer place for us than in the hand of God. The psalmist writes that God's hand was involved in our creation, our birth, and the planning of our life and our future. His hand is strong, trustworthy, and sure.

If you know Jesus as your personal Savior, you are in His grip. You rest in the hands that belong to the eternal God, the First and the Last. The One who overcame death. The One who knows your future. You can trust that He is guiding you every step of the way, and He is caring for every part of your life. You are in good hands.

A saint's life is in the hands of God like a bow and
arrow in the hands of an archer. God . . . goes on
stretching till His purpose is in sight, then He lets fly.

OSWALD CHAMBERS

THINK "ENCOURAGEMENT"

*Their hearts may be encouraged, being knit together in
love, and attaining to all riches of the full assurance of
understanding, to the knowledge of the mystery of God.*

COLOSSIANS 2:2

Jonas Salk, the great scientist and discoverer of the vaccine against polio, understood how to think and work with confidence. He was once asked, "How does this outstanding achievement, which has effectively brought an end to the word 'polio' in our vocabulary, cause you to view your 200 previous failures?"

"I have never had 200 failures in my whole life," he is reported to have said. "My family didn't think in terms of failure. They taught in terms of experiences and what could be learned. I just made my 201 discovery, and I couldn't have made it without learning from the previous 200 experiences."

Salk's example is illustrative of the Christian life. In order to support and encourage others, we have to stay encouraged ourselves, and we have to learn to think, believe, and live with assurance and conviction. Based on the promises of God, we have every reason to be optimistic. It's the uplifting "can-do" attitude of a biblical encourager that stokes the flames of God's work in the lives of others.

Learn to think "encouragement."

I have not failed. I've just found 10,000 ways that won't work.

THOMAS EDISON

"I ALWAYS SAY YES"

Be kindly affectionate to one another . . .
in honor giving preference to one another.
ROMANS 12:10

Several years ago, journalist Larry King interviewed television personality Art Linkletter, who had just turned ninety. King, who has famously been married several times, asked Linkletter the secret of longevity in marriage. At the time of the interview, Linkletter and his wife had been married sixty-six years. Linkletter simply replied, "I always say yes to anything she says."

"So how do you stay happy?" asked King in surprise.

Linkletter replied, "She's happy—when she's happy, I'm happy."*

There's a lot of truth in that little bit of wisdom. Of course, the real secret is when both partners begin practicing the habit of saying yes. The place where encouragement is most needed is the home, where our flaws are exposed and our selfishness is most likely to exert itself. But marriage works best when spouses are less selfish and more selfless. Marriage works when spouses understand that it's not about making themselves happy but about making the other person happy—in honor preferring one another. God's plan for marriage works!

Biblical love is not emotions or feelings, but attitudes and actions that seek the best interests of the other person.

JERRY BRIDGES

---

*Larry King interview with Art Linkletter on July 26, 2002, taken from a CNN transcript at http://www-cgi.cnn.com/TRANSCRIPTS/0207/26/lkl.00.html, accessed March 7, 2011.

LOSING THAT LOVING FEELING

*You shall love the L*ORD *your God with all your heart, with all your soul, with all your strength, and with all your mind.*

LUKE 10:27

Have you ever noticed how newlyweds can't do enough for each other? He brings her flowers. She writes him sweet notes. They take the necessary time to express their love for each other. Do you still feel that way about your relationship with God?

In Romans 12, Paul instructs believers to grow in their love for Jesus Christ so that they become living sacrifices, dedicated to Him. In the book of Revelation, there is a warning to the believers at Ephesus: they are falling short in their passion for Him. But when Christ gives a diagnosis, He also provides a prescription. He exhorts the Ephesians to repent and return to their first love, worshiping and serving Him as they did at the beginning (Revelation 2:4-5).

A married couple who feel they have lost the feeling of their first love can rekindle their passion by spending quality time together, sharing their goals, talking about their feelings, or praying together. You can rekindle the spark of intimacy with Jesus Christ by daily spending time with Him as you did in the beginning. Relish the joy of being near Him.

The mind grows by taking in, but the heart grows by giving out; and it is important to maintain a balanced life.

WARREN W. WIERSBE

AFFIRM TO MAKE FIRM

*Fathers, do not provoke your children,
lest they become discouraged.*
COLOSSIANS 3:21

The word *affirmation* is related to the word *firm*. In affirming others, we firm up their morale and confidence, and we encourage them in their decisions and direction.

Children need affirmation, for their self-esteem depends on the feedback they receive from us. Fortunately, there are lots of ways to affirm them. We can strengthen the children in our lives by using phrases like "Good job!" or "I'm so proud of you!"

We can also affirm by appropriate touch. A pat on the back or tousle of the hair can convey lots of love.

We can affirm with eye contact too. Try smiling at a child with your eyes. We often convey discipline through our eyes, but we can also communicate warmth and affirmation.

We also affirm children by spending time with them and praying for them.

Children who are praised are like young plants lifting their leaves to the sun. Children who receive praise are drawn to its warmth. No matter our age, we are all a bit like children. We should accept and love those around us—even as Christ Himself unconditionally loved and received us by His grace. Affirm someone today.

Praise your children. Do not for ever find fault with them. Whenever you can, praise them.

UNKNOWN

THE LOST ART OF LETTER WRITING

*[Paul wrote,] "To all who are in Rome, beloved of
God, called to be saints: Grace to you and peace
from God our Father and the Lord Jesus Christ."*

ROMANS 1:7

It's no accident that God chose the written form of epistles or letters to convey the teachings of the Christian life to the earliest believers. Paul, Peter, John, Jude, and James wrote personal letters to churches and individuals, and this body of correspondence makes up the richest source of our understanding of the Christian walk. Paul and the other authors could have compiled volumes of sermons or books of systematic teachings. But instead the Lord led them to use the medium of letter writing to leave a lasting legacy for all of Christian history. Letters are personal, readable, informal, enduring, and quotable.

Though our correspondence isn't inspired in the scriptural sense, don't underestimate the power of the written note. It's easy to pat someone on the back and say, "Good job." We need to frequently do that. But there is also great value in taking time to write encouraging words. They are durable and distance-proof.

Rediscover the lost art of letter writing. To whom can you send a letter today?

> Letter writing, in its ideal form, is really
> nothing else but indirect conversation.
>
> **C. H. CHARLES**

JOB'S PALS

I have heard many such things;
miserable comforters are you all!

JOB 16:2

Humorist Arnold H. Glasgow quipped, "A loyal friend laughs at your jokes when they're not so good and sympathizes with your problems when they're not so bad."

Job's pals seemed to start that way during his crisis, for we read in Job 2:11, "When Job's three friends heard of all this adversity that had come upon him, each one came from his own place. . . . For they had made an appointment together to come and mourn with him, and to comfort him." Job's friends began well. They sat with him on the ground seven days and seven nights and grieved with him. Few words were spoken. The friends were sensitive to Job's despair as he unburdened his heart.

But then they opened their mouths and spouted opinions—most of which were laden with misinformation—and their well-meaning visit took a wrong turn. That led an exasperated Job to call them "miserable comforters."

How many times have we resembled Job's friends? With our friends, let's sit where they sit, weep when they weep, and laugh as they laugh. But when we open our mouths, let's ask God for wisdom to reflect His truth into their lives in a way that builds them up, lest we, too, be miserable comforters.

Friends are relatives you make for yourself.

EUSTACHE DESCHAMPS

HIDDEN MESSAGES

*Let us consider one another in order to
stir up love and good works.*

HEBREWS 10:24

When Kellogg's introduced their Rice Krispies Treats with write-on wrapping, parents who packed lunches for their youngsters (or spouses) could use a permanent marker to jot a little note for their loved one: *I love you! Have a good day! Hugs and kisses!*

The new packaging prompted a Canadian group to survey how many parents actually add little personal notes to their children's lunch bags. Researchers found that although children desperately need encouragement at school, over half of Canadian parents never send notes along with their children's sandwiches.

While it was a great idea to utilize the write-on packaging, we can't wait for food that reminds us to be affirmers. There are countless little ways every day to boost your child, your spouse, your friend, and even a total stranger. It's up to us to begin cheering one another now. Why not think of a way you can snap, crackle, and pop with encouragement for someone today?

We need to encourage one another to fix our
eyes on the risen Jesus and thus to stir each
other up toward love and good deeds.[*]

IAIN M. DUGUID

---

[*] Iain M. Duguid, *Numbers: God's Presence in the Wilderness* Wheaton, IL: Crossway, 2006), 369.

AUGUST

THE WATCHING WORLD

By this all will know that you are My disciples,
if you have love for one another.

JOHN 13:35

When it comes to showing love in our Christian walk, there is no room for discrepancy! No one likes Christians who do not "walk the talk." They are like a carpet-cleaning product that claims to work miracles but only makes the stain worse. We must be consistent in our ability to love others in all kinds of circumstances.

The world is watching to see how God makes a difference in the lives of His own. What we profess must be lived out in the way we treat others. Jesus taught us that the one way we show the watching world that we belong to Him is by demonstrating our love for one another. Christians are to be known by the mark of love.

Is there a person in your life whom you find difficult to love? Is there a situation you often get into that makes it difficult for you to love? Commit your concern to the Lord in prayer. When you allow the powerful love of Jesus Christ to work through you, you can show a watching world that you belong to Jesus!

Love means to love that which is
unlovable; or it is no virtue at all.

G. K. CHESTERTON

GOD POTENTIAL

*Humble yourselves in the sight
of the Lord, and He will lift you up.*

JAMES 4:10

In Mark 9:33-35, we read about a group of disciples who had traveled to Capernaum to meet Jesus:

> After they arrived at Capernaum and settled in a house, Jesus asked his disciples, "What were you discussing out on the road?" But they didn't answer, because they had been arguing about which of them was the greatest. He sat down, called the twelve disciples over to him, and said, "Whoever wants to be first must take last place and be the servant of everyone else" (NLT).

God operates in ways opposite to the world. Even Jesus' disciples struggled with this concept. The world promises ladder-top fame, the chance to climb our way to a better place in life. But where does that leave us? We are confined to our own potential.

God says the first will be last and the last will be first. Let us remember that, in God's eyes, those who serve faithfully are the most successful. God will do immeasurably more than we could ever ask or imagine If we will choose to let go of the world's agenda for recognition. With God, we have access to divine potential.

Humility is the only soil in which the graces root.

ANDREW MURRAY

SPEAK NO EVIL

Do not speak evil of one another, brethren.
He who speaks evil of a brother and judges his brother,
speaks evil of the law and judges the law. But if
you judge the law, you are not a doer of the law but
a judge. There is one Lawgiver, who is able to save
and to destroy. Who are you to judge another?
JAMES 4:11-12

We have all crossed paths with overly critical people. These people are the ones who always have something negative to say about everyone and never give a compliment or an encouraging word.

Most of the time, people are critical because they want others to think they are witty, clever, or discerning. Ultimately, this kind of attitude is nothing more than a very effective repellent.

Who would want to be friends with a negative person who reproaches the people around him or her? No one wants to worry about being the next target of criticism.

James challenges us to avoid speaking evil about each other in order to bolster our self-image or hurt someone. God alone stands as the Judge, and He commands us to love each other as He loves us.

God has set a double fence before the tongue,
the teeth and the lips, to teach us to be wary
that we offend not with our tongue.

THOMAS WATSON

FIERY FAITH

*I will be with him in trouble; I will deliver him
and honor him. With long life I will satisfy
him, and show him My salvation.*

PSALM 91:15-16

When faced with death, three courageous men demonstrated their confidence in God. Shadrach, Meshach, and Abed-Nego already had a fiery faith in God before they faced the furnace. They knew that regardless of what the king might do, they would see their trial through and remain faithful to the almighty God.

It's not likely that you will ever have to face a consuming fire like Shadrach, Meshach, and Abed-Nego, but God will certainly give you the privilege of facing trials and difficulties. "Privilege?" you ask. Yes, it's a privilege to experience trials and testing because it is often at those moments when our faith takes on a new meaning and we grow deeper in our walk. We also have the reassurance that God Himself is with us in our trials, preserving us and strengthening us.

God knows exactly what you are going through. And, best of all, He is walking through it with you. Trust in Him to give you courage to handle every trial. Trust in Him to stay near to you in every difficulty you experience.

Rather than begrudge your problem, explore it.
Ponder it. And most of all, use it. Use it to the glory of God.

MAX LUCADO

REWARDING REST

*Surely goodness and mercy shall follow me all the days of
my life; and I will dwell in the house of the LORD forever.*

PSALM 23:6

King David was a godly man who knew what it meant to suffer. Sometimes his suffering came at the hand of an enemy, and sometimes it came as a result of his own sin. Throughout his trials, David sought the Lord and placed his faith squarely in the God who had proven Himself to be true.

In today's psalm, David reveals beautiful images of comfort and security. He paints a picture of refreshment and protection. David knew the contentment of complete trust in the Lord. He knew the refreshment of forgiveness of sin. He knew the protection God provides, having narrowly escaped a pursuing enemy, dodged a well-aimed spear, and evaded a soldier searching him out in a darkened cave.

King David writes of the bountiful blessings God brings when His people follow Him through the dark days as well as the bright ones. And he concludes this beautiful psalm with the best news of all—that God rewards those who remain faithful to Him. Let this great news encourage you to stay close to God!

God's promises are like the stars; the darker
the night, the brighter they shine.

DAVID NICHOLAS

COMPROMISE? NEVER!

My little children, these things I write
to you, so that you may not sin.

1 JOHN 2:1

When a race car driver climbs into his car, he expects the tires, brakes, and safety equipment to be sound and reliable. He wants to know that no compromise has been made in the manufacture of his gear. He stakes his life on the fact that the car is safe and strong.

During the earliest days of the church, compromises began to creep in. Believers faced the huge challenge of living holy lives while surrounded by a sinful society. They wanted to remain sound and pure, true to the original message of the gospel; however, the original standard of holy living gradually became compromised. False teaching crept in, and many Christians became casualties to the lies of false doctrine.

Today, there are many beliefs that run counter to the Scriptures. Many of them tempt us to compromise our faith. We need to fill our minds with the truth of God's Word. When we stay close to God, we are protected from the invasion of compromise. Consider your beliefs, and make sure they are based solely and soundly on God's truth. It matters what you believe.

A soft and sheltered Christianity, afraid to be lean and
lone, unwilling to face the storms and brave the heights,
will end up fat and foul in the cages of conformity.

VANCE HAVNER

WISE CONVERSATIONALISTS

*Speaking the truth in love, may [we] grow up in
all things into Him who is the head—Christ.*

EPHESIANS 4:15

A Chinese proverb says, "A single conversation across the table with a wise person is worth a month's study of books." Let's be like that wise person.

Colossians 3:17 tells us that whatever we do *in word*, we should do in the name of the Lord Jesus. In other words, we should speak as Jesus would on all occasions. The method and manner of expressing oneself matters. What we say should always be true, and our words should be lovingly motivated and delivered. Speaking the truth without love is harsh. Speaking in love without truthfulness is hypocritical.

We don't have to say everything we think, and we don't have to have the last word in every conversation. A harsh word stirs up anger, so we should rejoice when we restrain ourselves from speaking unkind thoughts. As British writer Dorothy Nevill put it, "The real art of conversation is not only to say the right thing at the right place but to leave unsaid the wrong thing at the tempting moment."

The man who lives right, and is right, has more power
in his silence than another has by his words.

PHILLIP BROOKS

THE DO-GOODERS

*By grace you have been saved through faith . . . it is the
gift of God, not of works, lest anyone should boast.*

EPHESIANS 2:8-9

How hard do you work at trying to be "good"? Technology can help you! Families can now view movies in their homes using a television filter, muting unacceptable language, behavior, and violence. There are also Internet filters that block pornography and foul content. And if you're trying to make good nutritional choices, you can use apps on your smartphone for counting calories. So technology can help you be good. But is it good enough?

God asks us to live in obedience to His Word, and our behavior should imitate Christ's. But how liberating it is to know that we don't need to be "good enough" for God's love! In the book of Galatians, the apostle Paul's anger toward the Judaizers was justified. They were trying to change the gospel of grace by adding required works (Galatians 1:9; 2:16). Paul's message is clear: either it's the gospel of grace or it's not the gospel at all.

Do you worry about being good enough for God? Filling your hands with good works is not the answer. Show Him empty hands, and ask Him to fill them with His grace.

I have a great need for Christ;
I have a great Christ for my need.

CHARLES H. SPURGEON

INTERCEPTED BY GRACE

They glorified God in me.
GALATIANS 1:24

Perhaps you're familiar with the Christian authors Josh McDowell and Lee Strobel, former atheists whose research led them to the One they sought to discredit. Their transformed lives now lead other truth seekers to God. Nothing gets your attention like someone who holds a strong position and then refutes it.

God has a way of getting people's attention. Take the apostle Paul: summa cum laude among Jewish scholars, impeccable credentials, zealous observer of every Jewish tradition (Philippians 3:5-6; Galatians 1:14). Paul was convinced that killing Christians was a noble service to God, and he took his gruesome assignment seriously (Acts 8:3). So how does a former terrorist of the church change his mind? Did he just wake up one morning and say, "I wonder what it would be like to be an apostle of grace"?

That's the miracle of being intercepted by grace. No one can look at the life of Paul—or any believer transformed by the gospel—and not see God's glory. Paul testified that when people heard his radical testimony, they didn't glorify him. All they could do was glorify God (Galatians 1:24).

This week, pray that others will see God in you and be amazed at His glory.

Grace must find expression in life, otherwise it is not grace.

KARL BARTH

STANDING ROOM ONLY

Now, Lord, look on their threats, and grant to Your servants that with all boldness they may speak Your word.

ACTS 4:29

Have you noticed schoolyard bullies have morphed into cyber-space bullies? Teenage peer pressure has followed us into adulthood via the media. But it is our Christian faith and morality that places us in the line of fire for stigmas of intolerance and prejudice. Do we shore up or retreat?

As our Lord's return draws near, bold believers are needed to stand up, speak up, and not shut up for the defense of the gospel! There is no better example for our critical mission than the apostle Paul. An outstanding freedom fighter, Paul fearlessly took on the Judaizers—a movement of people seeking to discredit his reputation for the sake of subverting the true message of the gospel (Galatians 2:4-8).

We are free in Christ to say what we want to say, do what we want to do, and go where we want to go. Why should we take a stand? Because we know and love our Savior, we want to say what *He* would say, do what *He* would do, and go where *He* would go.

Now is the time to stand up and be counted as followers of Christ. Strategize a way to take a stand for the gospel, and do it fearlessly!

Stand up, stand up for Jesus!

GEORGE DUFFIELD

ONE INSIGNIFICANT ACT

You have done foolishly. You have not kept the
commandment of the LORD your God.

1 SAMUEL 13:13

King Saul, a man chosen to lead God's people, found himself in a bind. It was time for a burnt offering, but the prophet, already seven days late, had not yet arrived. Taking matters into his own hands, Saul offered the burnt offering himself. As a result, he was met with harsh words by the prophet: "You have done foolishly. You have not kept the commandment of the Lord. . . . Now your kingdom shall not continue" (1 Samuel 13:13-14).

As it did for Saul, one seemingly insignificant choice has the potential to destroy your testimony. King Saul no doubt thought that making an offering was an insignificant act, but it cost him his kingdom, and more importantly, it damaged his relationship with God.

How can you keep your testimony strong and unblemished? Keep purity foremost in your heart and mind. Tune your heart to the Holy Spirit's gentle voice, and obey when He speaks to you. Keep a consistent prayer life so that your heart remains sensitive to the things that are important to the Lord. And above all, take the advice of the apostle Paul to the Thessalonians, "Test all things; hold fast to what is good. Abstain from every form of evil" (1 Thessalonians 5:21-22).

Things insignificant to man may be great in the sight of God.

UNKNOWN

A STEADFAST SPIRIT

Renew a steadfast spirit within me.

PSALM 51:10

While a family was on a camping trip, a storm struck. The winds were so strong that the parents spent the entire night clinging to the center pole of their old tent while their children slept. Had they not held fast to that center pole, the tent would have surely blown down, and their outing would have been spoiled.

For those of us seeking to remain steadfast in our faith, the Word of God is our center pole! The world we live in will buffet us with winds of temptation, false doctrine, and compromise. To remain true to God and His call on our lives, we must hold fast to the Word. When we look to the Word rather than the world, we can be assured that our doctrine will be correct and our faith will be pure.

Make it your aim to hold fast to the Word. Read it daily, and let it pervade your thoughts and actions. Consult your Bible in decisions large and small. In moments of confusion or trial, turn to the Scriptures for insight and guidance. Like the parents holding on to their tent's center pole, hold on to the Word of God.

Our strength is shown in the things we stand for.
Our weaknesses are shown in the things we fall for.

HUGH A. COWAN

SPIRITUALLY FRESH

[Samson] awoke from his sleep, and said, "I will go out as before, at other times, and shake myself free!" But he did not know that the LORD had departed from him.

JUDGES 16:20

When you purchase flowers to cheer up a loved one, it's important that the flowers be fresh and colorful, rather than wilted and brown. When it comes to showing love and support with blooms, freshness counts! We want today's bouquet, not something stale and wilted.

When we rely on the spiritual accomplishments of our past, we risk becoming *spiritually* wilted.

Samson thought he could live on his past victories. During his life, he slew a lion, defeated a thousand Philistines, and carried away the gates of Gaza. One day he woke up bound and roared, "I will shake myself free." He'd done it before. He'd do it again. But during the night the Lord had departed. Samson's spiritual strength was drained.

How can you stay fresh in your Christian life? Start each day dependent on the Lord in every part of your life—your workplace, your home, your church, and your neighborhood. Ask Him each day for a fresh perspective and a new start. Seek out believers who share what they're learning and how it applies to their lives. These steps will keep your spiritual life vibrant!

Complacency is a deadly foe of all spiritual growth.

A. W. TOZER

CHRIST IS ENOUGH

Walk worthy of the Lord, fully pleasing Him,
being fruitful in every good work.

COLOSSIANS 1:10

Have you smiled at someone today? Held a door open? Let someone slip ahead of you in traffic? Changed a diaper? Written a check to a charity?

Do any of those things make you more acceptable to God?

There's a biblical balance when it comes to good deeds. Our lives should be filled with them, but we don't labor for the Lord because we have to. We do good things out of our love for Him. We are already fully accepted by God through the blood of Christ. When we're justified by grace through faith, the righteousness of Christ is credited to our account. Thereafter we live a life of service because we love Him.

Never worry about whether God loves you. If you know Christ as your Savior, don't feel you have to win God's favor. You have all His grace for all your needs. Just serve Him with a desire to please Him in all you do and say.

Good works cannot put us right, but they necessarily
follow when we are right; they are the natural fruit and the
ordained sphere of the new creature in Christ Jesus.*

BERNARD H. NADAL

---

*Bernard Harrison Nadal, *The New Life Dawning* (New York: Nelson & Phillips, 1873), 321.

WHAT WE CANNOT SEE

*Now faith is the substance of things hoped
for, the evidence of things not seen.*

HEBREWS 11:1

Many of us claim that we have faith in God, trusting that He is real and that His promises are true. But if God asked us to act on our faith—trusting in what we cannot see—could He count our faith as righteousness?

Abraham believed God's promises. Even as he sat at the foot of Mount Moriah preparing to go and sacrifice Isaac, he turned to his traveling party and said, "The lad and I will go yonder and worship, and *we* will come back to you" (Genesis 22:5, emphasis added). He trusted that God would somehow intervene, and they would *both* come back. He knew this because God had told him that in Isaac his seed would be blessed. He didn't know how God was going to do it, but he believed God's promise.

Was Abraham righteous because he went up the mountain? No. Was he righteous because he raised the knife to take his son's life? No. Abraham was righteous for one reason: he believed, and his faith was counted unto him as righteousness.

Faith is believing what God says is true—even when we don't understand how it will ultimately work out.

Faith and obedience are inescapably related. There is
no saving faith in God apart from obedience to God,
and there can be no godly obedience without godly faith.

JOHN MACARTHUR

TEST YOURSELF

You must continue in the things which you have learned and been assured of, knowing from whom you have learned them.
2 TIMOTHY 3:14

The best way to ensure the long life of an automobile is to regularly maintain it and change its oil. Car owners who want a smoothly running vehicle for many years develop the habit of routinely checking its basic systems.

Do you regularly check and maintain your spiritual health? If not, use 2 Timothy 3 as a test to discern your spiritual condition.

First ask yourself, "Do I exhibit any of the qualities of godless people listed in 2 Timothy 3:2-5?" They are described as "lovers of themselves, lovers of money, boasters, proud, blasphemers, disobedient to parents, unthankful, unholy, unloving, unforgiving, slanderers, without self-control, brutal, despisers of good, traitors, headstrong, haughty, lovers of pleasure."

Second, determine if the qualities found in verses 10-12 are part of your life. Have you carefully followed sound doctrine, emulating Paul's manner of life, purpose, faith, longsuffering, love, perseverance, etc.?

What did you discover as you checked your heart? When you find a quality that does not belong in your life, eliminate it through confession and prayer. Regularly take a diagnostic look at your spiritual condition.

When you drink from the stream, remember the spring.
UNKNOWN

BLAND BELIEVERS

*I will search Jerusalem with lamps, and punish
the men who are settled in complacency.*

ZEPHANIAH 1:12

Have you ever sipped yesterday's coffee? Or slurped warm ice cream? Both are tepid. Neither one tastes the way it should! They disappoint because they aren't what you expect.

Sometimes the same thing can happen with our zeal for God. Perhaps before you knew the Lord, you were very cold to spiritual things. Then, when you finally came to the Truth and began your walk with the Lord, you were on fire—burning hot, perhaps. But eventually your fire cooled down and your walk with God became lukewarm.

Sadly, many believers over time become complacent. Complacency is a serious spiritual condition. In fact, God looks at apostasy with anger, but it is indifference that makes Him sick.

Do you settle for what is convenient and comfortable, instead of being bold and speaking the truth? Do you compromise your beliefs and behavior because you fear offending others?

Perhaps your faith has become lukewarm. Ask God to ignite His fire within your heart so He can revive the lukewarm parts of your spiritual life. You will become zealous and committed in your walk. Rekindle your spiritual zeal by drawing near to Him in prayer and worship.

God can't stomach lukewarm faith. He is angered by
a religion that puts on a show but ignores the service.

MAX LUCADO

HOPE-FULL

Let us hold fast the confession of our hope
without wavering, for He who promised is faithful.
HEBREWS 10:23

Be honest: How often do you catch yourself feeling hopeful? Hope is one of those emotions that we seem to know more by its absence than by its presence. (Not that it should be that way, but it often is.) Even though you may not recall the last time you felt hope-*full*, you can probably remember the last time you felt hope-*less*.

Hope, often taken for granted, is nothing more than rock-solid assurance that what God has said is true and that it will come to pass—even when there is nothing except His Word to back up that hope. Hope is not dependent on circumstances. Seeing is not believing. *Hoping* is believing! Hope is the confidence that wells up as a result of our believing God. There's a fine line between the two, and the transition is almost imperceptible. But you have to believe before you can hope, and hope happens as soon as you believe. So if you are walking confidently today in your relationship with Christ—at peace about today and the future—you are hope-*full*.

The Bible says to "hold fast the confession of [your] hope." Stay hopeful by staying faithful, just as God is faithful.

Hope means expectancy when things are otherwise hopeless.

G. K. CHESTERTON

A CONCEIT-FREE HEART

*I say, through the grace given to me, to everyone who
is among you, not to think of himself more highly
than he ought to think, but to think soberly, as God
has dealt to each one a measure of faith.*

ROMANS 12:3

The apostle Paul tells us to view ourselves and the success of our lives in light of the "measure of faith" God has allotted us. What is your "measure of faith"? According to Paul, it is the spiritual gifts God has given you, and they have one purpose only—to build up His body, the church of Jesus Christ.

When it comes to measuring our achievements, there may be times when we are tempted to feel pretty good about ourselves. We may momentarily believe that we have special value to the church.

Each of us is indeed valuable! But the apostle Paul reminds us repeatedly that if we boast in anything, it is to be in the Lord and all that He has done in our lives. That includes our giftedness, our proficiency, and our good works. Pride has no place in the Christian's life. With a humble heart, recognize the gifts God has given you, and put aside any temptation toward conceit or pride.

There is no spirit in man more opposed to the
Spirit of God than the spirit of pride.

JOHN BLANCHARD

A SIGN FROM ABOVE

The rainbow shall be in the cloud, and I will look on it to remember the everlasting covenant between God and every living creature of all flesh that is on the earth.

GENESIS 9:16

Its appearance stops you in your tracks. As you look up to see the rain, clouds roll back and the sun breaks through. Suddenly a rainbow fills the sky with color. Do you marvel every time you see a rainbow? For the Christian, it is far more than a visual phenomenon.

Scripture tells us that the rainbow is a sign from God. After the flood that covered the earth, He sent the rainbow as His promise to Noah, his family, and all who came after that He would never again destroy the earth with a flood.

This covenant—a binding pact that God promises He will never break—still holds today. God's promises are unchanging; they are everlasting. He is faithful to keep every covenant.

The next time you see a rainbow, stop for a moment and look up. Remind yourself of the beauty of God's mercy in your life, and the overarching ways He has forgiven and cleansed you of sin. Thank Him for the sign of the rainbow, and for its message of mercy and faithfulness.

God's promises are not mottos to hang on the wall. They are checks to take to the bank.

ADRIAN ROGERS

OUR HELP

Then she came and worshiped Him, saying, "Lord, help me!"
MATTHEW 15:25

A few years ago, a black bear in Vermont got himself into trouble. As he was nosing around where he shouldn't, he got his head stuck in an old-fashioned milk can. The bear lumbered around for hours, bumping into trees and boulders before being spotted near the highway to Reading. It took quite a while for biologists, firefighters, and police to figure out how to help him. They used soap to lubricate his head, but that didn't work. Finally, they managed to cut the can off his head.

Problems happen to all of us from time to time. We probably won't be walking around with a milk can on our heads, but we will need help to get out of our problem. The good news is that we have a God who is a very present *help* in trouble (Psalm 46:1). Our *help* comes from the One who made heaven and earth (Psalm 121:2). We need to simply pray to Him. When we pray, we're coming to the throne of grace to obtain mercy and grace to *help* in time of need (Hebrews 4:16). Then we can rest, knowing that He will provide. "Happy is he who has the God of Jacob for his *help*, whose hope is in the LORD his God" (Psalm 146:5, emphasis added).

O God, our help in ages past, our hope for years to come . . .
ISAAC WATTS

WORSHIP AT THE THRONE

*Your throne, O God, is forever and ever; a scepter
of righteousness is the scepter of Your kingdom.*

HEBREWS 1:8

When you think of the center of command and control for the United States of America, the White House quickly comes to mind. When you think of the focus of all authority and power in heaven, you think of the throne of God.

Just as the White House is a busy hub of constant activity, there is much that takes place at the throne of God. From His throne, God lovingly rules over the affairs of the earth. He exercises His authority over all people, and He asserts His control over time—past, present, and future. God's throne is also the seat of His judgment. He discerns between good and evil, and He administers reward and punishment alike.

The best thing that happens at the throne of God, however, is worship! All the saints, elders, angels, and creatures surround Him, singing praises and exalting Him in all His glory.

Will you be there, worshiping with all the others at the throne of God? Our occupation for all eternity will be to exalt and adore Jesus Christ. Knowing that, doesn't it seem worthwhile to worship the Lord now?

We are called to an everlasting preoccupation with God.

A. W. TOZER

MIRROR ANGST

He who looks into the perfect law of liberty and
continues in it, and is not a forgetful hearer . . .
this one will be blessed in what he does.

JAMES 1:25

When a fashion retailer commissioned a study of what women thought of their appearance in the mirror, researchers found that 90 percent of women in their forties and fifties were unhappy with the way they looked and suffered from "midlife mirror angst syndrome." According to the report, middle-aged women were four times unhappier than teenage girls with what they saw in the mirror.

Not so fast. For Christians, time enhances our appearance because the joy of the Lord shines through. As we age, let us seek to take on the "incorruptible beauty of a gentle and quiet spirit, which is very precious in the sight of God" (1 Peter 3:4).

But how much better to gaze into the mirror of God's Word! James says that the law is a mirror to show us what we're like. Without Christ, all we see are the wrinkles of wickedness and ghostly pallor of despair. But with Christ, looking into God's Word doesn't bring condemnation or judgment.

Study His Word today and see the mirror image of Christ.

The mirror of the Word not only examines us and
reveals our sins, but it helps to cleanse us as well.*

WARREN W. WIERSBE

---

*Warren W. Wiersbe, *The Wiersbe Bible Commentary: The Complete New Testament* (Colorado Springs: David C. Cook, 2007), 859.

WAYFARING STRANGERS

I instruct you in the way of wisdom and
lead you along straight paths.

PROVERBS 4:11, NIV

In 1936, a young Hungarian-born man found a job as an interpreter for a French shipping line. As he traveled around, he noticed tourists who were interested in where to eat and sleep and sightsee. This fellow, Eugene Fodor, put together a guidebook for them, thus launching the line of Fodor's travel guides, the largest such enterprise in the English-speaking world.

Travel guides are helpful as we prepare for a trip, but they can't replace the trip itself. No matter how much you read about Westminster Abbey or the Great Wall of China, it's not like seeing them in person.

The law of God is like a travel guide. We can see how we should walk, where we should go, how we should live, and what we should be. But no amount of cramming will actually get us there. Grace, on the other hand, is a trip to heaven with all expenses paid.

Don't just look at the pictures and read the text. Let Christ bring it alive in your life. He has come that you might have life, and that you might have it more abundantly!

Leader of faithful souls, and guide of all who
travel to the sky, come, and with us, even us,
abide, who would on Thee alone rely.

CHARLES WESLEY

TIME TO GROW UP

Therefore you are no longer a slave but a son,
and if a son, then an heir of God through Christ.

GALATIANS 4:7

Family experts advise parents to teach their children from the get-go to put away their playthings. As soon as toddlers can walk, they should learn to pick up after themselves. Cleaning up can be part of a bedtime routine, along with a bath, prayers, and a story. The idea is that as we grow older, we'll do the same—but not because we're told. As we mature, we internalize the spirit of cleanliness and maturely want to live well-ordered lives.

In the same way, the law was given when God's people were in their childhood. The law treats people like babies. Everything is spelled out. But with the coming of Christ, Christians are free to live as mature sons and daughters in Christ and not under the supervision of the law. It's time to grow up. We're under grace.

Christianity under grace isn't about legalistically following a set of rules. We've been set free from all such man-made rules and regulations. Now we walk in the Spirit and live out our faith with confidence and freedom.

God's gifts put man's best dreams to shame.

ELIZABETH BARRETT BROWNING

AUGUST 26

THE OFFENSE OF THE CROSS

*God forbid that I should boast except in the cross
of our Lord Jesus Christ, by whom the world has
been crucified to me, and I to the world.*

GALATIANS 6:14

In 2011, a sixty-four-year-old electrician in England faced dismissal because he displayed a small cross on the dashboard of his work vehicle. The man said, "I have worked in the coal mines and served in the Army in Northern Ireland and I have never suffered such stress." Company officials justified their demand by claiming the small cross might cause offense. But the electrician wouldn't back down. "I have never been so full of resolve," he told a newspaper. "I am determined to stand up for my rights. If they sack me, so be it. But I am standing up for my faith."*

As children of God, we enjoy intimacy and security in Him, but we must also endure pressure and sometimes persecution for our faith. Yet we should never be discouraged. We have liberty in Christ, the promise of eternal life in Him, and we are a blessed people.

Let's be full of resolve and full of rejoicing, no matter what persecution may come.

We don't want to be personally or institutionally offensive,
but we cannot buffer the offense of the Cross.**

JOHN MACARTHUR

*"Electrician Faces Sack for Displaying Christian Cross in His Van," *Telegraph,* April 18, 2011.
**Marshall Shelley, ed., *Growing Your Church Through Evangelism and Outreach* (Nashville: Moorings, 1996), 162.

WORSHIP IN OBEDIENCE

Oh come, let us worship and bow down;
let us kneel before the LORD our Maker.

PSALM 95:6

When we teach children obedience, we tell them that it is good for them. We expound on the rewards they will reap when they do as we wish: they will be kept safe from danger, they will learn new skills, and most of all, they will live a blessed and meaningful life. We teach our children to obey because their doing so will bring them joy!

It's the same with our worship of God. You may not think of worship as a command to be obeyed, but it is! In Psalm 95, we read the joyful command to *come, sing, shout, worship, bow,* and *kneel.* Scriptures tell us to worship so we will be blessed in return.

When we open our hearts to God, proclaiming His worth and thanking Him for His rich provision for us in Christ, it brings Him pleasure.

In worship, we recognize that God *is God,* and we are not. We acknowledge that there is no one higher, no one more powerful or worthy of our praise than our holy God. Through worship we receive the amazing blessing of meeting with our Maker.

God wills to be displayed and known and
loved and cherished and worshiped always
and everywhere and in every act.

JOHN PIPER

CONFIDENT IN YOU, IN THE LORD!

I have confidence in you, in the LORD.

GALATIANS 5:10

The German writer Johann Wolfgang von Goethe once observed, "Correction does much, but encouragement does more."

Yes, but correction and encouragement, wisely combined, do the most.

When he wrote to the Galatians, Paul devoted a bottle of ink to correcting and reproving his readers for theological carelessness. But along the way, he sought to encourage them and express his love and confidence toward them. Constant correction tears us down and demoralizes our hearts. When we're the object of nagging, harping criticism, things only get worse. We change our ways more quickly when surrounded by people who are both honest and uplifting.

Notice that Paul doesn't just say, "I have confidence in you." He adds an intriguing qualification: "I have confidence in you, in the LORD." He means, "I have confidence in the Lord that He can work in you what is pleasing to Him."

Don't just be on people's backs all the time. Don't harp and criticize too much. Add a spoonful of sugar. Learn to say, "I have confidence in you, in the Lord!"

Few things help an individual more than to place
responsibility upon him, and to let him know that you
trust him. . . . Every individual responds to confidence.*

BOOKER T. WASHINGTON

---

*Booker T. Washington, *Up from Slavery* (New York: A. L. Burt Company, 1901), 172.

AIM FOR PERFECTION

Aim for perfection, listen to my appeal,
be of one mind, live in peace.
2 CORINTHIANS 13:11, NIV

In the King James Version, 2 Corinthians 13:11 says, "Be perfect." The New King James Version says, "Become complete." Other translations capture the spirit of Paul's advice by saying, "Aim for perfection." Every day we're to grow more like Him who is perfect in every way.

The Bible gives us many examples of what a perfect God looks like. It says that God's works are perfect and that He is perfect in knowledge (Deuteronomy 32:4, NIV; Job 37:16). The law of the Lord is perfect (Psalm 19:7). His love and even His hatred are perfect (1 John 4:18; Psalm 5:5). He is able to keep us in perfect peace (Isaiah 26:3). We can experience His good and perfect will and enjoy His good and perfect gifts (Romans 12:2; James 1:17).

Sinless perfection may not be possible in this life, but the psalmist testifies, "The LORD will perfect that which concerns me" (Psalm 138:8). We can aim at perfection. Without Christ, our efforts in trying to achieve perfection are wasted; but in Christ, He who has begun a good work in us will carry it on to completion (Philippians 1:6, NIV).

Although it is true that we will never achieve a
sinless perfection until we reach heaven, this should
never keep us from striving and saying with Fanny
Crosby, "Take the world, but give me Jesus."*

KENNETH W. OSBECK

*Kenneth W. Osbeck, *Amazing Grace* (Grand Rapids, MI: Kregel, 1990), 240.

STANDING FAST

*Stand fast therefore in the liberty by which Christ
has made us free, and do not be entangled
again with a yoke of bondage.*

GALATIANS 5:1

The expression "stand fast" conjures up an ironic picture of opposing actions. To readers of Paul's epistles, the words were a reminder of the hardened and disciplined Roman soldiers who would stand fast, locking shields together and digging their feet in the ground to provide a solid front against the enemy. Paul uses this powerful image to show believers how serious he is about defending their freedom in Christ against false doctrine.

Over and over again, Paul uses this phrase to call believers to persevere against the winds of persecution: stand fast in your faith (1 Corinthians 16:13), in one spirit (Philippians 1:27), in the Lord (1 Thessalonians 3:8), and in the traditions you have been given (2 Thessalonians 2:15). It's a crucial command for believers today.

Be aware of encroaching enemies to the faith. You may find them in the media, in a curriculum, or in your relationships. God will give you the strength to stand fast. With no apologies, we need to put our shields together, dig our feet in, and say, "Not here, not now, not this time."

We never become truly spiritual by sitting
down and wishing to become so.

PHILLIPS BROOKS

REFLECTING GRACE

If we live in the Spirit, let us also walk in the Spirit.

GALATIANS 5:25

Brilliantly reflecting light from seventy-four facets, the pear-shaped Regent diamond is considered to be the most beautiful diamond ever seen. This gemstone adorned the crowns of kings and was worn in a hat by Marie Antoinette. Napoleon Bonaparte showcased the diamond in his sword. It now resides at the Louvre. Imagine the colorful stories of adventure and mystery this jewel could tell.

Have you ever thought of the many facets of God's jewel of grace? It's no ordinary grace that planned a way for sinful man to be redeemed through the death and resurrection of God's only Son. It's no common grace that sent the Holy Spirit to reside in all believers, giving us resilience and joy for life. It's no passive grace that reflects God's brilliant love wherever it rests—in a royal palace, at a kitchen table, in a lonely room, or at the end of a devastating phone call. God's grace is brilliant. It heals, illuminates, and understands.

Grace is not a one-way experience. Feed your spirit with God's Word and by ministering to others. When you do, the brilliant facets of His grace will touch the people you connect with every day.

Grace does not grant permission to live in the flesh; it supplies power to live in the Spirit.

JOHN MACARTHUR

SEPTEMBER

THE FAITH OF JOB

You have heard of the perseverance of Job
and seen the end intended by the Lord—that the
Lord is very compassionate and merciful.
JAMES 5:11

Job was one of the most afflicted figures in the entire Bible. He lost his children, his wealth, and even his own health. In the face of devastating circumstances, Job still maintained, "Though He slay me, yet will I trust Him" (Job 13:15).

It may seem difficult to attribute compassion and mercy to a God who would allow one of His own to suffer so intensely. But we must remember that the Lord's work in our lives has a purpose and that while we may feel defeated, we have the assurance that every adversity in our lives is sifted through God's hands.

Our hope amid personal catastrophe is in knowing that God sees the end before there is a beginning. He knows the purpose of the heartache even before we feel the pain. With resolute faith in the unchanging character of God, we can trust Him through the problems.

If you are facing a trial today, unsure of why God is allowing your life to be disrupted, take time to focus on His attributes. When we see God for who He is, we are better able to cope with where we are.

Trials are medicines which our gracious and wise
Physician prescribes because we need them.
JOHN NEWTON

HEALING FOR THE SOUL

Confess your trespasses to one another, and pray
for one another, that you may be healed.

JAMES 5:16

Admitting you are struggling with a sin is always the first step to overcoming it. What is hidden is destined to remain in darkness, but confessing sin exposes it to the light.

In the parable of the Pharisee and the tax collector, the Pharisee points to his own righteousness, while the tax collector confesses his sin (Luke 18:9-14). It is the tax collector that Jesus commends for his humility.

Just putting our sins into words often removes the power they hold over us. The second step, as outlined by James, completes the process. When we follow up an initial confession with prayer, we receive divine help that can lead us to victory over sins that once held us in bondage. And when we seek the prayers of godly believers, our opportunity for victory increases.

Regardless of your past record, you do not need to be defeated by sin's strongholds again! You can request the prayers of a trusted friend, Christian counselor, or pastor. Today is the day to take that first step toward spiritual healing. It begins in confession and sounds something like this: *Lord, I confess that I am a sinner. . . .*

In weighing our sins let us not use a deceitful balance,
weighing at our own discretion . . . but rather recognize
what has been already weighed by the Lord.

AUGUSTINE

THE SECRET PLACE

*When you pray, go into your room, and when you have shut
your door, pray to your Father who is in the secret place;
and your Father who sees in secret will reward you openly.*

MATTHEW 6:6

While He was here on the earth, Jesus talked to His Father
in prayer. He prayed publicly, as when He prayed with the
crowds. He also prayed privately. The Scriptures often describe the
times when Jesus withdrew from the masses to talk to His Father.

The importance of corporate prayer is indisputable. Numerous biblical references cite the times the early believers met
together for prayer. Yet Jesus first taught the disciples to have a
secret place for prayer. We, too, need a secret place and a quiet
time where we can enter into the Master's presence. He encouraged us to make prayer private—not as an act to be ashamed of,
but as something to be protected and cherished. We safeguard
our privacy with God because we treasure that intimacy.

Have you met God today in a secret place? Find a spot where
you can have uninterrupted time with Him. Your commitment to
find God through private times of prayer will result in rewards
straight from His hands. He promises He will bless you!

Don't pray when you feel like it. Have an
appointment with the Lord and keep it.

CORRIE TEN BOOM

BURYING A GRUDGE

Love your enemies, bless those who curse you,
do good to those who hate you, and pray for those
who spitefully use you and persecute you.

MATTHEW 5:44

When Methodist pastor Charles Allen was in the fourth grade, a school official mistreated him. The man, who had a falling-out with Allen's father, took it out on the son. Years later, during Allen's first pastorate, he heard that his old antagonist was seeking a job with area schools. Allen knew that as soon as he told his friends on the school board about the man, they would not hire him.

He later wrote, "I went out to get in my car to go see some of the board members and suddenly it came over me what I had done. Here I was out trying to represent Him who was nailed to the Cross and me carrying a grudge. That realization was a humiliating experience. I went back into my house, knelt by my bedside, and said, 'Lord, if you will forgive me of this, I will never be guilty anymore.'"*

The concept of grace is hard to understand because it's so far removed from how we as fallen people relate to each other. But we do know that grace changes things. Just as God offered us grace and forgiveness through the Cross, we can offer grace and forgiveness to those who have hurt us.

Every cat knows some things need to be buried.

RUTH BELL GRAHAM

---

*Charles Allen, *The Miracle of Love* (Old Tappan, NJ: Fleming H. Revell Co., 1972), 38.

FOLLOW THE LEADER

*For as many as are led by the Spirit
of God, these are sons of God.*
ROMANS 8:14

Directionally challenged people everywhere were thrilled when navigation systems became available. No longer would the embarrassing "I'm lost" phone call have to be made. Now we travel worry-free, allowing the system to do the work for us—until it leads us astray. Though there are many appreciative GPS users, occasionally drivers may circle a block three times before realizing there's not a restaurant in sight, or far worse, find themselves teetering on the edge of a cliff that their navigator insists is the safe route.

As Christians, we have an internal guide—the Holy Spirit—that serves as our life navigation system. But unlike our GPS, He can be trusted even when He's taking us down an uncertain road, because ultimately His way is best.

So the question is simple—will you follow? If we trust our GPS to guide us on a cross-country automobile adventure, shouldn't we follow the Holy Spirit through the journey of life? We may not always know where we are, but we will always be exactly where the Lord intends us to be.

When led of the Spirit, the child of God must be as ready
to wait as to go, as prepared to be silent as to speak.

LEWIS SPERRY CHAFER

TO THE RESCUE!

Rescue me speedily! Be a rock of refuge
for me, a strong fortress to save me!

PSALM 31:2, ESV

A thief is usually not happy to see law enforcement arrive at the scene of the crime. But a burglar who became trapped while trying to climb through the small window of a fifth-floor apartment was probably relieved when the police and fire crews arrived. It took firefighters thirty minutes to get the bungling burglar to safety—where he was promptly arrested.

The botched burglary is a great example of sin's trap and the need for rescuers. No one plans on getting trapped. The sin itself snags us, and we need rescuers. Those walking in the Spirit are responsible to rescue and humbly restore their brothers and sisters in Christ. What does that look like? The Greek language of the New Testament provides a graphic illustration. The word used for "restore" is *katartizo*, describing the setting of a broken bone.

So instead of having the attitude of a legalist, who seeks to exploit fallen brothers and sisters, and make them a topic of discussion, gently rescue others from their sin traps. You may share a house, an office, or a pew with someone who needs you to mend his or her brokenness with the spirit of love. Isn't that how you would hope to be rescued?

[Contrary to] people-pleasers,
only people-lovers are able to confront.*

EDWARD T. WELCH

---

*Edward T. Welch, *When People Are Big and God Is Small* (Phillipsburg, NJ: P&R Publishing, 1997), 41.

THE GIFT OF GRACE

This is a faithful saying and worthy of all acceptance, that Christ Jesus came into the world to save sinners, of whom I am chief.

1 TIMOTHY 1:15

Every adult has experienced it—being a dispenser or recipient of grace. Your child acts up and deserves to be punished, but you break his or her rebellious spirit with a loving hug. Or you treat your spouse badly but receive a smile and an "I love you" in return. Or you feel your actions displeased God, and then read in your Bible that His mercies are new every morning.

When God extends His grace to us—sinners and enemies—it ought to melt our heart. It's hard to be angry with someone who has every reason to turn away from us but who comes toward us with open arms instead. The Prodigal Son's heart melted when he experienced the loving arms of his father wrapped tightly around him in a welcoming embrace (Luke 15:20-21). Grace is receiving a present we know we don't deserve, we never thought we would receive, and we never saw coming. Grace is a gift, pure and simple. The love of God is shown in His grace to people who deserve nothing.

Grace is the love that gives, that loves the unlovely and the unlovable.

OSWALD C. HOFFMAN

THE WORDS OF MY MOUTH

*When you pray, do not use vain repetitions as
the heathen do. . . . For your Father knows the
things you have need of before you ask Him.*

MATTHEW 6:7-8

When you are with loved ones, how do you talk with them?
The heartbeat of any thriving relationship is the honesty
and transparency of the communication. When we spend special time with those we love, we share our lives with them, and
we listen as they share with us. We allow ourselves to be vulnerable and open because we know that relationships will not grow
unless we are willing to verbalize our deepest feelings.

When we commit to speaking with God in a way that is honest and transparent, we will be heard. But, more importantly, we
will be changed. We will experience the dynamic transformation
that takes place when we freely give the Father open access to
our most intimate praises and pains.

Allow yourself to speak the honest words that will open your
heart to the Lord. Ask Him to help you find the words . . . words
of thanksgiving, words of petition, words of repentance. He is
just waiting to show you the potential of perfect communication!

True prayer is measured by weight, not by length.
A single groan before God may have more fullness
of prayer in it than a fine oration of great length.

CHARLES H. SPURGEON

HOLY HARVEST

Do not be deceived, God is not mocked;
for whatever a man sows, that he will also reap.

GALATIANS 6:7

Have you ever heard of a farmer who planted corn yet harvested wheat? Or have you seen tomato seeds grow into watermelons? Few things in life are as certain as the agricultural principle that whatever seed you plant, that's what you'll reap. The same is true in technology: garbage in, garbage out. And in finance, if you don't invest, you won't get a return.

The same, of course, is true in the spiritual life. Through the books we read, the company we keep, the movies we watch, and the music we listen to, we are sowing either to the Spirit or to the flesh. When we sow to the Spirit, we set our affections on things above—seeking first God's Kingdom and His righteousness. By praying, studying God's Word, sharing our faith, and bearing one another's burdens, we sow to the Spirit. But if we sow our lives and money to the flesh, according to the apostle Paul, we reap corruption.

Holiness is a harvest gained by careful sowing. Will you reap the reward of holy sowing? Or will you be surprised by what your harvest yields?

Why would we want fame, when God promises us glory?
Why would we be seeking the wealth of the world
when the wealth of heaven is ours? Why would we
run for a crown that will perish with time, when we're
called to win a crown that is imperishable?

PAUL WASHER

A WORTHY FOCUS

Let us run with endurance the race that is set before us,
looking unto Jesus, the author and finisher of our faith.

HEBREWS 12:1-2

It's hard to believe the average attention span can be as short as eight seconds. If someone's cell phone rings, we hear it but then move our attention quickly on. When it comes to sustained attention—staying on task to accomplish goals—most people stay focused for about twenty minutes. We can then choose to repeatedly refocus on that same task. So with scores of distractions in our busy schedules, how do we stay focused on God?

One way is daily devoting time to spend with God by reading His Word and praying. Have you ever attended a church camp or retreat that stirred you to repent and set spiritual goals? Unfortunately, we can get distracted by our daily routines and responsibilities and forget those goals soon after we've returned home. But if we commit to meeting with God each day, we can stay focused on Him and on the spiritual goals we've made.

Let's not be "out of sight, out of mind" Christians. Continually refocus on God by spending time daily in His Word and in prayer. It's a focus worth repeating!

Turn your focus to God's love.*

RICK WARREN

---

*Rick Warren, "When Things Fall Apart, Focus on God's Love," *Daily Hope with Rick Warren*, May 21, 2014, http://rickwarren.org/devotional/english/when-things-fall-apart-focus-on -god-s-love.

CONTENTED BY GRACE

He makes me to lie down in green pastures;
He leads me beside the still waters.

PSALM 23:2

Few images convey the concept of peace like a flock of sheep lying under shady trees with their legs tucked under them, chewing the cud beside still waters. Sheep don't lie down to eat. They only lie down after they've eaten, and then they relax and enjoy again what they've previously eaten. Nor do they lie down if they're nervous or frightened. They only relax when they feel secure, content, and at peace. In Psalm 23, green pastures and still waters are symbols of the psalmist's contentment.

The provisions of God's grace include overflowing blessings accompanied by contentment and joy. God's grace enables us to enjoy His fields. When the Lord is our shepherd, we have everything we need. We shall not want. We're blessed, sustained, led, protected, and content with our Good Shepherd.

Jesus said, "The thief does not come except to steal, and to kill, and to destroy. I have come that they may have life, and that they may have it more abundantly. I am the good shepherd" (John 10:10-11). Rest in the fields of grace.

If you have the Shepherd, you have grace for
every sin, direction for every turn, a candle
for every corner, and an anchor for every storm.*

MAX LUCADO

---

*Max Lucado, *Safe in the Shepherd's Arms* (Nashville: J Countryman, 2002), 23.

FEELING ICKY?

If we confess our sins, He is faithful
and just to forgive us our sins.
1 JOHN 1:9

Though his bedtime had long passed, the five-year-old boy hollered for his mother: "I have an icky feeling inside!" The tired mother trudged up the stairs to her son's bedroom. Opening the door, she heard a long list of little-boy sins spill out of her child's troubled soul. They had talked about sin before, but this time the boy understood what sin felt like—icky.

Do you ever get that icky feeling? Maybe you've gotten so used to it that you hardly notice anymore. The Bible tells us how Moses needed to remove sin from the Israelites' camp near Mount Sinai (Exodus 32). The revival that had occurred only days earlier had radically turned into outright rebellion. Gross sin was present, and many of the Israelites were not convicted. It took the slaying of three thousand men to purge the sin that had entered their camp.

The heaviness of sin weighs us down and keeps us from being used by the Lord to our fullest potential. Repentance is needed. Confess your sin now, and ask God to bring renewal to your heart.

It is when we notice the dirt that God is most present in us.

C. S. LEWIS

ONE DAY AT A TIME

Give us this day our daily bread.

MATTHEW 6:11

When the children of Israel journeyed in the wilderness, they awoke every morning to find that manna, bread from heaven, had been provided for them to eat. God gave the Israelites specific instructions never to hoard more than a single day's ration, except on the day before the Sabbath, when they gathered twice as much.

By His grace, God provided for the Israelites' physical needs, but the spiritual lesson they learned was an even greater gift. God was intent on teaching His people to trust Him through their reliance on Him for daily needs.

As it was in the Old Testament, God's physical provision for His people is still a tangible reminder of His spiritual provision. When we pray for tangible as well as intangible provision, we are choosing to eliminate pride, materialism, and worry. We are making a conscious effort to acknowledge that God has not promised us anything but to meet our needs.

Do you have a significant need in your life—family, finance, health, or job related? In His Word, God has told us that He does not want us to worry about tomorrow, and the way we give tomorrow to God is through the process of prayer.

We have to pray with our eyes on God,
not on the difficulties.

OSWALD CHAMBERS

BOOKENDS OF PRAISE

Enter into His gates with thanksgiving,
and into His courts with praise.

PSALM 100:4

Jesus taught us through the Lord's Prayer to begin and end our prayers with praise. In a sense, our praises to God are to be like bookends to our prayers.

A bookend is used to straighten and support. While it is often a beautiful decoration, it is also very functional. And our praise to God should be no different. While we worship Him with beautiful words, those words have a distinct purpose.

When we place the bookends of praise against our prayers, we tell God that who He is and what He means to us supports us and straightens and guides our lives.

If your life needs guidance, remember that starting and finishing your prayers with the bookends of praise will be a beautiful way to identify God's attributes and remind you of God's work in your life.

Without praise, we remain focused on our own requests and worries. But when we recognize God's greatness before and after our own needs, the problems in our lives begin to look a little smaller.

It is in the process of being worshipped that
God communicates His presence to men.

C. S. LEWIS

SEPTEMBER 15

GRACE TO SEE

*[The man said,] "One thing I know: that
though I was blind, now I see."*
JOHN 9:25

Seemingly miraculous advances are being made toward restoring sight to the blind. One amazing tool is a tiny electronic lens that receives light waves (images) and transmits them to the brain, allowing the blind to "see"—at least partially. But one kind of blindness will never be cured on the operating table, and that is the spiritual blindness of the human heart.

Jesus said He came to restore spiritual "sight to the blind" (Luke 4:18) and went about restoring physical sight to the physically blind as an object lesson to show the reality of the Kingdom of God (John 9:1-7). Jesus physically healed a paralytic to show that He also had power to forgive sins (Mark 2:1-12)—and healing eyes proved He could heal hearts. The people of Israel collectively lost their spiritual sight in the Old Testament for their failure to believe God (Isaiah 6:9-10), and Jesus came to restore sight—if only the people would believe.

Because we are born spiritually blind, it takes an act of God's grace for our eyes to be opened. If you have believed, thank God for His grace. If you want to believe, ask God to open your spiritual eyes so you can see Jesus.

Faith is the sight of the inward eye.
ALEXANDER MACLAREN

A GOD OF HIS WORD

The grass withers, the flower fades,
but the word of our God stands forever.

ISAIAH 40:8

Ecclesiastes 5:5 says, "Better not to vow than to vow and not pay." While that passage deals primarily with human promises made to God, it certainly applies to promises made from person to person as well. In fact, Jesus said something similar when He said, "But let your 'Yes' be 'Yes,' and your 'No,' 'No'" (Matthew 5:37). In other words, "Say what you mean and mean what you say."

What would life be like if we had to wonder whether God would keep His promises? They certainly would not be "great and precious promises," as Peter described them (2 Peter 1:4). No promise made by an untrustworthy God would be worthy of human belief. Think of what would be lost if we couldn't trust God: salvation, forgiveness, eternal life, reconciliation, daily bread—everything God has promised and on which we depend. What if we made our way to God's "throne of grace" only to find we could not "obtain mercy and find grace to help in time of need" as promised in His Word (Hebrews 4:16)? But God *is* trustworthy, and we can believe He will keep His promises.

God spoke through His prophet Isaiah and said that while creation passes away, His Word stands forever. If you need grace and mercy today, take God at His Word and receive these gifts.

Let God's promises shine on your problems.

CORRIE TEN BOOM

BRIDGING THE GAP

Between us and you there is a great gulf fixed,
so that those who want to pass from here to you
cannot, nor can those from there pass to us.

LUKE 16:26

Massive steel bridges are monuments to the knowledge, determination, and capability of humanity to reach across great gulfs. For example, when touring the Florida Keys, one can literally drive across the ocean for miles on one of these bridges, speeding from island to island.

Some gulfs, however, cannot be bridged. In the parable of the rich man and the beggar (Luke 16:20-31), the rich man, suffering torment in Hades, looked up to heaven and asked if Lazarus could bring him a drop of water. His request was denied with a reminder that the gulf between them could not be bridged.

Despite our best efforts, none of us can span the gulf between heaven and hell. While many religions attempt to reach God through human effort, God is the One who bridged that gulf through the sacrifice of His Son, Jesus Christ.

By God's initiative, Jesus stretched out His human body so that we might have a bridge that will take us to heaven. While our efforts to reach God fall woefully short, we can turn to Jesus and find not only God, but heaven, too.

If there were no hell, the loss of heaven would be hell.

CHARLES H. SPURGEON

SPIRITUALLY SANITIZED

*As He who called you is holy, you also
be holy in all your conduct.*

1 PETER 1:15

When we were children, our mothers always reminded us to wash our hands. But sales of hand sanitizer have skyrocketed since it was introduced to the public in the late '90s. A recent study showed hand sanitizers containing ethanol to be more effective at removing rhinovirus (a cold virus) than washing with soap and water! And sanitizers with both ethanol and organic acids significantly reduce recovery of the virus from hands for up to four hours after application.

Wouldn't it be nice to have a spiritual sanitizer that could remove our ability to sin for several hours at a time? The theological term *sanctification* describes the process of becoming more holy—clean. Sanctification is a continual process, living each day in awe and remembrance of Jesus' blood sacrifice on the cross. King Hezekiah led the nation of Israel to repentance and a return to sanctification (2 Chronicles 29). He cleansed Israel's place of worship, the temple, and the nation was spiritually renewed.

Today we don't have a designated temple for worship. Worship is represented by our personal holiness before God. And when God brings revival, He starts cleaning the rubbish out—like spiritual sanitizing.

Holiness is nothing less than conformity
to the character of God.

JERRY BRIDGES

FERVENT IN SPIRIT AND SERVING

[Be] fervent in spirit, serving the Lord.
ROMANS 12:11

Revivals are launching pads for each new generation of Christian workers. A limited revival touched parts of our world after World War II, and many Christian organizations, missionary agencies, and parachurch groups trace their origins to the late 1940s. There was a stirring of revival on college campuses in the early 1970s. *Time* called it the "Jesus Movement." Today many pastors and workers trace their conversion or call to ministry back to that era.

When revival comes, it immediately revives God's work in the world. Revival is like water falling on a wilted plant. It perks us up and produces in us fruitfulness for God's glory. When the church experiences renewal, we don't have to beg for volunteers. We don't have to pressure people to serve against their will. We don't have to struggle to support our missionaries. The incoming tide of revival lifts all the boats.

We don't have to wait for national or global revival to be renewed ourselves. Get excited about the Lord, and let His excitement fuel your passion.

The best is yet to be.

JOHN WESLEY

OUT OF FOCUS

*One's life does not consist in the abundance
of the things he possesses.*

LUKE 12:15

Many people mistakenly believe that wealth is fulfilling simply because it provides a way to accumulate possessions. But in His parable of the wealthy fool (Luke 12:13-21), Jesus warns us that true satisfaction is not found in the abundance of belongings.

How do we make our lives fulfilling and not just simply filled? In Philippians 4:18, Paul thanks the Philippians for their generosity to him: "I am full, having received from Epaphroditus the things sent from you, a sweet-smelling aroma, an acceptable sacrifice, well pleasing to God." The material gifts in themselves did not give Paul as much satisfaction as the spiritual goodness that prompted the gesture.

In John 10:10, Jesus points to Himself as the ultimate way to find fulfillment: "I have come that they may have life, and that they may have it more abundantly."

We can find our lives satisfying when we focus on Christ. As we let His Spirit fill our lives and take priority, we find ourselves learning how to be generous and caring. The stuff of life simply matters less. It's in our relationships with God and others that we discover true satisfaction.

God is most glorified in us
when we are most satisfied in Him.

JOHN PIPER

CREDITWORTHY

God said to him, "Fool! This night your soul will be required of you; then whose will those things be which you have provided?" So is he who lays up treasure for himself, and is not rich toward God.

LUKE 12:20-21

What does God, who has everything, *need* from us? Nothing, really. He reminds us in Psalm 50:12, "The world is Mine, and all its fullness." So, what does Luke 12:21 mean when it suggests that we should be "rich" toward God?

Paul tells us: "Let them do good, that they be rich in good works, ready to give, willing to share, storing up for themselves a good foundation for the time to come, that they may lay hold on eternal life" (1 Timothy 6:18-19).

The size of our bank balance doesn't determine our ability to be "rich" toward God. Whatever we have, we should recognize that it is God's and we are only stewards of it for a time. Good stewards in God's economy share their possessions with the church, the poor, the unfortunate, and the hungry.

True riches are found in giving, and God's Word says the giver will also be credited in heaven.

In this world, it is not what we take up,
but what we give up, that makes us rich.

HENRY WARD BEECHER

GRATEFUL FOREVER

*We, Your people and sheep of Your pasture,
will give You thanks forever; we will show
forth Your praise to all generations.*

PSALM 79:13

Our English word *gratitude* is derived from the Latin word *gratia,* which was associated with the ideas of grace and gratefulness. For the Christian, a lifetime of experiencing the grace of God should result in a lifetime of gratitude, expressed in praise and worship to God.

According to the *Handbook of Positive Psychology,* a grateful person will be characterized by behavior that is costly, expressions of gratitude that are valuable to the recipient, and intentionality—the choice to be grateful. Those three characteristics are consistent with biblical traits of praise and worship: we are to "continually offer the sacrifice of praise" (Hebrews 13:15). God is "enthroned in the praises of Israel" (Psalm 22:3), and we are exhorted to intentionally "give unto the LORD the glory due to His name; worship the LORD in the beauty of holiness" (Psalm 29:2).

If you are a follower of Christ, you have experienced the grace of God. So how have you responded? Sacrificially, in a way that pleases HIm, by your own choice? Make today a grateful day of praise.

God is never less than generous, even
when we are less than grateful.

JOHN BLANCHARD

THE SURPRISING EDGE

Her sins, which are many, are forgiven, for she loved much.
But to whom little is forgiven, the same loves little.

LUKE 7:47

To train for competition, many athletes strap extra weights to their arms and legs to build their endurance and stamina. As they become stronger and remove the weights for competition, they are able to move with increased speed and agility.

We all start out running the race of the Christian life with a surprising edge. When we are freed from the burden of sin, it is like a weight is lifted off our backs. We feel like we can run faster and jump higher than ever before.

The woman who anointed Jesus' feet with fragrant oil and her tears, drying them with her hair, is an example of great devotion energized by God's great forgiveness (Luke 7:44-47). God stands ready to lift the burden of sin and shame from our lives. When we ask for forgiveness, He forgives us fully and completely.

When you are weighed down by unconfessed sin, remember that the Lord wants to take that burden away. He promises that He will if you will only ask for forgiveness.

Either sin is with you, lying on your shoulders, or it is lying on Christ, the Lamb of God. . . . Now choose what you want.

MARTIN LUTHER

BIBLE-BASED REVIVAL

*Hezekiah gave encouragement to all the Levites
who taught the good knowledge of the LORD.*

2 CHRONICLES 30:22

The book of 2 Chronicles is the Bible's handbook on revival, describing the periodic waves of revival that swept over Judah. One of the greatest revivals of that time occurred during the reign of King Hezekiah, who had the sense to encourage those who were teaching the "good knowledge of the Lord." By promoting sound teaching for his nation, Hezekiah fanned the flames of revival so it wouldn't die down.

Genuine revival is rooted in solid biblical teaching. A revival that doesn't rest on the Word of God will either fade out or turn into an ostentatious display of emotionalism and sensationalism. Nothing except a return to Scripture can arouse a nation, a church, or an individual to return to God from a backslidden condition. We must have the power and authority of God's truth.

For personal revival, open your Bible. Encourage those who teach and preach God's Word, and respond to the Word with humility and obedience.

God has promised to respond with revival fire for any
person who will hear, love, trust, and obey Him.*

BILL BRIGHT

---

*Bill Bright, *The Coming Revival* (Orlando: NewLife Publications, 1995), 90.

A READY WORD

Take the helmet of salvation, and the sword
of the Spirit, which is the word of God.
EPHESIANS 6:17

Well-trained soldiers know where to find appropriate weapons to fight their enemy. They store these weapons strategically in case retrieval is necessary in an instant.

In Ephesians 6:10-20, the apostle Paul instructs believers on how to guard themselves against Satan's attacks. Paul describes the full armor of God, calling attention to each piece and how it works. Paul identifies only a single piece as an offensive weapon—the sword, which is the Word of God.

To fight off temptation, we need to take up that offensive weapon, the Word of God, in a heartbeat. Some conflicts will require instant rebuttal. Only Scripture that has been committed to memory will be a ready weapon in this battle. In the midst of the conflict, applicable Scripture will stand at attention in our minds, called forward at the command of God's Spirit to aid us.

Soldiers of Christ need never be weaponless when Satan attacks. If we discipline ourselves to commit God's Word to memory, we'll always have the sword of the Spirit at our immediate disposal.

The Bible is an armory of heavenly weapons.

THOMAS GUTHRIE

THE NOURISHED SOUL

If you instruct the brethren in these things,
you will be . . . nourished in the words of faith and of
the good doctrine which you have carefully followed.

1 TIMOTHY 4:6

In his 1729 Christian classic, *A Serious Call to a Devout and Holy Life*, William Law gave us the secret to a spiritual and productive life. "Nourish [your soul] with good works," he wrote, "make it wise with reading, enlighten it by meditation, make it tender with love, sweeten it with humility, humble it with penance, enliven it with Psalms and Hymns, and comfort it with frequent reflections upon future glory."*

The vibrant Christian life is one of continual revival. While longing for a global revival to sweep the earth or a local revival to touch our church, we can personally nourish our soul every day. We can grow wise by reading God's Word, becoming enlightened by meditating on memorized Scripture, learning to treat others with the tenderness of agape love, and displaying the sweet traits of humility and confession. We can bolster our spirits with hymns and songs, and we can comfort and strengthen our hearts by reflecting on heaven and on things above.

For renewal to take place, we have only to study God's blessed Word and let It do its work in our lives.

This regularity of devotion, this holiness of common life . . .
is a devotion, that is the duty of all orders of Christian people.**

WILLIAM LAW

---

*William Law, *A Serious Call to a Devout and Holy Life* (Grand Rapids, MI: Eerdmans, 1966), 45–46.
**Ibid., 87.

NEEDING THE KNEE

Pray without ceasing.

1 THESSALONIANS 5:17

A strange phenomenon swept over Washington's Union Station on the morning of June 6, 1944. No announcements came across the speakers. No one made a loud pronouncement. But suddenly the hustle and bustle of thousands of people criss-crossing the vast terminal came to a quiet moment of silence and stillness. One person after another dropped to a knee, folded their hands, and prayed. A few minutes later, the phenomenon passed, and people returned to their feet and scurried toward their trains or taxis. What had happened? It was D-day, and news of the Allied invasion of Normandy flashed from person to person. Everyone felt the need for prayer.

You may see football players dropping to their knees in prayer at the end of a game. Many biblical figures knelt when they prayed—not always, but sometimes. And kneeling is a godly habit that represents our reverence to the Lord.

But whether we're kneeling literally or figuratively, our hearts should always be in an attitude of prayer. We can pray at all times, even amid the hustle and bustle of life. Even now.

Prayer isn't limited to a slot in our schedule. It's living
in the Lord's presence and being open to Him.*

CHERI FULLER

---

*Cheri Fuller, *When Mothers Pray* (Sisters, OR: Multnomah, 1997), 38.

OUT ON A LIMB

If I have defrauded anyone of anything, I restore it fourfold.

LUKE 19:8, ESV

Making restitution is a wonderful privilege. In a sense, it allows us to change the past. While we can never turn back the clock, we often have the opportunity of correcting past mistakes, making up for them, and turning them to good. If we've taken, we can return. If we've defrauded, we can restore. If we've injured, we can affirm. If we've broken, we can mend.

Zacchaeus was a diminutive man who crawled out on a limb for a glimpse of Jesus. Our Lord paused under the tree, looked up, and told him to come down. So moved was Zacchaeus that he received Christ into his heart and home, offered to give liberally to the poor, and promised to make restitution to anyone he had defrauded. Jesus replied, "Today salvation has come to this house . . . for the Son of Man has come to seek and to save that which was lost" (Luke 19:9-10).

Look for ways to make restitution or amends for any wrongs you have done—and consider it a liberating privilege. It's evidence of Christ's life-changing power.

Restitution is evidence to others that one has made
a transaction with God. Be committed to making
restitution when needed, in God's timing.*

ROBERT A. HANSON

---

*Robert A. Hanson, *Transforming the Trials of Life* (2006), 238.

FROM PRAISE TO PRAISE

Yours is the kingdom and the power
and the glory forever. Amen.

MATTHEW 6:13

Many of us remember seeing our mothers buy dress patterns to aid in sewing. Perhaps you've done the same yourself. A pattern is a paper template from which the parts of the dress are traced onto the fabric before it is cut and stitched together at the sewing machine.

The Lord's Prayer is a pattern that allows us to trace and assemble a beautiful prayer life. Hardly any parts of life are excluded in this prayer. It covers all our needs and relationships, and it encompasses matters affecting both time on the earth and eternity.

One of the most useful observations is that the Lord's Prayer begins and ends on a note of praise. Left to ourselves, we'd probably begin and end our prayers with our own needs. But Jesus taught us to begin with a respectful attitude: "Our Father in heaven, hallowed be Your name." And He showed us to end with a powerful proclamation: "For Yours is the kingdom and the power and the glory forever. Amen."

When we begin and end our prayers with praise, we keep the focus on Him, and that's the pattern for joy.

Holy, holy, holy, Lord God Almighty! All Thy works shall praise Thy name in earth and sky and sea. Holy, holy, holy! Merciful and mighty! God in three Persons, blessed Trinity!

REGINALD HEBER

TAKE HEART

Then He spoke a parable to them, that men
always ought to pray and not lose heart.

LUKE 18:1

When we lose heart, we lose our passion. When we don't have the heart for a battle, we're tempted to give up and surrender. The widow in the Luke 18 parable stands before an unjust judge, pleading for justice from her adversary. The Scripture tells us that the judge does not fear God, nor does he have a regard for man. But the widow's passionate, persistent pleas convince him that she won't give up—and he is the one who surrenders. In the face of her great passion, he complies with her wishes.

We see that this uncaring city official responds not out of mercy, but because he doesn't want to be bothered any further by the woman's pleas. This parable asks the question, How much more will our loving, caring heavenly Father respond to our pleas?·

In troubling times, prayer can be a place of serene refuge where we can come to grips with God's willingness to intervene on our behalf. Our willingness to continually surrender our heartfelt concerns to God is evidence of our faith in Him.

No prayer will ever prevail with God more surely than
a liquid petition, which, being distilled from the heart,
trickles from the eye, and waters the cheek. Then is
God won when he hears the voice of your weeping.

CHARLES H. SPURGEON

OCTOBER

GOD IS IN CONTROL

In the beginning God created the heavens and the earth.

GENESIS 1:1

One of the themes of the famous 1968 film *2001: A Space Odyssey* was the idea of a man-made computer (named HAL) taking on human characteristics—even taking on a will of its own. At a time when computers were not common, it was a revolutionary thought. Unlike HAL, human creations in real life are subject to their creators.

That reflects a principle set in motion by the God who created the world out of nothing and remains supreme over it. Humans, the pinnacle of God's creation, attempt at times to rise up against the Creator and replace God's will with their own. God's response, in human terms, is to "laugh [and] . . . hold them in derision" (Psalm 2:4). Yes, humanity has a will that can be exercised, but only within limits. God is the Creator who never relinquishes control of this world to human or spiritual beings.

When you next read a headline that makes you worry and wonder if God is still in control, remember that in the beginning God created everything by His word—a word that never fails to accomplish the purpose for which it was spoken (Isaiah 55:11).

Biblical patience is not rooted in fatalism that says
everything is out of control. It is rooted in faith
that says everything is in God's control.

JOHN BLANCHARD

PRESENCE, PROTECTION, AND POWER

*Many are the afflictions of the righteous, but
the Lord delivers him out of them all.*

PSALM 34:19

Cindy left the doctor's office in a state of shock. Tests had confirmed that her illness was very serious. She was frightened and on the verge of hysteria. Conflicting thoughts overwhelmed her. *Why, Lord? I thought I would live till I was old. Who will take care of my family? Will I have to depend on them? Lord, I'm afraid.*

We may have our life planned out with a road map for where we want to go and how we're going to get there. But then something happens that short-circuits our plans. We become very vulnerable when we lose control.

The Bible offers encouragement for when we feel powerless. Psalm 73:26 says, "My flesh and my heart fail; but God is the strength of my heart and my portion forever." After all is said and done, God is the only One we can put our trust in. Only He knows the reasons for and results of our situation. When our security is shaken, He is always a secure and strong rock to cling to.

God is in control, and therefore in *everything* I can
give thanks—not because of the situation but because
of the One who directs and rules over it.

KAY ARTHUR

YOUR HEART CONDITION

Do not judge according to appearance,
but judge with righteous judgment.

JOHN 7:24

Appearances don't always tell the whole story. Take John Wesley, the founder of Methodism. In his early years, he appeared to be everything a Christian should be. He memorized the Greek New Testament. He took the gospel to the American Indians. Yet, according to Wesley, he did these things outwardly because inwardly he hoped to gain God's acceptance. One day, he realized he needed to trust Christ for salvation. When he made his heart right with God, Wesley began his true ministry.

Outwardly, we can look like we have everything together in the Christian life. We can know every song in the hymnal, dress immaculately on Sundays, and participate in community service. But God sees what humans cannot. He looks at the condition of our hearts.

What is the condition of your heart? Are you following Jesus with a sincere heart, or simply going through the outward motions of being a Christian? Although we may be able to fool our friends, God always knows our true motivation for spiritual service. Take time for a heart-to-heart conversation with Him today.

Beware you be not swallowed up in books! An
ounce of love is worth a pound of knowledge.

JOHN WESLEY

SURPRISING CONVERSIONS

It is hard for you to kick against the goads.

ACTS 9:5

As a mighty awakening rolled across New England in 1737, Rev. Jonathan Edwards compiled a pamphlet of revival stories titled *A Narrative of Surprising Conversions*. More than a hundred years later, William C. Conant wrote an updated version designed to include stories from the revivals of the 1800s. He used a similar title: *Narratives of Surprising Conversions*.

In a sense, every conversion is surprising. That God would reach down in infinite mercy and save any of us is a story of amazing grace. But the conversions of some souls are particularly surprising. No one expected Christianity's greatest enemy, Saul of Tarsus, to turn to Christ and become a great missionary. Paul later called himself the chief of sinners, adding "For this reason I obtained mercy, that in me first Jesus Christ might show all longsuffering, as a pattern to those who are going to believe" (1 Timothy 1:16).

Perhaps God will reach down and convert some strident anti-Christian voice today. Those who are the loudest may be the ones most secretly longing to believe. Let's pray for some more "surprising conversions."

It is wonderful that persons should be so
suddenly and yet so greatly changed.

JONATHAN EDWARDS

UNDER NEW OWNERSHIP

Therefore, if anyone is in Christ, he is a new creation.
2 CORINTHIANS 5:17

Imagine daily driving by an old, run-down store, only to one day find it restored with a fresh sign overhead reading, "Under New Ownership."

That's a picture of our lives before and after we meet Christ. Before we meet Christ, we are left to perish in sin. After we find forgiveness in Christ, He gives us a new lease on life. You could say we are under new ownership. God wants to hang His sign of ownership over our lives for the world to see as a testimony of His love.

It's like the farmer who brands his cattle with a unique mark. The farmer makes a physical mark so there can be no question about who owns the cattle. In the same way, God wants to place His mark on those who are His. Do you have God's seal of ownership on your life? If so, can others clearly see that you are under new ownership?

Don't hide God's presence in your life by keeping it a secret. Wear the mark of Christianity with pride. It cost the Savior His very life to own you.

God doesn't save people on the installment
plan, as one buys furniture.
BILLY SUNDAY

THIS CLATTERING TRAIN

God reigns over the nations; God sits on His holy throne.

PSALM 47:8

When Winston Churchill was trying to awaken the world to the Nazi threat, he quoted a poem by Edwin J. Milliken: "Who is in charge of the clattering train? The axles creak and the couplings strain; and the pace is hot, and the points are near, and Sleep has deadened the driver's ear."

When we look at our world today, we're apt to wonder who's in charge of this clattering train. Wars raging. Morality collapsing. Infections spreading. Weapons proliferating. Economies faltering. Hearts failing. Is anyone in control?

We can rest assured that however chaotic things appear on earth, God is still in charge, ruling and overruling, moving this world toward its preappointed end. The Bible declares, "The Lord is in control. . . . Yours is the mighty power and glory and victory and majesty. Everything in the heavens and earth is Yours, O Lord. . . . We adore You as being in control of everything" (1 Kings 20:13, CEB; 1 Chronicles 29:11, TLB).

Regardless of the headlines we read or the heartaches we feel, we can rest assured that the Lord is our stability and peace.

The God of Abraham praise, who reigns enthroned above; Ancient of Everlasting Days, and God of love.

DANIEL BEN JUDAH

TRUSTING GOD

*Faith is the substance of things hoped for,
the evidence of things not seen.*

HEBREWS 11:1

The American Heritage Dictionary says faith is (among other things) "belief that does not rest on logical proof or material evidence." Is Christianity illogical, or is there material evidence for our faith? *We* didn't see Jesus' empty tomb, but His disciples did—and more than five hundred others saw the risen Lord (1 Corinthians 15:6). So there *is* material evidence on which to base our faith.

But, if we're honest, we have to admit that the Christian life is a walk based on what is unseen rather than seen. So how do we strengthen our faith? We do so by reading and taking to heart the promises of God. The same God who performed and provided for eyewitnesses in the past has promised to perform and provide for us. His "exceedingly great and precious promises" are the basis of our partaking of His "divine nature" (2 Peter 1:4). Faith in promises *not* based on evidence is truly blind faith; faith in promises based on evidence is biblical faith.

Maintain your familiarity with God's promises to strengthen your faith and prepare for life's next challenge.

You never test the resources of God until
you attempt the impossible.

F. B. MEYER

PICTURE PERFECT

The LORD has His way in the whirlwind and in the storm, and the clouds are the dust of His feet.

NAHUM 1:3

When a tornado destroyed the home of Mike and Freida Evans of Hackleburg, Alabama, a photograph of their 1982 wedding was among the items lost. Imagine their surprise when a family in Lincoln County, Tennessee—120 miles from Hackleburg—found the photo in their yard and had it printed in the local paper to find the owners. The Evans family said the picture appeared to be completely undamaged.

"When we go through trials, it makes us stronger," said Freida Evans, who had been involved in a serious car accident years earlier. "I am [a] survivor. I had depended on my faith and church family to get us through after the accident, and that's what we'll do now. We'll be able to build back."*

Sometimes our lives feel like a whirlwind, but we have confidence in the future because we have a God who rides above the storms.

What have I to dread, what have I to fear,
leaning on the everlasting arms.

ELISHA A. HOFFMAN

---

*United Press International, "Tornado Carries Photo 120 Miles," May 30, 2011, http://upi.com/Odd_News/2011/05/30/Tornado-carries-photo-120-miles /73191306788936.

FALSE ALLIANCES

*A man devoid of understanding shakes hands in
a pledge, and becomes surety for his friend.*

PROVERBS 17:18

A Wikipedia article titled "List of Treaties" cites all the treaties and agreements formalized between nations and groups from 2100 BC through the present. There are hundreds and hundreds of them. Comparing this long list of agreements with a list of wars, arguments, and broken treaties between nations and groups in the same time period calls into question the usefulness of human agreements. As the saying goes, "Treaties are made to be broken."

One of the worst mistakes Joshua made as the leader of Israel came shortly after the nation entered the Promised Land with the mandate to clear out the pagan residents. A certain group of men, representing the town of Gibeon, came to Joshua deceptively posing as travelers from a city outside of Canaan. They asked Joshua to make a covenant with them to ensure their protection, which Joshua did without consulting the Lord. Because of that treaty, the men of Gibeon remained a thorn in Israel's side.

Scripture warns against making alliances with unbelievers, whether for affection or protection (2 Corinthians 6:14-18). Our hearts should belong to God alone.

Division is better than agreement in evil.

GEORGE HUTCHESON

CHECK IT OUT

Guard the good deposit that was entrusted to you—
guard it with the help of the Holy Spirit who lives in us.

2 TIMOTHY 1:14, NIV

We like to think our banks are safe and our deposits are secure, but 414 banks failed during the Great Recession. In the United States, the FDIC bailed out one large bank to the tune of over $38 billion. Hundreds of banks have been placed on the FDIC's confidential problem list.

But let's not forget that we ourselves are living banks into which the Lord is depositing His Son, His Spirit, His Word, and His grace. The Bible says that God has "put his Spirit in our hearts as a deposit, guaranteeing what is to come" (2 Corinthians 1:22, NIV).

We're to guard the good deposit entrusted to us. That means we must be shrewd and disciplined managers of our time, treasure, and talents. We must guard our hearts carefully so the enemy cannot creep in to steal, kill, or destroy. Treasure the deposits that God is making into your life. The banks of the world may fail, but God's investments are secure and limitless.

When you "deposit" your life with God, you have
nothing to fear; for He is able to keep you.

WARREN W. WIERSBE

GOD HAS A PLAN

The Word became flesh and dwelt among us,
and we beheld His glory, the glory as of the only
begotten of the Father, full of grace and truth.

JOHN 1:14

Deism is the worldview that says the universe was created and set in motion by God, who then abandoned it, exerting no control over its outcome. Deism compares God to a highly skilled watchmaker who creates a mechanical marvel, then winds it up and sets it to ticking before walking away.

There is no revelation, biblical or scientific, to support such a theory; those who hold it do so on the basis of reason alone. Besides being unsupported, it is a highly impersonal, even depressing, view of God, creation, and human existence and destiny. The Bible's view of God is totally different: He created us in His image with a plan to spend eternity with us. In spite of the disruption of sin, the second member of the Godhead, Jesus Christ, came to earth to "fix" the problem of sin and bring us back into relationship with God, making it possible for God's original design for eternal fellowship to be ultimately realized.

The day of the Incarnation—when God became a man to dwell among us—is the day God proved His promise: "I will never leave you nor forsake you" (Hebrews 13:5).

The atonement is the real reason for the Incarnation.

JAMES MONTGOMERY BOICE

THE HERD

Take heed to yourselves, lest your hearts be weighed down with carousing, drunkenness, and cares of this life, and that Day come on you unexpectedly.

LUKE 21:34

In his blog post "Why Economists Missed the Crises," Barry Ritholtz observed that most of the world's financial and political leaders overlooked the warning signs of the Great Recession. Some saw it coming, and a few on Wall Street sounded the alarm. But, wrote Ritholtz, "the vast majority of professional economists, strategists and analysts—the 'Herd'—totally missed it."*

It's interesting that Ritholtz described them as the *Herd.* It's easy to be stampeded by our society. Groupthink takes over, certain opinions form in the popular culture, morality is prescribed by Hollywood, and our spending habits are influenced by the number of commercials we see.

We can't go with the Herd. The majority of people in this world are missing the warning signs. But as Christians, we march to the beat of a different drummer. We handle our money, our morals, and our ministries as those who know that crises are ahead and that judgment is coming. Jesus told us to stay alert, lest the Day of the Lord come on us unawares. Watch for the signs and take heed.

There is a choice you have to make
in everything you do. So keep in mind that in
the end, the choice you make, makes you.

JOHN WOODEN

---

*Barry Ritholtz, "Why Economists Missed the Crises," *The Big Picture*, January 5, 2009, http://ritholtz.com.

NO REVISIONS NECESSARY

Forever, O Lord, Your word is settled in heaven.
PSALM 119:89

Imagine a college student sitting in his first session of American History. As he pulls out his textbook, he notices that his book looks different from everyone else's. On closer examination, he realizes he has purchased the wrong edition.

Books are constantly being updated as new information and research emerge. It's not uncommon to see the words *updated* or *revised* splashed across textbook covers. But there is one book that never needs altering.

The Bible is eternal and timeless. No revisions will ever be necessary. The Bible is the Book for all ages. Think about the impact the Word of God has made upon the human race. Remove from our lives every law that is founded on the Ten Commandments or the Sermon on the Mount, and you remove the very cornerstone of modern civilization.

As you read the Scriptures today, thank God for His everlasting message of love and salvation. Cherish this eternal Book that applies to every generation—past, present, and future.

This old Book is my guide, 'tis a friend by my side. It will lighten and brighten my way. And each promise I find soothes and gladdens my mind, as I read it and heed it today.

UNKNOWN

REMEMBER HIS GOODNESS

I will meditate on the glorious splendor of Your majesty.

PSALM 145:5

Imagine the excitement when Moses and the children of Israel crossed the Red Sea, escaping Pharaoh's hand. They sang, "He has triumphed gloriously! The horse and its rider He has thrown into the sea!" (Exodus 15:1).

The children of Israel remembered God's provision, and that caused them to praise.

Throughout the Old Testament, we see God's people worshiping Him for His mighty acts. King David declares in Psalm 145, "Men shall speak of the might of Your awesome acts, and I will declare Your greatness. They shall utter the memory of Your great goodness."

What wonderful works has God done in your life? Take a few moments to review God's work in your life. Remind yourself of His provision for you in your personal life, family, or work. If you keep a journal, read about the victories God has given you in the past. Verbalize your praise to God. When you remember God's goodness, isn't it easy to praise Him?

Now thank we all our God with heart and hands and voices,
Who wondrous things hath done, in whom His world rejoices,
Who from our mothers' arms hath blessed us on our way
With countless gifts of love, and still is ours today.

MARTIN REICHARDT

"I AM NOT SKILLED TO UNDERSTAND"

*Now I know in part, but then I shall
know just as I also am known.*

1 CORINTHIANS 13:12

An old hymn says, "I am not skilled to understand what God hath willed, what God hath planned." Sometimes we can't find explanations for our situations; we either trust our Lord or lose our minds. At such times, Jesus says to us as He did to Peter, "What I am doing you do not understand now, but you will know after this" (John 13:7). God, though personal, is eternal, transcendent, and omniscient. He possesses total knowledge of all things visible and invisible, past, present, and future. He knows the end from the beginning. His perspective is as different from ours as ours is from an insect's.

He is also good, kind, and full of compassion. He has promised to work all things for good in the lives of His children. God moves in a mysterious way. Instead of always asking "Why?" let's learn to say with the hymnist, "I am not skilled to understand what God hath willed, what God hath planned; I only know that at His right hand is One who is my Savior."

I take Him at His Word indeed; "Christ died for sinners"—
this I read; for in my heart I find a need of Him to be my Savior.

DOROTHY GREENWELL

A PROPHET AND A PROSTITUTE

*I will have mercy on her who had not obtained mercy;
then I will say to those who were not My people, "You are
My people!" And they shall say, "You are my God!"*

HOSEA 2:23

Hosea probably would have never chosen the woman who would become his wife. In fact, when God instructed Hosea to marry Gomer, a prostitute, Hosea was probably tempted to run. But God wanted to paint a vivid picture of His mercy. And He wanted to use the unlikely marriage of a prophet and a prostitute as the canvas.

God told Hosea to marry a woman who would be unfaithful. As expected, she broke the marriage vows and became the slave of another man. So God told Hosea to go and buy her back and restore their marriage. And Hosea did.

This is the story of God's mercy—a mercy that hardly even makes sense. We enter into a relationship with God, but we make choices that violate our intimacy with Him. And instead of abandoning us, God runs after us like Hosea ran after Gomer.

Have you made mistakes that have caused you to believe God would never want you back? Open God's Word to the book of Hosea and find out for yourself just how much God wants you as His own.

Morning by morning new mercies I see. All I have needed Thy hand hath provided. Great is Thy faithfulness, Lord, unto me!

THOMAS O. CHISOLM

OUR REMARKABLE BOOK

*I have rejoiced in the way of Your testimonies,
as much as in all riches.*

PSALM 119:14

What a remarkable book is the Bible! It's just the right length— long enough to tell us all that God wants us to know, yet short enough to carry in our hands. Its verses are deep enough to puzzle scholars, yet simple enough for children to memorize. It's food for the soul.

The Bible is infallible in telling us about fallible people. It's as high as the highest heavens, but as down to earth as David's adultery, Noah's drunkenness, or Paul's argument with Barnabas. Without sugarcoating its heroes, it shows us how to live extraordinary lives as pilgrims in this world.

Though timeless, it's timely. Though written over a span of ages, its message is consistent and cohesive. It's without error, but it shows us our errors and helps us correct them. It reveals to us the holiness of God, the mercy of Christ, the power of Calvary, the way to heaven, and the life that wins. It contains all the answers we need even when we don't always understand the questions.

What a remarkable book is the Bible!

Christ and the Bible are the two impregnable
forces upon which Christianity stands or falls.

ROBERT P. LIGHTNER

EYE ON THE BALL

Therefore gird up the loins of your mind, be sober, and rest your hope fully upon the grace that is to be brought to you at the revelation of Jesus Christ.

1 PETER 1:13

Keep your eye on the ball" has its roots in baseball, but it also applies to Navy aviators as they approach an aircraft carrier for a landing—the "ball" being a glowing light that helps them line up and land safely on a pitching carrier deck. "Get your head in the game" is a similar exhortation, shouted by coaches to "wake up" drowsy players.

These and other similar sayings have the same purpose—to force active, intelligent awareness of one's surroundings and to keep from being lulled into complacency. While using different language, the New Testament certainly endorses that goal from a spiritual perspective. For example, handling finances requires attention and active involvement. Passivity can lead to destruction and the loss of assets. Christians, as good stewards of the money God has entrusted to them, need to take active steps to preserve what they have through wise management.

Take stock. Take action. And take heart! God blesses wisdom and diligence in every area, including financial management, for His glory.

True conversion gives a man security, but it does not allow him to leave off being watchful.

CHARLES H. SPURGEON

WRONG WAY!

He led them forth by the right way.

PSALM 107:7

Just after five o'clock on the morning of July 17, 1938, Douglas Corrigan, thirty-one, took off in an old secondhand plane from New York City on a nonstop solo flight across America, bound for Los Angeles. Turning into a cloud, Corrigan's plane disappeared into the eastern sky. Twenty-eight hours later, he landed—in Dublin, Ireland. "I'm Douglas Corrigan," he told onlookers. "Just got in from New York. Where am I? I intended to fly to California."

Known for the rest of his long life as "Wrong Way Corrigan," he blamed his error on a faulty compass.

If you're an aviator, a hiker, or a soldier, you want a compass that works with precision, one that reads accurately in the storms when the landmarks are altered, the sky is darkened, and the stars are blackened in the heavens.

It's sad to come to the end of our days only to realize we've gone the wrong way. God alone is our moral compass, and the Bible gives us the true directions for life.

Chart and compass come from Thee;
Jesus, Savior, pilot me.

EDWARD HOPPER

HOW HEALTHY IS YOUR HEART?

Search me, O God, and know my heart; try me,
and know my anxieties; and see if there is any wicked
way in me, and lead me in the way everlasting.

PSALM 139:23-24

Jeremiah 17:9 says, "The heart is deceitful above all things, and desperately wicked; who can know it?" In a world that wants us to believe in the decency and goodness of every person, it can be hard to accept that our hearts are truly wicked.

King David knew all about treachery after betraying his captain, Uriah, in order to wed Uriah's wife, Bathsheba, who was pregnant with David's baby. With the mask of deceit, David presumed he had slipped past God. His deception lasted until Nathan the prophet confronted him. David confessed and repented without excuses. Perhaps that's why God called him a man after His own heart.

We know from Scripture that we cannot discern the true state of our hearts without the help of God. With every new dawn and every new sunset, we need to whisper David's prayer. We need to open our souls for God to search the recesses of our hearts and then ask Him to wash us clean and lead us in His way.

Real change is an inside job. You might alter things a
day or two with money and systems, but the heart of the
matter is and always will be the matter of the heart.

MAX LUCADO

PUSHED TO THE EDGE

I am not ashamed of the gospel of Christ.
ROMANS 1:16

We've all experienced it: a clique of "cool kids" at school decides to reduce our significance. We aren't welcomed or included. We may even be called unpleasant names. In the workplace, a particular employee might not be invited to significant policy meetings or is excluded from social gatherings. This treatment is what the Bible is experiencing today in our culture. God's Word is being marginalized—pushed to the edges of our families and even our churches!

The gradual process of marginalization happens so slowly that we almost don't notice societal shifts until after the fact. We wake up one day and the Bible has moved from a central position of education and authority to a shelf next to books by leading atheists, trivializing its content and intimidating its readers.

You and I can't control how others view or treat the Bible. But there's one place we can stop its marginalization: our own lives. When we do that, the Bible will gain new traction in our homes, churches, and communities. Don't miss the significance of living in this particular moment of history. Nothing could be more dangerous than to wander thoughtlessly down the path of marginalizing the Bible.

Men do not reject the Bible because it contradicts
itself but because it contradicts them.

UNKNOWN

PLUGGED IN

I am the vine, you are the branches.
He who abides in Me, and I in him, bears much fruit;
for without Me you can do nothing.

JOHN 15:5

Imagine what would happen if someone unplugged all your home appliances. Your refrigerator, microwave, and oven would be utterly useless. How long could you live that way, with no ability to make food? It wouldn't be long before you figured out the problem and plugged everything back in to the power source.

Like those appliances, we, too, are dependent on a power source. Jesus used the example of the vine and the branches to illustrate this principle. Branches are powerless to bear fruit if they are not connected to a vine. The vine provides the nutrition that the branch must have for growth and development.

Today, are you counting on Christ to make you a productive or "fruitful" Christian? Or do you find yourself relying on your own talents and abilities? The Bible says that without Christ, we can do nothing. Enjoy the benefits of being plugged in to God's power by depending on Christ daily, reading God's Word, and praying.

I know I have needs, but that's not my responsibility.
My response is to rest in the vine's ability to
provide. I don't produce the fruit. I just bear it.

ADRIAN ROGERS

BUILT TO LAST

You are God's building.

1 CORINTHIANS 3:9

Have you ever seen a building after a massive fire? Blackened walls, burned-down sections, charred remains. A fire devastates everything in its path, leaving very few things to salvage.

Did you know that the Bible compares us to a building that will be tried by fire? We have the choice to either build on the foundation of Christ or build our lives on earthly desires. The apostle Paul gives one of the greatest motivations for pure Christian living: *someday we will stand before God and give an account for how we built our lives* (Romans 14:12).

As we're told in 1 Corinthians 3:9-15, there will come a day of judgment for our lives—our building—when our works will be exposed by fire. When we stand before God, His fire will reveal the foundation of our building. Have we been building with wood, hay, and stubble, which are perishable? Or have we been using gold, silver, and precious stones, which are permanent?

Is it your heart's desire to stand before God one day and present an enduring building, built on Jesus Christ? Then live your life with eternity in mind. Read and obey God's Word. Witness to your friends and family. Build with the things that last.

A Christian has one foundation: Jesus Christ!
On that he must build for eternity.

FRANCIS SCHAEFFER

FACES NOT PLACES

*These who have turned the world upside
down have come here too.*

ACTS 17:6

Did Jesus send a church building into the world to make disciples of all the nations? Of course not. He sent people. But this question helps clarify the definition of *church*. The New Testament uses the Greek word *ekklesia* (literally, "called-out ones") for *church*, referring to those who are called together by God. The word always specifies people—the followers of Jesus—not buildings.

Our culture is questioning the relevancy of the church. Unsavory things have happened to people "in church" or in the name of Christ throughout history. But that doesn't negate the good that has been done. Nor does it make the church irrelevant. The pundits may rail against our stand on immorality, but they cannot deny our compassion for the poor, orphans, and widows. The church's relevancy is based on the message we preach of "Jesus Christ and Him crucified" (1 Corinthians 2:2).

Is the church making an impact on the world? Before you answer that question, there is one place you must look: the mirror. If we're going to be ridiculed by the world, let it be for turning the world upside down with the gospel as the early apostles did (Acts 17:6).

Now the church is not wood and stone, but the
company of people who believe in Christ.

MARTIN LUTHER

311

GOD BLESS YOU

*I will bless those who bless you . . . and in you all
the families of the earth shall be blessed.*

GENESIS 12:3

When someone sneezes we say, "God bless you." We might use the same phrase to appreciate someone who gives needed help. Sometimes we close our correspondence with it. But more than a figurative expression, the concept of *blessing* carries great significance. We read in Scripture that when God blesses, it is a sign of His relationship with a person or nation and His grace.

God created a people for Himself, the nation Israel, to *bless* the world through the gift of the Savior and Messiah, Jesus Christ, and His plan of redemption. Genesis 12:3 promises that God blesses those who bless Abraham's descendants. Conversely, the history of nations that have abused the Jewish people proves the inevitable doom that comes to those who don't choose to bless Israel. The promises of God toward Israel cannot be compromised or renegotiated at the political bargaining table. God has a plan for Israel, and His words never fail to accomplish their purpose (Isaiah 55:11).

As we wait for God's ultimate new world order, pray for your pastor and political leaders. And God bless you, friend, as you pray for "the peace of Jerusalem" (Psalm 122:6).

Anything is a blessing which makes us pray.

CHARLES H. SPURGEON

RESPOND WITH LOVE

I beseech you therefore, brethren, by the mercies of God,
that you present your bodies a living sacrifice.

ROMANS 12:1

The fact is, if we have to ask someone to tell us "I love you," it's not going to mean as much as the spontaneous version. These universally desirable words are usually not something you have to teach. It's just natural to respond with love to those we care about. Why, then, are we sometimes slow to verbalize and show our love to the One who loves us the most?

When the apostle Paul offered his appeal, "I beseech you," in Romans 12:1, he didn't command his readers to present themselves to God because it's an imperative, crucial step toward salvation. Instead, "beseech" implies an urging to *respond* to what God has already done—mercifully delivering us from sin and graciously bestowing blessings we don't deserve. We can't help but respond to what God has done for us. Without hypocrisy or envy, Paul's counsel models a true spirit of love toward God.

The only spiritual service that honors and pleases God is the heartfelt devotion of His children who give themselves totally to Him. Tell God you love Him, and think of some ways you can pour His love into those around you.

Every Christian would agree that a man's spiritual
health is exactly proportional to his love for God.

C. S. LEWIS

CHOOSE PEACE

Blessed are the peacemakers, for they
shall be called sons of God.

MATTHEW 5:9

A word. A slight. A look. A forgotten birthday or anniversary. A piece of gossip about us. Things happen to us every day, from minor to major, that could serve as an excuse for vengeance. And each time something hurtful happens, we have a choice to make: Will we be a peacemaker or a revenge seeker? Will we inflame the event with the fire of revenge, or will we smother it with the blanket of peace?

Let's assume you've been hurt purposefully. What should you do? God said, "I have no pleasure in the death of the wicked, but that the wicked turn from his way and live" (Ezekiel 33:11). Substitute whatever you're tempted to do in retaliation for the word "death" in that verse, and you'll get God's counsel on your course of action. God said that vengeance is His; He will repay (Romans 12:19). Paul writes that we are to do everything possible to "live peaceably with all men" (Romans 12:18). When we choose to forgive instead of fight, we become peacemakers.

If you are faced with the choice of seeking peace or seeking vengeance, choose peace and receive the blessing of God.

The noblest revenge is to forgive.

THOMAS FULLER

STEP INTO THE LIGHT

Everyone practicing evil hates the light and does not come to the light, lest his deeds should be exposed. But he who does the truth comes to the light.

JOHN 3:20-21

Many tourists have visited the Carlsbad Caverns in New Mexico. At a certain point in the tour, all the lights are turned off. The result is absolute darkness. It's eerie to be unable to sense your surroundings.

Sin in the life of a believer creates this same eerie phenomenon. As Christians, we claim that we do not want to be unequally yoked with the works of darkness. But when we choose sin, darkness enters our lives, and we become shut off from God, our light source. Like the psalmist tells us, when we live with the darkness of sin in our lives, our communication with God is broken (Psalm 66:18).

So how can we turn the lights back on, spiritually speaking? Confessing our sin to God is the only way to bring His light back.

Is God convicting you to evaluate a relationship, a habit, or maybe an attitude? Before you do anything else, take a moment to clear out the darkness in your life. Confess your sin and step into the light!

It is no advantage to be near the light if the eyes are closed.

AUGUSTINE

OCTOBER 29

THE HOLINESS OF GOD

*They do not rest day or night, saying: "Holy, holy, holy,
Lord God Almighty, who was and is and is to come!"*
REVELATION 4:8

Sometimes we as Christians take God's holiness for granted.
Along the pilgrimage of life, we become casual and careless;
and often the reverence for a holy, almighty God dies in the routine of daily living. A verse tucked away in the book of Job is a
reminder of how awesome God really is. We limit Him when we
forget His omnipotent ability to create out of nothing. Just think
about it! "He stretches out the north over empty space; He hangs
the earth on nothing" (Job 26:7).

To some He seems unreachable, and yet He reached down
to us through the sacrifice of His only Son to bring us across the
bridge of darkness into pure light! As believers we have no claim
to holiness, and yet the Bible says that God sees us through glorious, white robes of righteousness (Isaiah 61:10). Isaiah 1:18
says, "Though your sins are like scarlet, they shall be as white as
snow; though they are red like crimson, they shall be as wool."

Christ's finished work *is* our holiness!

My holiness is not in me,
Oh blessed Lord, it is in Thee!
CLAUDIA RUSSELL WARD

WHAT GOD PUTS IN OUR HEARTS

I told no one what my God had put in my heart to do.

NEHEMIAH 2:12

In the book that bears his name, Nehemiah relates his burden for rebuilding the walls of Jerusalem. The moment he heard of the distress of his city, he began praying, fasting, and seeking God's will (Nehemiah 1:4). His concern deepened until King Artaxerxes noticed it on his face (2:2). Traveling to Jerusalem, Nehemiah surveyed the ruined walls and devised a plan for their rebuilding. At first, he told no one what God had put in his heart to do. But at the right moment he revealed his plan, mobilized the people, and persevered until the work was done.

Have you seen a need? Have you prayed for a burden? Our work for Him isn't a personal ambition we seek. It's a vision He places on our hearts—perhaps to become involved in orphan care, to minister to the homeless, to work with nursery children, to evangelize the lost, to plan a missions trip.

What has God put in your heart to do? What can you do today to make your vision a reality?

It is a terrible thing to see and have no vision.

HELEN KELLER

OCTOBER 31

A VERSE IN THREE DIMENSIONS

*Blessed be the Lord, who daily loads us with
benefits, the God of our salvation!*

PSALM 68:19

If you've ever been hiking, you know those backpacks can get mighty heavy after a while. Packed with supplies (or books, if you're a student), backpacks can make your shoulders ache and your back hurt. But step onto a bus or into a taxi, and, oh, the relief of letting the burden slip from your shoulders as it's carried by the same vehicle that is carrying you. You still have your backpack. You've not lost your burden. But now something else is bearing it.

The New International Version renders Psalm 68:19, "Praise be to the Lord, to God our Savior, who daily bears our burdens."

The English Standard Version puts it a little differently: "Blessed be the Lord, who daily bears us up; God is our salvation."

And the New King James Version says, "Blessed be the Lord, who daily loads us with benefits."

Which translation is best? Why not choose all of them and praise our Savior who daily bears our burdens, bears us up, and loads us with benefits?

Commit to God whatever burden He has placed on you.
Don't just cast it aside, but put it over onto Him and
place yourself there with it. You will see that your burden
is then lightened by the sense of companionship.

OSWALD CHAMBERS

NOVEMBER

TEAR DOWN THE WALLS

*Then Jesus, looking at him, loved him, and said to him,
"One thing you lack: Go your way, sell whatever you
have and give to the poor, and you will have treasure in
heaven; and come, take up the cross, and follow Me."*

MARK 10:21

The Great Wall of China is a barrier so huge it can be seen from space. This ancient wonder is an engineering feat. Spanning 4,500 miles, it was built to protect the Chinese empire from invading tribes. While physical barriers are often built to protect, spiritual barriers can separate us from the things we need.

The young man in today's reading had many good things in life, and he hoped to add eternal life to his list. His heart was pointed in the right direction, but a barrier kept him from accepting Christ. Jesus understood this barrier, and He cut through the conversation with a prescription for its removal. In telling him to sell his possessions, Jesus helped the young man see that he valued his earthly possessions more than eternal reward. Until the young man put God first, the barrier to heaven would be insurmountable.

What barriers keep you from complete fellowship with the Lord today? Be honest with yourself and Him. Examine your life and confess the barriers that have been built. Tear them down in heartfelt prayer to God.

A man wrapped up in himself makes a very small package.

UNKNOWN

SEEING AROUND THE BEND

The LORD, He is the One who goes before you.
He will be with you, He will not leave you nor
forsake you; do not fear nor be dismayed.

DEUTERONOMY 31:8

Imagine you're driving at night through a mountainous area. There are no lights on the winding, narrow road. As you slowly approach another sharp turn in the road, your headlights shine straight ahead into the dark. The road bends, but your headlights don't. You can see what's on this side of the bend, but around the curve, there is only darkness and the unknown.

That's how we often feel when we approach bends in the road of life. And it surely must be how Moses and Joshua felt as they prepared to take the children of Israel into the Promised Land. On their side of the Jordan River, they could see clearly, but the Canaan side was a mystery. Moses told the people not to fear, that God would be with them, that He would never leave them nor forsake them. And God later told Joshua the same thing (Joshua 1:5).

If your knowledge of the future only goes so far, and you are approaching a sharp curve, know that God is with you now and will be with you on the other side.

Saving faith is resting faith, the trust which
relies entirely on the Savior.

JOHN R. W. STOTT

NOW I BELONG TO JESUS

When Christ who is our life appears,
then you also will appear with Him in glory.
COLOSSIANS 3:4

Have you ever been in the middle of a group of people but somehow still felt alone? Maybe that group was a throng of strangers or casual acquaintances at work, perhaps even family members. Just because you're surrounded doesn't mean you always feel connected.

But Jesus Christ offers a connection and a belonging that works from the inside out. You see, once He comes into your heart—infiltrating your life—you never have to be disconnected again.

The hymn "Now I Belong to Jesus" is a reminder of that ultimate belonging you can experience with your Creator and Savior. "Joy floods my soul, for Jesus has saved me, freed me from sin that long had enslaved me; His precious blood He gave to redeem. Now I belong to Him."

And the best part is the confidence in knowing that belonging to Jesus is *not for the years of time alone, but for eternity!*

Have you made that commitment to Christ so that you can say that you belong to him? Experience the greatest sense of belonging possible through new life in Him when you ask Him to become your Savior and Lord. Then you will say, "Now I belong to Him!"

He gave His life to ransom my soul;
Now I belong to Him.

NORMAN J. CLAYTON

GUARDIAN ANGELS?

*Their angels always see the face
of My Father who is in heaven.*

MATTHEW 18:10

When a construction worker in Austria went to take his lunch break, he slipped on some tiles and plunged off a roof, falling twenty-six feet. Despite landing on concrete, he was unhurt. He got up and went off to enjoy his lunch. An Austrian newspaper, reporting the story, speculated that his guardian angel must have been watching over him.*

For centuries, theologians have debated whether everyone has a guardian angel. We get excited thinking about the prospect, and there are a couple of verses that may indicate the possibility (Matthew 18:10; Acts 12:15). We don't know everything about how angels sometimes protect people. We do know for certain that a host of angels are available to do God's bidding on our behalf. Elisha was surrounded by many angels in 2 Kings 6:17, and several angels carried Lazarus to heaven in Luke 16:22. According to Psalm 91, God gives His angels (plural) charge over us to keep us in our ways.

Whatever we believe about guardian angels, we know that angels are involved in our lives every day and at every juncture of life.

Through the long night watches may Thine angels spread
their white wings above me, watching round my bed.

SABINE BARING-GOULD

---

* "Worker uninjured after eight-metre plunge," *Austrian Independent*, July 14, 2010.

PROBLEMS AND PERSPECTIVE

*It is good for me that I have been afflicted,
that I may learn Your statutes.*
PSALM 119:71

You and your friend have been close for years—never a cross word between you. But suddenly, you find yourself reacting with harsh, impatient words. Whoa! Where did that come from? And your friend looks at you with a puzzled expression as if asking the same thing. If you will look beneath the problem, perhaps you will find a wound that needs healing, a jealousy that needs confessing, or a resentment in need of repentance.

Problems in life are tools in the Holy Spirit's hands to reveal things to us we might never have otherwise considered—truth about God, about others, and especially about ourselves. If we respond to the perspective God allows us to see, we can come out more mature on the other side. Remember how Paul asked God to take away his problem—and God said no? Paul saw something new. He realized that God's grace is sufficient—so much so that he began opening his arms to problems in order to experience more grace (2 Corinthians 12:7-10).

The next time you experience a problem, pray for a new perspective—and open your heart to embrace what God reveals.

Life can only be enjoyed as one acquires a true perspective
of life and death and of the real purpose of life.

SPIROS ZODHIATES

ANGELS UNAWARES

*Do not forget to entertain strangers, for by so doing
some have unwittingly entertained angels.*

HEBREWS 13:2

"I always have one extra plate at my table," said a Christian
woman long ago. "The command is, 'Be not forgetful to
entertain strangers, for thereby some have entertained angels
unawares.' As I never know when the angels will come, I think it
wisest to be always ready and waiting for them."*

For centuries, Hebrews 13:2 has inspired Christian hospitality, and it used to be a common custom to set an extra plate at
supper in case someone dropped by.

In Genesis 18, we read that three strangers showed up at
Abraham's tent. They appeared to be human, but they were
not. One was the Lord Himself (the pre-incarnate Christ), and
the other two were angels on a mission to judge Sodom and
Gomorrah. Abraham and Sarah entertained them and set an
example for us. Could it be that in helping a stranger, smiling
at a visitor, or befriending a newcomer, we are ministering to an
angel? The Bible supports that possibility. It's a good reason to
be kind to everyone you meet today.

Messengers from God brought a greater blessing
than they received. Whoever entertained a servant
of the Lord entertained the Lord himself.

HOLMAN NEW TESTAMENT COMMENTARY ON HEBREWS 13:2

---

*Quoted from an anonymous homemaker in *Anecdotes Illustrative of New Testament Texts*
(New York: A. C. Armstrong & Son, 1887), 322.

LIVE IN THE SPIRIT

Set your mind on things above,
not on things on the earth.
COLOSSIANS 3:2

When Jesus walked this earth, no one would have considered Him a success. He wasn't wealthy or politically powerful. Yet no life has been more influential, for Jesus taught people a new way to live. "Success" to Him was not wealth or power, but a deep and abiding love for God.

His message was unique: *Love your enemy. Pray in secret. Turn the other cheek.* His listeners had never heard this before. Jesus told them not to be satisfied with external conformity to Old Testament law, but to move toward an internal conformity to the character of God. Jesus presented a whole new paradigm to that first-century audience. Some of them struggled and rejected His message, but others embraced His words and placed their faith in Him.

Jesus' message has not changed. His plan for our lives is unique, especially amid a culture that does not follow His truth. As His messengers to a lost world, we must be willing to live our lives according to His principles. In all we do, we must choose words and actions that reflect the transforming power of His Word.

There are three secrets to the success of our work:
prayer, prayer, and more prayer.

BILLY GRAHAM

CONSTANT CHARACTER

He honors those who fear the LORD; he who
swears to his own hurt and does not change.

PSALM 15:4

In the 1960s, an Episcopal priest named Joseph Fletcher developed a theory of Christian ethics known as "situational ethics." He said that the highest biblical law was selfless (agape) love and that other, lesser laws could be disobeyed if necessary in the pursuit of love. Therefore, the ends can justify the means. And one's circumstances or situation can determine which of God's laws one keeps.

This unbiblical approach to God's laws can also lead to "circumstantial character"—character that is dictated by one's circumstances. If God says He does not change (Malachi 3:6), and if it is God who lives in us (Galatians 2:20), it's hard to see how we could be justified in changing who we are—our character—as a response to our circumstances. One of the characteristics of those who dwelt in the presence of God in the Old Testament was a willingness to suffer loss rather than compromise their character (Psalm 15:4).

Character has often been described as what people do when they know no one is looking. Because God's eyes are always open, our character needs to be constant before Him.

A person's character is accurately measured
by his reaction to life's inequities.

UNKNOWN

PREACH THE WORD!

*We do not preach ourselves,
but Christ Jesus the Lord.*

2 CORINTHIANS 4:5

The apostle Paul preached the Word because he couldn't do anything else and still remain in the will of God (1 Corinthians 1:17; 9:16). If Paul were with us today, he would likely show us the amazing work God did through his ministry in Corinth. He would help us see that our goal should be to share the same message.

What did Paul preach? First, he revealed what a sinner is. Sinners and their sin made it necessary for Christ to go to the cross. Second, Paul revealed what a Savior is. When he preached Christ, he preached the doctrine of a Savior who died on a cross. Third, he preached what sin is—something so heinous that it would nail the Son of God to the cross. Fourth, he preached what salvation is—everlasting life in heaven with the Lord.

In light of the Second Coming, the world needs to hear the message of the Savior who came to redeem us from our sins. Have you spoken that message of hope to someone lately?

If when I get to heaven the Lord shall say to me,
Spurgeon, I want you to preach for all eternity, I would
reply, Lord, give me a Bible, that is all I need.

CHARLES H. SPURGEON

BREAK THOU THE BREAD OF LIFE

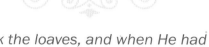

Jesus took the loaves, and when He had given
thanks He distributed them to the disciples,
and the disciples to those sitting down.

JOHN 6:11

You've probably seen accounts of people who see spiritual images in unlikely places. For example, a couple in South Carolina claimed that a dark gray mark on their Walmart receipt was the image of Christ. When they got home from their shopping trip, the receipt fell on the kitchen floor. Picking it up, they noticed it had acquired a stain of some kind. They were struck with how the stained image resembled the face of the Lord, and the local media picked up their story.

We can see Jesus on the printed page, all right—but only by looking into the pages of the Bible. Someone once said that the Bible is simply "Jesus in print." In times of suffering, we can open the Word, find His promises, and fellowship with Him there. He knows our burdens, and He brings rest and peace to our hearts. He gives a Scripture for every situation and a promise for every problem.

In times of illness, loneliness, or low spirits, seek Him in His Word and rest in His promises.

Beyond the sacred page I seek Thee, Lord;
my spirit pants for Thee, O living Word.

MARY LATHBURY

DEFINING DEATH

We are confident, yes, well pleased rather to be absent from the body and to be present with the Lord.

2 CORINTHIANS 5:8

Perhaps the one thing that unites diverse cultures through-out history is the near-universal belief in life after death. The ancient Egyptians are a good example. Archaeologists have revealed that the Egyptians buried their dead with pets, food, and even boats by which to navigate to the next life.

If nearly all worldviews hold to some sort of life after death, Christianity is the one that defines it with specifics. For the Christian, physical death is simply the temporary end of the life of the body. God created humans to live forever—physically and spiritually. But once sin entered the world, both body and spirit were subject to death. It was necessary for both to be reborn. Spiritual rebirth takes place at the time we place our faith in Christ, while physical rebirth will occur at the resurrection of the dead after we leave this earth (or at the Rapture for those who are alive when that event occurs). Christians have no reason to fear death since their conscious spirit will always be in the presence of the Lord (2 Corinthians 5:8).

Make sure your fear of death is removed by faith in the Christ of the Resurrection!

Is it wise to leave massive questions about life, death, and eternity hanging in the air?

JOHN BLANCHARD

MINISTERING SPIRITS

Then an angel appeared to Him
from heaven, strengthening Him.

LUKE 22:43

T he phrase "there for me" has entered the cultural conversation in recent years, appearing everywhere: song titles,
tributes, testimonies, eulogies, and the like. Rarely is the phrase
illustrated by specific examples, but when we hear a person
say that someone was "there for me," we get the idea that one
person stepped in to bring aid, comfort, advice, or resources to
another person in need.

While it may sound trite to apply it to them, we could say that
the angels were always there for Jesus. At least twice in His life
that we know of, in moments of weakness and stress, one or
more angels appeared to support Jesus: following His forty days
of fasting and temptation in the wilderness, "angels came and
ministered to Him" (Matthew 4:11); and during the hours of His
agony in the garden of Gethsemane, an angel appeared in the
garden to strengthen Him (Luke 22:43). While it is hard for us to
imagine Jesus needing ministry or strength, in His humanity He
suffered the same tests as we do, even though He was without
sin (Hebrews 4:15; 5:8).

Fortunately, angels are there for us as well, "sent forth to
minister for those who will inherit salvation" (Hebrews 1:14).

Beside each believer stands an angel as
protector and shepherd leading him to life.

BASIL THE GREAT

COUNTING OUR DAYS

*Surely goodness and mercy shall follow me all the days
of my life; and I will dwell in the house of the L<small>ORD</small> forever.*

PSALM 23:6

It is hard to conceive, but there are only forty-eight days left in this calendar year. Where did another year go? As we progress toward the end of the year and the beginning of another, it is important that we evaluate how our time is being spent. Our days on this earth are finite. Innately we know that—but do we really think about what that means?

There are 168 hours in a week, and if you sleep 8 hours a night, 56 hours of your week's allotment are already gone. When you add getting ready for work, commuting to work, being at work, and eating, the hours quickly dwindle away. You must have time for your friends and family, but what about time for God? How can you be sure to make enough time for the Lord of the universe?

I believe the answer can be found by walking with Christ throughout every moment of your life. In all of your activities, great or small, He should be your ever-present guest. Invite the King of glory to share the days allotted to you now, and look forward to enjoying His presence throughout eternity.

Outside of Christ, I am empty; in Christ, I am full.

WATCHMAN NEE

BE PATIENT IN TRIALS

Count it all joy when you fall into various trials,
knowing that the testing of your faith produces patience.

JAMES 1:2-3

Have you ever witnessed a fight between young siblings? For no apparent reason, one will begin pulling the other's hair or pinching his or her skin. Little children also like name-calling. Mostly, it is done to see if they can get a reaction out of the other child, and often they do. It takes great restraint for the child not to start a fistfight or a screaming match.

Sad to say, it's not just children who pick on each other. Grown adults often do the same thing. The pain they inflict upon one another goes much deeper. They seem to throw daggers instead of spit wads.

Do you know what it is like to be mistreated? Has a coworker ever spread lies about you? Have you ever been the target of unjust insults and ridicule? Perhaps someone else got the promotion you clearly deserved.

How does God want us to respond when we are treated unjustly? He wants us to respond with patience. Being patient means not retaliating. It means holding your spirit in check. The next time you are mistreated, look at it as an opportunity to grow in patience.

Patience is the ability to idle your motor when
you feel like stripping your gears.

BARBARA JOHNSON

MYSTERIOUS STRANGERS

He shall give His angels charge over you,
to keep you in all your ways.

PSALM 91:11

Edward King entered the ministry in 1854 in the village of Wheatley, England. One night he was called to visit a dying man a mile or two away. The night was dark, but King trudged on, only to discover that no one was sick at all. He returned home perplexed. Years later, King made another visit, this time to a condemned prisoner. The man asked King if he remembered his useless, nocturnal walk of yesteryear. "It was I who gave the false message . . ." said the man, "to lure you out, that I might rob you." King asked why he hadn't carried out his plan. "When you came near," said the man, "I saw you were not alone. . . . There was a mysterious looking stranger walking close behind you, and he followed you to your home and then disappeared."*

Perhaps if angels were always visible, we'd be tempted to worship them. People would flock to them as to idols. But though usually invisible, these mysterious strangers are close at hand. The angels are watching over us.

The angels know each saint on earth more intimately than the saints themselves are known by their nearest friends.**

NORMAN MACLEOD

---

*Alida Stanwood, *Reinforcements* (New York: R. R. Beam & Co., 1915), 148.
**Ibid., 140.

STATIC ON THE LINE

If I regard iniquity in my heart, the Lord will not hear.

PSALM 66:18

Cell phones can be a blessing and a curse. Their convenience is a benefit, but they can prove to be very frustrating when we move out of the signal range. The phrase "Can you hear me now?" originated for moments like these. It is difficult to have effective communication when a call is interrupted.

Just as static makes talking on the phone difficult, sin hinders our communication and fellowship with God. God does not listen to our prayers when there is iniquity in our hearts. It is also impossible for us to hear His voice when we harbor unconfessed sin. It is as if there were static on the line.

In Old Testament times, God withdrew His Spirit when there was sin in a person's life. When Saul rejected and disobeyed God, he forfeited his intimacy with God, and the Spirit of the Lord left.

Today the Holy Spirit indwells every believer permanently, but He can be grieved. Then we lose fellowship with God. Is there static on your line? Is there some sin you need to confess? Take the time to reconnect with the Lord—He is never out of range.

Confession is the first step to repentance.

ENGLISH PROVERB

BEING GOD'S ROAD SIGN

The Son of Man has come to save that which was lost.

MATTHEW 18:11

There is nothing worse than being lost in unfamiliar territory. The roads all begin to look alike, and each turn seems to lead you farther from where you need to go. Have you ever experienced that frustrating feeling?

Did you know that as you drive down the street today, you will pass many people who are lost? These lost folks aren't just looking for their next turn; they are *spiritually* lost. Living in this world apart from God, they are traveling toward a destination of destruction—and they may not even know it.

Fortunately, the lost are not without hope. Jesus left us a Guidebook with directions. His Word tells us that He came to this world to save the lost. His death and resurrection made it possible for us to get on the road to eternal life. This is good news! It is our responsibility to share this good news with those who are lost and wandering through life, turning every which way in hopes of finding fulfillment.

Be a road sign, pointing others toward Christ. Share the good news with those around you!

Jesus Christ did not say "Go into all the world
and tell the world that it is quite right."

C. S. LEWIS

ALONE . . . WITH GOD

The Lord stood with me and strengthened me.

2 TIMOTHY 4:17

Lonely. You may *feel* the word even as you read it. It's an ache inside, almost to the point of nausea. Some understand the anguish of loneliness more than others. But there's One who understands it more acutely than any of us.

Testimonies of men and women in Scripture like Job, Hagar, Moses, David, and Paul express the crushing weight of loneliness. But Jesus was separated from God as He hung on the cross for our sins. Though He was the one who needed to be strengthened in the hours leading up to His crucifixion, Jesus comforted the lonely disciples as they feared His imminent departure, saying, "Let not your heart be troubled. . . . I go to prepare a place for you" (John 14:1-2).

We may feel lonely here on the earth, but Jesus is preparing a place for us, and He will return to take us there if we have accepted His gift of salvation. Even now, we are not truly alone. The One who bore the loneliest moment in history promises, "I will never leave you nor forsake you" (Hebrews 13:5). Live in the assurance of His promise. See with eyes of faith the One who listens to your heartfelt cries and cares for you.

O Thou who changest not, abide with me.

HENRY LYTE

BEARING BURDENS

Bear one another's burdens,
and so fulfill the law of Christ.

GALATIANS 6:2

Medal of Honor recipient Leroy Petry was in a 2008 firefight in Afghanistan. Though already wounded in both legs, he grabbed a live grenade that landed amid his team and attempted to throw it away. It exploded before he could release it, destroying his right hand and forearm and shredding him with shrapnel. Putting a tourniquet on his arm to stop the bleeding, he continued to direct his men until the fight was over. His actions saved his fellow soldiers from death and injury.

Sergeant Petry took upon himself the burden of injury that his fellow soldiers would certainly have suffered—not unlike what Christ did on the cross to spare us from certain death for our sins. The power one individual has to come alongside and bear the burden of a discouraged soul is amazing—perhaps even the power of life and death. We are in a spiritual battle, after all. And it may be a word of encouragement from the sword of the Spirit (Ephesians 6:17) that saves a friend from the attack of the giant of despair.

Be a burden sharer and bearer today in the life of one who needs a word of encouragement from a friend like you.

No one is useless in this world who
lightens the burdens of another.

CHARLES DICKENS

SATISFACTION GUARANTEED

O God, You are my God; early will I seek You; my soul thirsts for You; my flesh longs for You in a dry and thirsty land where there is no water.

PSALM 63:1

Have you ever bought something—perhaps a car or expensive outfit—hoping that it would bring satisfaction? If so, you know the disappointment that ultimately follows. It may satisfy for a few days, but then your heart is left with the same emptiness again.

Are you trying to find satisfaction in things that this world has to offer? Are you trying to fill the void with approval from others, possessions, a career, entertainment, or education? Let me assure you that these things will ultimately leave you feeling empty. They are not the source of lasting satisfaction.

If you are thirsty, turn to the Living Water. Seek the Lord and call upon Him. Drink from His Word and dwell in His presence. Your thirst will be quenched, and your soul will be satisfied.

Where your pleasure is, there is your treasure;
where your treasure is, there is your heart;
where your heart is, there is your happiness.

AUGUSTINE

HIGH PRAISE

Praise Him in the heights!
PSALM 148:1

How high is Mount Everest? For years, we've been taught that the highest peak in the world tops out at 29,028 feet. But critics have recently claimed that the exact height is 29,008 feet. Others have suggested the summit rises to 29,035 feet. Even the government of Nepal chimed in and announced a new measurement would be made using the most modern satellite technology. Those few disputed feet are important to the thousands of brave souls who have conquered the summit since Sir Edmund Hillary stood there in 1953.

Most of us will never hike to the top of Mount Everest, but we ascend to even greater heights whenever we're caught up in the joy of thanksgiving and praise. We're in rare air when we're breathing in the lofty atmosphere of joy and gratitude. We're dwelling above the heads of 99 percent of the world when we learn to see blessings amid the problems, count our mercies instead of our miseries, and thank God in all things, knowing that this is the will of God in Christ Jesus concerning us.

Live in the heights today. Be thankful.

From the depth of sin and sadness to the heights
of joy and gladness Jesus lifted me.

JULIA H. JOHNSTON

ANGELS OF LIGHT

Satan himself transforms himself into an angel of light.

2 CORINTHIANS 11:14

Paul warns us to be wary of false prophets claiming to be apostles. Satan pretends to be an angel of light, and "his ministers also transform themselves into ministers of righteousness, whose end will be according to their works" (2 Corinthians 11:15).

Our society is captivated by angels. In fact, many religions boast of their "angels of light." We mustn't get caught up in mystic speculations or false prophets in our pursuit of knowledge about angels. The study of angels isn't a fanciful leap into the realm of the supernatural. The true understanding of angels comes by rightly dividing Scripture.

It isn't a false worship of angels we need, but the Word of God with its reassuring truth that angels are ministering spirits sent to serve those who inherit salvation (Hebrews 1:14).

The acknowledgment of angels is needful in the church. Therefore godly preachers should teach them logically.*

MARTIN LUTHER

---

*Thomas S. Kepler, ed., *The Table Talk of Martin Luther* (Grand Rapids, MI: Baker, 1952), 278–79.

THANKING GOD FOR OTHERS

I thank God upon every remembrance of you.

PHILIPPIANS 1:3

When was the last time you told someone, "I thank God for you"? The apostle Paul regularly expressed his gratitude for his friends in his letters. It seems that the more Paul suffered (he was jailed, shipwrecked, beaten), the more his letters dripped with thanksgiving. He thanked God for those who stood with him, he thanked God for those who served alongside him, and most of all he thanked God for those who had come to faith in Christ through his ministry.

For whom are you thankful? Use this Thanksgiving week to think of the family and friends God has brought into your life. Do you know what will happen when you do that? You'll find yourself sitting down to write someone a note of encouragement. Maybe you'll pick up the phone and call someone to say, "I've just been thinking about how God has blessed my life because of you. I thank God for you today and want you to know that."

Let the celebration of Thanksgiving remind you of the importance of gratitude. Don't miss the opportunity to tell your loved ones why you're thankful for them today!

Gratitude is one of those things that cannot be bought. It must be born with men, or else all the obligations in the world will not create it.

LORD HALIFAX

IT'S A MATTER OF PERSPECTIVE

*Whoever is wise will observe these things, and they
will understand the lovingkindness of the LORD.*

PSALM 107:43

A woman once approached a man who had a sour expression on his face. She encouraged that grumpy-looking man to be thankful. He replied, "Thankful for what? I don't even have enough money to pay my bills." The woman thought for a moment, then said, "Well, then be thankful you're not one of your creditors."

If we try, we can always stop and find something to be thankful for! Helen Keller noted, "I have often thought it would be a blessing if each human being were stricken blind and deaf for a few days at some time during his early adult life. Darkness would make him more appreciative of sight; silence would teach him the joys of sound."

We continually experience so many blessings in our lives that it becomes easy for us to take them for granted. God's mercies to us are new every morning. Even in the midst of difficulty or heartache, we can find so many reasons to thank God. It's just a matter of perspective. Make thanksgiving the theme of your prayers today.

Keep your face to the sun and
you will never see the shadows.

HELEN KELLER

BE THE ONE

Jesus answered and said, "Were there not
ten cleansed? But where are the nine?"

LUKE 17:17

Are you familiar with the story of Jesus and the ten lepers? These ten lepers cried out to Jesus for healing and were miraculously healed of their terrible disease. But only one came back to say thank you. Ten miracles. One thank-you.

The ratio probably hasn't changed much over the years. A spirit of ingratitude pervades our society. In fact, the Bible tells us in 2 Timothy that one of the characteristics of the end times is that people will be ungrateful.

Imagine how you would feel if no one ever thanked you for your kind actions. In the same way, God's heart is broken when we do not thank Him for touching our lives with His love. In light of God's magnificent grace, ingratitude is a grievous sin.

Don't allow the spirit of ingratitude to sneak into your life. Be the one who, like the lone leper, returns to give thanks. Be the one who remembers to say, "Thank You, Lord."

Praise the Savior, ye who know Him!
Who can tell how much we owe Him?

THOMAS KELLY

NEVER LONELY AGAIN

He Himself has said,
"I will never leave you nor forsake you."
HEBREWS 13:5

Even with the many "friends" people enjoy today through social media, there is a longing for a friend, loved one, mentor, teacher, or other important person to be there for us on a consistent basis away from the computer screen. But "always" is a relative term—no human friends can measure up to "always." One day, they will not be there for us.

There is another who is definitely always there: God's Holy Spirit. The Holy Spirit is sent by God to indwell all who have a relationship with Him through faith in Jesus Christ. It is the Spirit who makes real the life of Christ in us (Romans 8:11). And it is the Spirit who gives us love, joy, peace, longsuffering, kindness, goodness, faithfulness, gentleness, and self-control (Galatians 5:22-23). What more could a person want in a time of loneliness or discouragement? The Holy Spirit is also our Counselor, or Helper (John 14:16-17). So in lonely moments, when we need comfort and counsel, the Spirit is there, never to leave us nor forsake us.

If you know Christ today yet are in a lonely place, remember this: the Spirit of God is with you—never to leave.

Loneliness is the first thing
which God's eye named not good.

JOHN MILTON

PRAY BOLDLY

Let us therefore come boldly to the throne of grace, that we
may obtain mercy and find grace to help in time of need.
HEBREWS 4:16

Telephone calls used to be routed by operators manually connecting circuits at a switchboard—plugging and unplugging wires all day long to keep conversations going. Today, think how many millions of calls are handled by computerized routers every second of the day. Better yet, imagine how many countless prayer "calls" God receives every moment from all over the world.

It would be easy to be dissuaded from praying by thinking of our individual prayer requests getting lost amid the millions God hears. Yet we are exhorted to "let [our] requests be made known to God" (Philippians 4:6) and to do so boldly (Hebrews 4:16). King David did (countless times in Psalms), and so did the apostle Paul—the same request three different times (2 Corinthians 12:7-8). They didn't feel bad or guilty for continually asking God for help, nor should we. In fact, not to pray is to portray God as less than He is—a generous Father (Luke 11:11-13).

If you are in a stressful place today, stop now and tell God. Because ultimately He is the answer to our prayers, meeting with Him is the beginning of your answer.

Anxiety and prayer are more opposed
to each other than fire and water.

J. A. BENGEL

AN URGENT MESSAGE

Behold, now is the accepted time;
behold, now is the day of salvation.

2 CORINTHIANS 6:2

Billy Graham sat incognito at an open-air crusade. He was scheduled to speak the next evening, but this day he was among the audience. When the speaker gave an altar call, Billy Graham tapped the shoulder of the gentleman in front of him. He asked, "Would you like to accept Christ? I'll be glad to walk down with you if you want to." The man said, "Naw, I think I'll just wait till the big gun comes tomorrow night."

Are you waiting for the perfect set of circumstances to fall into place before you accept Christ? Are you putting Him off until later, so you can party now? Are you waiting for a setting that is glamorous, exciting, or emotional? If so, you are treading on dangerous ground.

The overriding message that we should glean from events occurring around us is that salvation is an urgent matter. If the Holy Spirit is calling you to Himself, don't ignore His voice. Respond to Him today. Life promises no guarantee of tomorrow. Let today be the day of salvation. If you are saved, are you sharing the gift of salvation with others? You have the message of life in your hands. Give it to as many as you can.

You cannot escape the responsibility
of tomorrow by evading it today.

ABRAHAM LINCOLN

WHEN THERE IS NO PEACE

They have also healed the hurt of My people slightly,
saying, "Peace, peace!" when there is no peace.

JEREMIAH 6:14

The League of Nations (1920). The United Nations (1945). Countless regional, charitable, educational, and nongovernmental organizations with "peace" in their titles. None have actually promised peace, but they have all attacked the problem of war and discord as if peace were possible. Despite their efforts, none of them have achieved permanent success. At any time of the day, somewhere in the world, a war is being waged.

How are we to live in a warring world without being influenced by such ever-present discord? How can we live in peace when there is no peace around us? How can we quell the internal discord we feel in times of loneliness, discouragement, or despair? The Bible points to the Prince of Peace, Jesus Christ, as the answer (Isaiah 9:6-7). With Him living in us as Lord, the fruit of His Spirit in our life is peace (Galatians 5:22). When we commit our anxieties and discord to Him in prayer, we receive His peace (Philippians 4:6-7)—regardless of what is going on around us or within us.

Don't wait for the world to give you a peace it has no ability to provide. Take the peace of Christ that is available today to calm your troubled soul.

Peace reigns where our Lord reigns.

JULIAN OF NORWICH

PATIENT WITH ALL

Now we exhort you, brethren, warn those who are unruly,
comfort the fainthearted, uphold the weak, be patient with all.

1 THESSALONIANS 5:14

Have you ever had a mosquito bite? If so, you've experienced the nagging itch and redness it creates. It's difficult to focus on anything else because all you can think about is how much you want to scratch the bite. Sometimes you want to let out a scream because of the annoying irritation!

Have you ever felt this way about a person? He or she has crawled under your skin and become a source of irritation. Perhaps it is a family member who continually nags you. Maybe you have a young child who constantly asks you, "Why?" It may be a friend who has an annoying habit. Or it could be a store cashier who is particularly slow.

These irritants can become like an itch that won't go away. We long to react with biting words and explosive tempers, but God has laid out a better way for us. He wants us to apply the soothing ointment of His grace to our interactions with others. The next time a person's words or actions cause you irritation, ask God to help you respond with patience and love.

The times we find ourselves having to wait on others may be the perfect opportunities to train ourselves to wait on the Lord.

JONI EARECKSON TADA

DECEMBER

POSSIBILITY OF PEACE

They have seduced My people, saying,
"Peace!" when there is no peace.
EZEKIEL 13:10

There was a reason World War I was called "The Great War"—it was the largest, costliest war in human history. To ensure such a war never happened again, the League of Nations was created in 1920 to maintain world peace through negotiations, disarmament, settling of disputes through the justice system, and other means. Unfortunately, World War II proved the League lacked the ability to keep the peace, and it was replaced in 1945 by the United Nations—which has also failed to bring peace on earth.

There is nothing wrong with trying to create peace. Indeed, the apostle Paul wrote, "If it is possible, as much as depends on you, live peaceably with all men" (Romans 12:18). Whether others seek the same peace is beyond our control. But regardless of what is happening around us, we can have the peace of God "[guarding our] hearts and minds through Christ Jesus" (Philippians 4:7).

As you turn your attention to the birth of Christ this month, let His peace be birthed in your heart. What is impossible with man is certainly possible with God.

When there is a storm without, He will make
peace within. The world can create trouble
in peace, but God can create peace in trouble.

THOMAS WATSON

BOTH GOD AND MAN

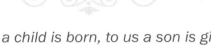

For to us a child is born, to us a son is given,
and the government will be on his shoulders.
And he will be called Wonderful Counselor.

ISAIAH 9:6, NIV

As Christmas approaches, we turn our attention to the One who came to deliver us from sin forever. Isaiah 9:6 tells us that He was *born*—speaking of His humanity—and that He was *given*—reminding us that He is deity.

In calling Jesus the Wonderful Counselor, Isaiah is reminding us that we can come to Him for the same kind of wisdom a loyal subject would seek from a ruling king.

When we enter into His courts, we recognize that we are the subjects of a Great Ruler who sees everything in His Kingdom and knows how to best rule over it all. We can bring our questions and concerns to Him, and we can seek His divine and eternal guidance with confidence that He will direct us in the very best way.

When we seek the Lord's royal wisdom and guidance, we participate with Him in changing our hearts and our emotions. When we consult with Him and allow Him to reign as our Wonderful Counselor, we gain an inside track to joyful and abundant living in Him.

Thou art coming to a King, large petitions with
thee bring; for his grace and power are such,
none can ever ask too much.

JOHN NEWTON

POINTING THE WAY

*When Jesus came to the place, He looked up and saw
him, and said to him, "Zacchaeus, make haste and
come down, for today I must stay at your house."*

LUKE 19:5

If you encountered someone who was lost and needed help
finding the way, would you offer that person a maze instead of
a road map? Of course not! Most of us would give detailed directions. We might draw a map. We might even offer to personally
escort the lost person to his or her destination.

While Zacchaeus was in the tree, Jesus discerned his lost
condition and need for direction in his life. So He stopped what
He was doing to talk with Zacchaeus and took the time to personally show him the way.

To always be ready and willing to share our faith means we
must first be aware that there are lost people around us. We
must look for those who are wandering aimlessly through life
and offer to help them find their way, even before we're asked.

To make ourselves available to the lost may interrupt our
schedule and take us out of our way. But in doing so, we tread
the path already mapped out by Christ, our Savior and our Lord,
who came to seek and save the lost.

The Gospel is not something we come to church to
hear; it is something we go from church to tell.

VANCE HAVNER

AMAZING GRACE

*Then he said to Jesus, "Lord, remember me
when You come into Your kingdom."*

LUKE 23:42

You may know some people who believe that the course they set out on early in life cannot be altered. These people don't do anything to change their circumstances because it seems to be too late. Their fates are sealed in their minds.

Others are exemplary and inspiring in their ability to see that it is never too late to change. Whether it is a hardened prisoner who finally turns to Christ, or an ailing senior citizen who resolves to get right with God before the end of his life, these people know something that the thief on the cross in today's passage knew—that change is always possible.

The repentant thief on the cross was so certain of Jesus' deity that he pleaded with the Lord to remember him when He entered heaven. After living a life of sin, he saw in an instant that there was another way. While it was very, very late in this man's life, it wasn't too late to turn to Jesus. It isn't too late for you, either.

Isn't it inspiring to know that Jesus loves you so much? What amazing grace that our Savior would offer eternity to all of us—no matter who we are.

God loves each of us as if there were only one of us.

AUGUSTINE

BLESSED DECEMBER

Let not your heart be troubled.

JOHN 14:1

Wouldn't it be wonderful if we could suspend all wars for the month of December in honor of Christ's birth? We've read about the amazing Christmas Truce of World War I when German and Allied soldiers sang carols, exchanged gifts, and played soccer on the battlefields of Flanders. Why can't the armies of the world declare December a month of peace? What if no diseases struck during December? No deaths occurred? No funerals were necessary?

We live in a deadly, disease-ridden, war-weary world, and there's no cessation of trouble. But the Lord Jesus Christ can give *inner* peace, and He can provide assurance of *eternal* peace. In one of His greatest promises, He said, "Peace I leave with you, My peace I give to you; not as the world gives do I give to you. Let not your heart be troubled, neither let it be afraid" (John 14:27).

How personal! Notice the phrases in the verse: *with you, to you, to you, your heart.*

We don't know how to suspend war or wickedness, but as Christians, we walk with the Lord and experience His peace every day of December and beyond.

Peace on the outside comes from knowing God on the inside.

UNKNOWN

WHY THE INCARNATION?

The Word became flesh and dwelt among us.

JOHN 1:14

Our heavenly Father yearned through the centuries and the rise and fall of civilizations to redeem His needy people. He never ceased to reach out to His prodigal family. He did this in every possible way: through the glories of His creation, through the immeasurable gifts He gave them, through the words of prophets and teachers. He dispatched His servants with countless messages that said the same thing in ten thousand ways: "Come home! Come home! You are loved now and forever."

In the end and at long last, in the fullness of time, God Himself made the journey. He poured His Godhead into flesh and blood and visited the earth as a man. He walked among us—a King in disguise, the Creator among His creatures. He entered our world through a doorway called Bethlehem, and our world was changed forever.

That's something to celebrate! That's the reason we have a *merry* Christmas. The Word became flesh and dwelled among us. He is your Emmanuel today—God with us . . . God with you.

He is God Incarnate; not man becoming God,
but God coming into human flesh, coming into
it from the outside. His Life is the Highest and
the Holiest entering in at the lowliest door.

OSWALD CHAMBERS

REST, NOT STRESS

*My peace I give to you. . . . Let not your heart
be troubled, neither let it be afraid.*
JOHN 14:27

"Cure stress permanently!" The advertisement is alluring. But do you notice there's no guarantee? Promises of natural cures for stress flood the market. So why are emergency rooms and doctors' offices overflowing with patients complaining of symptoms that are stress related? Causing numerous physical and emotional conditions, stress is the malady of our day.

But stress is not a modern-day phenomenon. The Jews of Jesus' day also experienced burnout. Feverishly, they worked in vain to meet the demands of the hypocritical scribes. Jesus saw the Jews struggling under the weight of that oppressive system and entreated them to come to Him and receive His rest. Those who responded felt the weight of their sin removed, and they experienced the promise of a new life and future.

Jesus' invitation calls out to us today. Are you burdened by unconfessed sin? Weary from responsibility, monotony, anxiety? Few things in life come with guarantees. Accept the lifetime guarantee that Jesus offers you now: "Come to Me, all you who labor and are heavy laden, and I will give you rest" (Matthew 11:28).

Rest in this—it is His business to lead, command,
impel, send, call, or whatever you want to
call it. It is your business to obey.

JIM ELLIOT

RUSTING OR TRUSTING

Do not fret. . . . Trust.

PSALM 37:1, 3

The Harbour Bridge and nearby Opera House are iconic images of Sydney, Australia. But engineers have recently grown alarmed that the famous bridge is showing serious signs of corrosion. In one year, city officials spent $12 million fighting an endless battle with rust.

Anxiety is like rust. It coats and corrodes the mind, weakening the entire structure. Worry dissolves our peace just as rust eats away the strength of a bridge—weakening the metal that was formerly strong.

Sydney's Harbour Bridge will be fine. Workers have been stripping the structure back to bare metal and starting the rust-proofing process all over again with special paints. But how do you rust-proof the heart?

You simply add a *t* and turn *rust* to *trust*. The writer of Psalm 37 said, "Trust in the LORD. . . . Delight yourself also in the LORD. . . . Commit your way to the LORD, trust also in Him. . . . Rest in the LORD, and wait patiently for Him; do not fret" (verses 3-5, 7).

Don't rust. Trust.

A loving parent would be sorely grieved if his child
could not trust him; . . . how unkind is our conduct
when we put so little confidence in our heavenly Father
who has never failed us, and who never will.

CHARLES H. SPURGEON

DEVOTION'S DIVIDENDS

Now on the first day of the week Mary Magdalene went to the tomb early, while it was still dark, and saw that the stone had been taken away from the tomb.

JOHN 20:1

Mary Magdalene was a devoted follower of Christ, and with good reason. In Luke 8:2-3 we read that she was part of a group that traveled with Jesus, devoting themselves to Him by serving Him and seeing to His daily needs.

What was the source of Mary's devotion? She had been healed of the debilitating spiritual condition of demon possession. Freed from that evil tyranny, she dedicated herself to showing gratitude and thanks to Jesus by ministering to Him out of her own resources.

It has been said that Mary Magdalene was the last at the cross and the first at the grave.

When Jesus was buried, Mary still wanted to show her love and dedication to Him. Her faithfulness was rewarded when she met the resurrected Lord in the garden. This privilege was hers alone because she rose early and went to the garden in devotion and service.

When we serve the Lord faithfully, we will be rewarded in large and small ways. In the daily faithfulness of time spent with the Lord, we can ask Him, "Lord, what would You have me do today?"

May Christ be our joy, our confidence, our all.

MATTHEW HENRY

JOSEPH: A JUST MAN

*Then Joseph . . . being a just man, and not wanting
to make her a public example, was minded to put her
away secretly. But while he thought about these things,
behold, an angel of the Lord appeared to him.*

MATTHEW 1:19-20

The word *just* means righteous, fair, and upright. When the Scriptures describe Joseph as a just man, they show us the qualities in his life that caused God to choose him to be the earthly father of the Lord Jesus.

Joseph was compassionate. When he learned Mary was pregnant before their marriage ceremony, he was entitled to divorce her in a public spectacle or a private ceremony. Choosing the gracious option, he decided to divorce her quietly. He didn't seek revenge but thought about what was best for Mary.

Joseph was thoughtful. While he was trying to decide how to handle his dilemma, he "thought about these things." His pause for thought gave God time to speak to him through an angel. Had Joseph acted rashly, the plan could have gone awry.

Parents, when you bring compassion into your parenting, you will raise tenderhearted children who can see with the eyes of Jesus. When you bring thoughtfulness, taking time to think before acting, you will raise children who act fairly and justly, giving honor to God.

The most valuable gift you can give another is a good example.

UNKNOWN

I AM GETTING OLDER

Multitude of years should teach wisdom.

JOB 32:7

An old prayer, purportedly from a seventeenth-century nun, says, "Lord, You know better than I know myself that I am getting older and will someday be old. Keep me from the fatal habit of thinking I must say something on every subject and on every occasion. Release me from craving to straighten out everybody's affairs. Make me thoughtful but not moody, helpful but not bossy. With my vast store of wisdom it seems a pity not to use it all, but you know, Lord, that I want a few friends at the end."

Sometimes we think young people are more susceptible to the temptations of life. But we encounter new sets of temptations at every age. Satan tempts senior adults as mercilessly as he tempts seniors in high school, though the allurements may be different. That's why it's so important to keep growing throughout life.

Job 32:7 says that as our years advance, our wisdom should increase. We can't outgrow temptation, but we can overcome it with increasing strength as we age gracefully in the Lord.

If any man thinks that he is strong enough to
resist the devil at any one point he needs special
watch there, for the tempter comes that way.

D. L. MOODY

THROWING STONES

He raised Himself up and said to them, "He who is without sin among you, let him throw a stone at her first."

JOHN 8:7

Imagine Jesus in the Temple, speaking to a crowd, when suddenly the scene is interrupted by the sound of loud voices and cries of protest. As the scuffle becomes louder, a woman is thrust at Jesus' feet. We can see her gasping for breath, heart pounding, with tear-streaked dirt on her face and arms. She has been caught in the sin of adultery.

Knowing Jesus' teaching on forgiveness, the Pharisees sought to trap Jesus into either validating the harsh capital punishment prescribed by the law or proclaiming a more lenient punishment. They planned to discredit Jesus, but they did not foresee His divine wisdom.

Jesus knew their sin and the sin of every person there in the Temple. So, without condemning any of them, He said, "He who is without sin among you, let him throw a stone at her first." One by one the accusers walked away.

The Pharisees had their eyes on Jesus and on the woman, refusing to look inward at their own sin. Where are our eyes focused? Are we looking at others and casting blame, or are we willing to look inward and see the truth about ourselves?

Unless you have never been tempted, don't pass judgment on someone who has yielded.

UNKNOWN

INDECISION IS A DECISION

*When they had gathered together, Pilate said to
them, "Whom do you want me to release to you?
Barabbas, or Jesus who is called Christ?"*

MATTHEW 27:17

Indecision is a decision. This thought sums up the choice Pontius Pilate made when he encountered Jesus Christ. Pilate believed he could postpone his decision about Jesus, but he was wrong because every action he took led to a choice, even though he sought to avoid one.

When Jesus came before Pilate, the Roman governor of that distant outpost, He discovered a man who was torn. Even Pilate's wife added to his confusion, warning her husband to "have nothing to do with that just Man" after having a dream about Him (Matthew 27:19). Pilate and Herod debated, and neither could find any wrong in Him. Yet the throng clamored for the release of Barabbas, so the expedient political decision was to send Jesus to His death.

We all come to a point when we have to make a decision about Jesus. We must accept Him as our Savior, or we reject Him. Once we take Him as our Savior, we must choose to enthrone Him as our Lord. If we think we can postpone and *not* decide, we have decided already.

I believe in my soul that there are more at this day being
lost for want of decision than for any other thing.

D. L. MOODY

DECEMBER 14

CONQUERING HERO

His name will be called . . . Mighty God.
ISAIAH 9:6

Modern-day warriors rarely engage in hand-to-hand combat. "Smart" missiles, radar tracking, and high-tech computers do the work that was once relegated to the foot soldier. However, when Isaiah prophesied that Christ would be called the Mighty God, we get the image of a powerful warrior—one who would defeat his enemies decisively one-on-one.

When Jesus appeared on the scene that first Christmas, He came as more than just a frail infant in a manger. The eyes that beheld Him in the manger may not have recognized it, but Jesus came to earth as a warrior. Clothed in the tender flesh of a newborn babe, He nevertheless was prepared to war with evil and vanquish the enemies of God. He would do it with the weapons of His warfare—love and peace, backed with the strength of forgiveness from an all-powerful God.

As Christmas approaches, draw on the strength that radiates from the manger. Jesus is our Mighty God, and we can take up His unique weapons. Using forgiveness to dispel anger, love to drive away hate, and goodness to counter wickedness, we show the power and strength of God to love the world into accepting His gift of eternal life.

Jesus Christ is not valued at all until He is valued above all.

AUGUSTINE

GOD ENABLES YOU

Then Mary said, "Behold the maidservant of the Lord!
Let it be to me according to your word."

LUKE 1:38

Have you heard the old saying "This is bigger than the both of us"? In the case of Mary and Joseph, this sentiment rings true. What started as a simple commitment to God and each other ended in enormous, earthshaking events.

Told by the angel Gabriel that she would have a child by the Holy Spirit, Mary submitted to God's plan with an obedience that was radiant in its simplicity: "Let it be to me according to your word."

Then, when an angel in a dream instructed Joseph, he committed himself fully to God's plan. He took Mary to be his wife. He named the baby Jesus. He complied with every detail.

When God targets you for a task that seems too big to handle, follow Mary and Joseph's example. Make a simple commitment to be faithful and willing. You aren't alone. God will enable you to accomplish whatever He has planned.

Today as I read the accounts of Jesus' birth
I tremble to think of the fate of the world resting
on the responses of two rural teenagers.*

PHILIP YANCEY

---

* Philip Yancey, *The Jesus I Never Knew* (Grand Rapids, MI: Zondervan, 1995), 31–32.

WHY THE STAR?

We have seen His star in the East and
have come to worship Him.

MATTHEW 2:2

What compelled the magi to put aside all they were doing to undertake a long and dangerous journey, following one shimmering star across the landscape? The wise men were astrologers, seeking to understand human events by reading the constellations. It was their habit to compare the skies to prophetic literature, including the Jewish Scriptures. Perhaps they had read Numbers 24:17, which says, "I see Him, but not now; I behold Him, but not near; a Star shall come out of Jacob; a Scepter shall rise out of Israel."

For the ancient magi, the message was clear: a great King, announced with the silent fanfare of a brilliant star, was on the way. And if such a King was foretold more than one thousand years earlier, He was worth traveling to see.

So they came, and so do we. Somehow this star, *our* star, broke through the galaxies to remind us that the intimate story of the Nativity is written on the widest of canvases. And when we see the promised Savior, every star dims by comparison.

He became like us, so we could become like him.

MAX LUCADO

PRINCE OF PEACE

His name will be called . . . Prince of Peace.

ISAIAH 9:6

Royal titles mean very little to Americans, but in some parts of the world they signify the privilege of birthright. By virtue of their parents and ancestors, royal people assume positions of power. It may be largely symbolic, but traditionally, royalty sets the rules.

Isaiah characterized the coming Messiah as Prince of Peace because of His birthright. As the Father's Son, Jesus had the right to reign over the earth. While many nations have been burdened by the tyrannical rule imposed by royalty, that's not the case in God's Kingdom!

Jesus' birth and subsequent sacrificial death made it possible for us to have eternal life and to have peace with God. Because we put our trust in Him, we have peace now. In the future He will establish a lasting peace.

This Christmas, celebrate the birth of our Savior and enjoy the rich blessing from the Prince of Peace.

He brought peace on earth and wants to bring it also into your soul—that peace which the world cannot give. He is the One who would save His people from their sins.

CORRIE TEN BOOM

GLORY CAME DOWN

The Word became flesh and dwelt among us,
and we beheld His glory, the glory as of the only
begotten of the Father, full of grace and truth.

JOHN 1:14

Once Adam and Eve had broken the heart of God with their fall into sin, God knew that there would be a need to atone for their sins. Jesus' birth accomplished that, for by sending Jesus to the world, He placed the Word, the divine Son of God, in the form of a man so that He could bring our salvation.

In Jesus we see both man and God. We relate to Him as a fellow human being, but we cannot forget that He is God. Proclaiming truth, He taught us how to live. Radiating grace, He showed us what it means to forgive. And as the only begotten of the Father, the unique Son of God, He came into our midst to show us that God planned for us to be with Him forever.

There is probably no better time than the Christmas season to envision the glory of God. Every pageant, each Nativity scene, and all the twinkling lights are our attempts to capture the glory. But ultimately we must remember that Christmas represents God's gracious plan of redemption.

The incarnation is in itself an unfathomable
mystery, but it makes sense of everything
else that the New Testament contains.

J. I. PACKER

OUR TIMES ARE IN HIS HANDS

Then He arose and rebuked the wind, and
said to the sea, "Peace, be still!"

MARK 4:39

Do you remember Hurricane John? It formed in the Pacific in 1994 and set a world record as the longest-lasting and farthest-traveling hurricane in recorded history. It was also one of the strongest hurricanes ever to sweep across the sea. It lasted a full month—thirty-one days—and traveled from the eastern Pacific to the western Pacific and back to the central Pacific. Fortunately it remained mostly at sea, so damage was minimal despite the duration of the storm, but it broke records everywhere it went.

Some storms seem to go on forever. A health crisis, a job disruption, a damaged relationship, a tough period at church. For the disciples, the storm lasted far too long. They feared death by drowning while their Lord slept peacefully in the stern. But Jesus knew the exact time to say, "Peace, be still." At that moment, "the wind ceased and there was a great calm" (Mark 4:39).

Let's learn to weather the storm by faith in Him. Our times are in His hands, and in His timing He will say, "Peace, be still!"

No waters can swallow the ship where lies the
Master of ocean, and earth, and skies.

MARY A. BAKER

DECEMBER 20

WHY BETHLEHEM?

Jesus was born in Bethlehem of Judea.

MATTHEW 2:1

Someone once said that the hinge of history is on the door of a Bethlehem stable. There were thousands of towns in the days of Christ. But Micah 5:2 predicted only one as the Messiah's birthplace: "But you, Bethlehem Ephrathah, though you are little among the thousands of Judah, yet out of you shall come forth to Me the One to be Ruler in Israel, whose goings forth are from of old, from everlasting."

The name Bethlehem means "House of Bread," and Christ is the Bread from heaven. Ephrathah means "fruitfulness." As Jesus later told His disciples, "By this My Father is glorified, that you bear much fruit" (John 15:8). In a forgotten corner of a forgotten town came the most unforgettable news the world has ever heard. In the House of Bread, Bread was served. In the town of fruitfulness, Someone came as the sweet fruit of heaven.

Just as Jesus quietly arrived in that town of towns, so He longs to be born again in the hearts of every one of us.

The greatest gift you will ever receive will never be found under a Christmas tree. It is far too valuable to be stored in any other place but in the depths of your heart.

UNKNOWN

KING, HIGH PRIEST, AND SAVIOR

*When they had opened their treasures, they presented
gifts to Him: gold, frankincense, and myrrh.*
MATTHEW 2:11

There is great joy in choosing a gift carefully, matching the selection to the interests and lifestyle of the one who will receive it. When we find a gift that has significant symbolism or meaning, we are especially pleased.

The wise men brought special gifts to young Jesus—gold, frankincense, and myrrh. Gold, a valuable, pure, and incorruptible metal, is the element of royalty. Frankincense, a resin requiring a slow and tedious extraction process, was burned by the priests to make a fragrant aroma pleasing to God. The leaves of myrrh were often used in embalming.

These gifts were special in their value, but they were also prophetic in their meaning, for in them we see the child Jesus being honored as the *King,* the *High Priest,* and the *Savior* who would die. Each of these roles was essential to Jesus' ministry on earth.

What good gifts are you giving to Jesus this season? He is your King, your High Priest, and your Savior. Return to Him the gift of your allegiance as His loyal subject, your sacrifices in holiness, and your humble praise to Him as the One who has rescued you from sin.

God gave a Person as a gift to every one of
us, and that Person is Jesus Christ.

BILLY GRAHAM

SOMETHING ABOUT THAT NAME

His name was called JESUS, the name given by the
angel before He was conceived in the womb.

LUKE 2:21

Jesus: There's just something about that name!* As He is King of kings, so His name is above all names. *Jesus* is a simple word. Yet somehow His name stirs the deepest passions in humanity. To believers it's a holy word; to others it's a curse.

The Bible says, "Call His name JESUS, for He will save His people from their sins" (Matthew 1:21). We're to forsake all for His Name, and though we'll be hated by all nations because of His name, the message of repentance and remission of sins is to be preached in His name to all nations (Matthew 19:29; 24:9; Luke 24:47).

Peter reminds us, "There is no other name under heaven given among men by which we must be saved" (Acts 4:12). And at the name of Jesus every knee will bow and every tongue confess that He is Lord (Philippians 2:10-11).

Jesus! Because of His Name, ours are written in heaven.

How sweet the name of Jesus sounds in a
believer's ear! It soothes his sorrows, heals
his wounds, and drives away his fear.

JOHN NEWTON

---

*The Bill Gaither Trio, "There's Something About That Name," in *There's Something About That Name*, Sony, 2006.

GOOD NEWS

Now there were in the same country shepherds living out in the fields, keeping watch over their flock by night. And behold, an angel of the Lord stood before them, and the glory of the Lord shone around them, and they were greatly afraid. Then the angel said to them, "Do not be afraid, for behold, I bring you good tidings of great joy which will be to all people."

LUKE 2:8-10

The darkened skies of that Middle Eastern night gave no hint of the explosion of light and splendor that was about to take place. As the watchful shepherds relaxed, the silence was interrupted with the occasional bleating of their flocks. An extraordinary God had chosen these shepherds on this night to observe His magnificent glory! God broke through simple circumstances with a fantastic display of unimaginable brilliance, direct from heaven.

If the thought has ever crossed your mind that you may be too insignificant, too poor, too *unworthy* to receive the gospel, think again. The Lord entrusted the lowly shepherds with the news of Christ. No matter your social standing, job, race, or role in life, you've heard the Good News because God wants you to know and to tell others.

The gospel is good news of mercy to the undeserving. The symbol of the religion of Jesus is the cross, not the scales.

JOHN STOTT

WHY BELIEVE?

Behold, now is the accepted time;
behold, now is the day of salvation.

2 CORINTHIANS 6:2

Someone's missing from your Nativity set. Among the shepherds, sages, and sheep, there should be a little figurine of yourself. The story of Jesus isn't just about Mary, Joseph, and the others. It concerns us just as if we had stood there, knelt by the manger, and marveled at the newborn child.

We should trust in Him because He believes in us and invites us to a life that makes sense. Through His teachings, Jesus showed us the only workable strategy for living a fulfilling life. And we should trust in Him because He can forgive us of every sin—past, present, and future—and impart eternal life. He lived a perfect life, then offered Himself as our substitute on the cross. He paid the price for every sin, and those who trust and follow Him become heirs of heaven.

Today is the best day of your life to trust Him as your Savior. Now is the time of salvation. Stand by His manger, gaze at His cross, and open the door of your heart to Him today. For "whoever calls on the name of the LORD shall be saved" (Romans 10:13).

[His love is] that which makes us live,
love, sing, and praise forever.

JOHN BUNYAN

GOD WITH US

The Lord Himself will give you a sign:
Behold, the virgin shall conceive and bear
a Son, and shall call His name Immanuel.

ISAIAH 7:14

The name Immanuel in Matthew 1:23 means "God with us." But what does it mean to have God with us? For starters, it means that God understands humanity. He has experienced firsthand the limitations of being human. He's felt the frailty of being a newborn, the fatigue of not having a place to lay His head, the pain of betrayal by one of His closest companions, and the burden of the sins of the *entire* world. God knows what it is like to be us—God *with* us is also one of us.

But it doesn't end there. God didn't just get down to our level. He brings us up to His. As we cling to Jesus, His majesty lifts us from the darkness of humanity to the glory of God.

On this Christmas Day, if you find dark places in your life, take hope. God knows. Christ will light the way, for He is with you.

When God chose to reveal himself, he did so through a
human body. The hand that touched the leper had dirt
under its nails. The feet upon which the woman wept were
calloused and dusty. And his tears . . . they came from
a heart as broken as yours or mine ever has been.

MAX LUCADO

THE SEARCH FOR JESUS

Now after Jesus was born in Bethlehem of Judea in the days of Herod the king, behold, wise men from the East came to Jerusalem, saying, "Where is He who has been born King of the Jews? For we have seen His star in the East and have come to worship Him."

MATTHEW 2:1-2

The word about Jesus spread far and wide shortly after His birth. In today's Scripture, we read that many months after the birth, men traveled great distances to inquire of King Herod where they could find this "King of the Jews."

To seek the Messiah shows true wisdom. The magi are remembered as wise men because they sought Jesus. It is still a wise person who takes the time and makes the effort to find Christ in Christmas.

So today, while Christmas is still with us, look at your December calendar and review the ways you have celebrated. Ask yourself, *Did I look for Jesus? Did I worship Him? Did I present Him with gifts?*

If you have been too busy or too preoccupied to find Jesus this Christmas, stop now and take some moments with Him. The wise men sought and found Him. What better time than now for you to do the same?

Let us not flutter too high, but remain by the manger and the swaddling clothes of Christ, "in whom dwelleth all the fullness of the Godhead bodily."

MARTIN LUTHER

TASTE OF PERFECTION

*Oh, taste and see that the L*ORD *is good.*

PSALM 34:8

If you knew you'd be wandering in a wilderness for forty years, would you panic, wondering how you would find food to eat? That's what the Israelites did even though God had just miraculously released them from slavery in Egypt. Why do we forget that God is bigger than our fears and difficulties?

Hungry, the Israelites woke up one morning wondering where breakfast would come from. As the dew lifted from the ground, there lay God's provision—manna—which sustained the Israelites for forty years until they entered the Promised Land (Exodus 16). No man-made solution could have provided an omer (six pints) of manna per person for two million people—every single day. God did it! He's always the answer for our needs.

Do you ever spend sleepless nights projecting your future and wondering how you will solve seemingly insurmountable problems? You may feel that life is pointless. You're in a wilderness experience, and the help you need is not from yourself or any other person. Jesus is your manna, all-sufficient for the ups and downs of your life. Have you tried Him? Have you tasted? Have you trusted? "Oh, taste and see that the Lord is good; blessed is the man who trusts in Him!" (Psalm 34:8).

He who has God and everything else has
no more than he who has God only.

C. S. LEWIS

NOTHING

You are my Lord, my goodness is nothing apart from You.

If you think you have nothing to offer the Lord, consider the early Freewill Baptist evangelist David Marks. One day, he rode his horse into Ancaster, Ontario, announcing that he was going to preach. Marks asked the gathered crowd if anyone had a suggestion for a topic. Mocking him, a man called out, "Nothing!"

Robert Morgan continues the story this way: "Marks immediately began preaching on 'nothing.' God created the world from 'nothing,' he said. He gave us laws in which there is 'nothing' unjust. But, Marks continued, we have broken God's law and there is 'nothing' in us to justify us. There will be 'nothing' to comfort sinners in death or hell. But, while Christians have 'nothing' of their own in which to boast, we have Christ. And in Him, we have 'nothing' to cause us grief, 'nothing' to disturb our peace, and 'nothing' to fear in eternity." Marks then got back on his horse and left the town.*

Sometimes when we're low in spirits, we feel we're nothing that really matters, that our lives amount to nothing at all. But when we feel our weakest, the Lord's power is the strongest. Even a sermon on nothing can save souls—for *nothing* is impossible with God.

In Christian service, the branches that bear
the most fruit hang the lowest.

UNKNOWN

---

*Robert J. Morgan, "May 13," in *On This Day* (Nashville: Thomas Nelson, 1997).

WHY HIS RETURN?

If I go . . . I will come again.

JOHN 14:3

The first appearance of Jesus was a mission of humility and sacrifice. The second will be a mission of triumph and transformation. Christ often described His return as the coming of a groom for his bride. The church, He said, is "the bride of Christ." And what an eager bride we are, awaiting our Lord to come take us home. According to 1 Thessalonians 4:16, He will break through the clouds "with a shout, with the voice of an archangel, and with the trumpet of God."

But He must also come to judge the world. Jesus spoke several times of the final judgment, when He would come to judge the living and the dead and to separate His faithful children from those who refuse to follow Him.

He'll also return to establish a new heaven and a new earth wherein dwells righteousness. How eagerly we're awaiting His new universe with its shimmering capital city, described in Revelation 21 as the New Jerusalem.

Whether He returns today or years from now, we can live for Him. Let's say with the hymnist, "Another year is dawning, dear Father, let it be, on earth or else in Heaven, another year for Thee!"

Standing before Him at last, trial and trouble all past, crowns at His feet we will cast. Jesus is coming again!

JOHN W. PETERSON

DECEMBER 30

STEWARDS OF HEALTH

You shall come to the grave at a full age,
as a sheaf of grain ripens in its season.

JOB 5:26

The English author Daniel Defoe may have said it first, but it's Benjamin Franklin's version that has become the standard: "In this world nothing can be said to be certain, except death and taxes." Setting aside taxes, we can agree regarding death that "it is appointed for men to die once" (Hebrews 9:27).

The picture of death painted for Job by one of his friends is a strange one to the modern reader. Eliphaz pictured life as a growing season, with the harvest of full fruit coming at the end. In a garden, harvest only happens when plants are nourished richly and consistently to encourage the bountiful fruit God intended.

Gardening is a matter of stewardship of soil and plants together. So are life and health a matter of good stewardship. As stewards of the gifts of God, we are called to care for our physical life just as faithfully as our spiritual life, nourishing our bodies with good food, exercise, and plenty of rest.

As you look toward the coming year, plan now to become a better steward of your health.

The fundamental truth in the matter of stewardship
is that everything we touch belongs to God.

JOHN BLANCHARD

FACING THE FUTURE

*Call to Me, and I will answer you, and show you great
and mighty things, which you do not know.*

JEREMIAH 33:3

As the new year approaches, we may be tempted to speculate about what the future holds. Will there be challenges and trials? Unexpected blessings and windfalls? Thinking about the future can seem like unraveling an intricate mystery plot, but the prophet Jeremiah assures us that God reveals exactly what we need to know!

As we look to the new year, we may try to gain a sense of control over the unknown by planning, setting goals, or making resolutions. But most of us realize that the future really lies outside of our control.

We can, however, trust God for what lies ahead. God sees everything that will happen, and He sees us as well. God, through Jeremiah, doesn't encourage us to try to set our course. God encourages us to call on Him as we face the future and to anticipate an answer.

God has promised that He will be faithful. Be encouraged that He goes before you and follows close behind. His hand is lovingly directing your course.

I do not know what the future holds, but
I do know who holds the future.

GEORGE W. TRUETT